LETHAL FORCE
and the OBJECTIVELY REASONABLE OFFICER

Law, Liability, Policy, Tactics and Survival

John Michael Callahan

43-08 162nd Street
Flushing, NY 11358
www.LooseleafLaw.com
800-647-5547

This publication is not intended to replace nor be a substitute for any official procedural material issued by your agency of employment nor other official source. Looseleaf Law Publications, Inc., the author and any associated advisors have made all possible efforts to ensure the accuracy and thoroughness of the information provided herein but accept no liability whatsoever for injury, legal action or other adverse results following the application or adoption of the information contained in this book.

©2015 Looseleaf Law Publications, Inc. All rights reserved. No part of this book may be reproduced, stored in a retrieval system, or transcribed, in any form or by any means, electronic, mechanical, photocopying, recording, or otherwise, without the prior written permission of the Copyright owner. For such permission, contact Looseleaf Law Publications, Inc., 43-08 162nd Street, Flushing, NY 11358, (800) 647-5547, www.LooseleafLaw.com.

Library of Congress Cataloging in Publication

Callahan, John M. (John Michael), 1943-
  Lethal force and the "objectively reasonable" officer : law, liability, policy, tactics and survival / John Michael Callahan.
     pages cm
  Includes index.
  ISBN 978-1-60885-132-4
  1. Police shootings--United States. 2. Reasonable care (Law)--United States. 3. Police--United States. I. Title.
  KF5399.C355 2015
  342.73'0418--dc23
                                                    2015020544

Digital ISBN 978-1-60885-133-1

Cover by *Tin Box Studio,* Cincinnati, Ohio

Table of Contents

Acknowledgments i

About the Author iii

Foreword v

Introduction ix

Chapter 1
DEADLY FORCE AND CONSTITUTIONAL LAW 1
    Legal Knowledge — An Absolute Necessity 1
    The Constitutional Standard for the Use of Deadly
        Force 2
    Summary of the Constitutional Standard 5
    Graham v. Connor — the "Objectively Reasonable"
        Officer 5
    Meaning and Importance of the Graham Decision 6
    The Fourth Amendment "Seizure" Requirement 7
    Summary of the Fourth Amendment "Seizure" 9
    The "Seizure" Issue—Shooting Innocent Hostages 9
    The "Seizure" Issue—Suspects Who Escape After
        Being Shot 12
    The "Totality of Circumstances" Test 16
    Federal Circuits Split on Scope of "Totality of
        Circumstances" Test 19

Chapter 2
IMPACT OF GRAHAM AND GARNER DECISIONS ON THE
    FEDERAL CIRCUIT COURTS 29
    The First Circuit (Boston, MA) —
        Bennett v. Wainwright 29
    The Second Circuit (New York, NY) —
        Salim v. Proulx 31
    The Third Circuit (Philadelphia, PA)—
        Lamont Estate of Quick v. New Jersey 33
    The Fourth Circuit (Richmond, VA)—*Noel v. Artson* . 40
    The Fifth Circuit (New Orleans, LA)—
        Elizondo v. Green 42
    The Sixth Circuit (Cincinnati, OH)—*Simmonds v.*
        Genesee County 44
    The Seventh Circuit (Chicago, IL)—*Marion v. City*
        of Corydon, Indiana 46

The Eighth Circuit (Saint Louis, MO)—
Lee v. Anderson 48
The Ninth Circuit (San Francisco, CA)—*Glenn v. Washington County* 51
The Tenth Circuit (Denver, CO)—
Thomas v. Durastanti 59
The Eleventh Circuit (Atlanta, GA)—
Penley v. Eslinger 64

Chapter 3
THE QUALIFIED IMMUNITY DEFENSE 67
The Officer's Shield Against Frivolous Constitutional Lawsuits 67
The Genesis of the Qualified Immunity Defense—*Harlow v. Fitzgerald* 68
The Development of the Qualified Immunity Defense after Harlow 70
Mitchell v. Forsyth 70
Anderson v. Creighton 72
Pearson v. Callahan 76
Qualified Immunity and Officer Involved Shootings—*Brosseau v. Haugen* 77
Qualified Immunity—Material Facts in Dispute—*Tolan v. Cotton* 82
Summary of the Law on the Qualified Immunity Defense 85

Chapter 4
GRAHAM V. CONNOR/CRIMINAL PROSECUTION FOR USING DEADLY FORCE 87

Chapter 5
THE "OBJECTIVELY REASONABLE" OFFICER DEFINED 91
The Inherent Danger of the Law Enforcement Job 94
Never Underestimate Your Adversary 95
The "Kill Zone" 96
Pre-Battle Precautions 100
Approach Vehicles with Extreme Caution 101
Protect Your Firearm 103
Wear Your Body Armor 103
Vital Equipment on Your Body or Within Your Reach 104

Chapter 6
FIREARMS AND DEADLY FORCE TRAINING 107
Mandatory Firearms Skill and Marksmanship
  Training 107
Firearms Training—Beyond Marksmanship 110
Training on Realistic Targets 111
Video Simulators and Force on Force Training 112
In the Line of Enemy Fire—Move and Shoot 114
Repetitive Regular Firearms Training—
  A Necessity 116
Firearms Training in Close Quarters 117
Regular Training on Constitutional and
  Departmental Deadly Force Standards 118
Inadequate Firearms Training and
  Municipal Liability 118
City of Canton, *Ohio v. Harris* 120
Connick v. Thompson 122
Failure to Train and its Consequences—The Zuchel
  Case 125

Chapter 7
**ACTION VERSUS REACTION—THE DEADLY
REACTIONARY GAP** 129
Reaction Time Components 130
Reaction Time Studies—"The Tempe Study" 131
Decision Time—Laboratory v. Reality 135
The Reactionary Gap Hypothetical 135
The Blair Reaction Time Study 136
The Blair Reaction Time Study Results 137
The Blair Study's Potential Impact on
  Civil Litigation 138
Action v. Reaction—The Bottom Line 143
How Long Does It Take to Stop Shooting? 145
Reaction Time / Knife and Edged Weapons Attacks . 147

Chapter 8
WOUND BALLISTICS 151
Most Gunshot Wounds Are Not Fatal 151
Deadly Force and Immediate Incapacitation—An
  Elusive Goal 152
Gunshot Wounds—Blood Loss—Physical
  Incapacitation 153
Non-Survivable Wounds and the Continuing
  Threat 154

Gunshot Wounds and the Immediate Fall— A
Hollywood Myth 155
Real World Reality—The FBI Miami Shootout 158
The Miami Shootout—Aftermath and
Lessons Learned 166
Changes After Miami 166
The FBI Handgun and Ammunition Transition 167
Other Lessons Learned from the Miami Shootout 172
Shooting to Wound—"A Fool's Errand" 175

Chapter 9
TENNESSEE V. GARNER—DEADLY FORCE AND THE
FLEEING FELON 179
Dangerous Fleeing Felons—*Forrett v. Richardson* ... 183
The Necessity of Shooting Forrett—A
Safe Alternative? 185
Fleeing Felons—The Fourth Amendment and
Deadly Force Policy 186
Dangerous Fleeing Felons—The Reactionary Gap /
Hide & Ambush 188
Case Law on Deadly Force and Armed
Fleeing Felons 193

Chapter 10
DANGEROUS VEHICLE PURSUITS—*SCOTT V. HARRIS* 199
Dangerous Vehicle Pursuits—*Plumhoff v. Rickard* .. 203
Plumhoff's Progeny 208

Chapter 11
DEADLY FORCE—THE BODY'S PHYSIOLOGICAL RESPONSE 213
Avoiding "Condition Black"— Stress Inoculation 217
Avoiding Condition Black — Tactical Breathing 218
Winning the Gunfight—Physical Fitness 219
Physical Exhaustion—Officer Survival—Use of
Deadly Force 221

Chapter 12
POLITICS AND THE PATROL RIFLE 225

Chapter 13
"THE OBJECTIVELY REASONABLE LAW ENFORCEMENT
OFFICER" — SUMMATION 235

Index 239

Acknowledgments

My work on this book is the product of years of training, research, practical experience, personal interest, and the generous assistance and help from friends and former law enforcement colleagues.

No one undertakes and successfully completes a work of this nature by themselves. Accordingly, I now wish to take this opportunity to recognize, thank and salute those persons who provided extremely valuable assistance to me along the way. Not only in the writing of this book but also in helping me to develop as a law enforcement trainer and writer.

I would like to recognize and sincerely thank my former Unit Chief at the FBI Academy at Quantico, Donald "Don" McLaughlin for helping me to develop and hone my writing, teaching abilities and skills while serving under him in the Legal Instruction Unit at the Academy. Don was an outstanding FBI Supervisor and a fine mentor to me at the FBI Academy. Under his guidance, I left the Legal Instruction Unit at the FBI Academy with far greater writing skills than when I entered.

I would also like to thank in a special way Don McLaughlin and three of my former colleagues, John Hall, Bob McGuiness, and Dan Schofield in the Legal Instruction Unit at the FBI Academy for giving me the support and confidence I needed to handle the challenging job as an Instructor of Law at the FBI Academy. I left the Academy a far better law trainer than when I entered. My growth and development as an Instructor and writer was no doubt enhanced because of the guidance, direction and advice provided by these four special men.

With respect to this book in particular, special thanks goes to my lifelong friend from Dorchester, Massachusetts, Joe Driscoll. Brilliant and successful in his health care field career, he agreed without hesitation to become my main proof reader for the book. Joe provided excellent practical suggestions and positive regular feedback for me during the writing of the entire book. His contributions were invaluable.

I would also like to thank my former FBI partner from the Phoenix FBI office, retired Special Agent Pete Lanthorn for his review of the book. Pete was one of the finest and hardest working FBI Agents I ever worked with, and his advice with the book was exceptional. Pete could always be counted on to back me up when I needed help. In this instance, he backed me up once again.

Another individual who took the time to review a draft of the book was retired Superintendent of the Boston Police Department, John Gallagher. John, a graduate of the FBI National Academy, who rose through the ranks from Patrolman to Superintendent during his most productive career, provided valuable insight from a police officer perspective on the content of the book. Many thanks go to John for his invaluable contribution.

Finally, great thanks must be directed to John Hall, my former FBI Academy colleague and mentor, for his review, advice and suggestions regarding this book. John was not only the finest Law Instructor that the FBI Academy ever had, in my humble opinion, but also the principal architect of the FBI deadly force policy that was dramatically altered in 1995 because of his work. John and his former colleague in the Firearms Training Unit at the FBI Academy, Urey "Pat" Patrick are the authors of a fabulous book on law enforcement use of deadly force that I cite numerous times in this book. Both Patrick and Hall are recognized deadly force experts in the field of officer-involved shootings.

I would also be remiss if I failed to mention the outstanding and tremendous work in the field of officer-involved shootings that has been accomplished by Colonel Dave Grossman, Professor William Lewinski, and Professor Pete Blair. The work of these fine men is referenced frequently in the pages of this book. Law enforcement officers across America and the world are far better off and safer due to their exceptional contributions.

I would also like to give special thanks to my beloved Father, "Jack" Callahan, a retired FBI Agent and FBI firearms instructor who taught me how to shoot, kindled my lifelong interest in law enforcement, and provided extremely valuable guidance to me along life's journey. He was recently taken home by God but I know I will see him again on the other side.

About the Author

John M. "Mike" Callahan Jr. served in the field of law enforcement for 44 years. He was appointed as a Special Agent with the United States Naval Criminal Investigative Service (NCIS) in May 1968. He conducted criminal investigations on U.S. Naval bases in Boston, Massachusetts and Quonset Point/ Davisville, Rhode Island. During his tenure with NCIS, Mr. Callahan investigated criminal matters involving arson, rape, assault with a deadly weapon, robbery, larceny, drug violations, and child molestation.

In October 1969, Mr. Callahan was appointed as a Special Agent with the FBI. He served in four FBI field offices including Detroit, Richmond, Phoenix, and Boston. During his FBI career, Mr. Callahan conducted a wide range of criminal investigations, which included such diverse crimes as bank robbery, kidnapping, extortion, government fraud, crimes on U.S. military bases (including murder, armed robbery, burglary, theft, drug violations, child molestation, etc.), car theft rings, and bribery of city officials. He was also involved in the apprehension of numerous individuals who were fugitives from justice and wanted for committing violent crimes including murder and armed robbery.

While serving in both the Phoenix and Boston FBI offices, Mr. Callahan was appointed to the position of Chief Division Counsel and handled all legal matters for those FBI Divisions. His legal duties included assisting in the legal defense of lawsuits directed toward FBI Agents, FBI Supervisory Officials, and the FBI as an agency; Training FBI Agents and FBI Management Officials regarding current legal matters and FBI policies; Training State and Local Law Enforcement Officials on legal matters of interest to them, including use of deadly force; reviewing and approving all electronic surveillance affidavits; reviewing and approving all undercover operations; providing legal advice on all investigative operations and legal advice to FBI Supervisory Officials on management decisions and disciplinary matters. During his tenure as FBI Boston Division Chief Counsel, Mr. Callahan served for three years as a Special Assistant United States Attorney handling legal matters related to the FBI.

Mr. Callahan also taught constitutional criminal procedure at the FBI Academy, Quantico, Virginia for several years and wrote numerous legal articles for the FBI Law Enforcement Bulletin.

During his FBI Academy assignment, he authored the FBI Legal Monograph on the Law of Entrapment. While serving at the FBI Academy, he taught criminal law and procedure to hundreds of new FBI Agent Trainees and hundreds of police officers who attended the FBI National Academy from across America and from different countries around the world. Mr. Callahan retired from the FBI in 1999 and at that time held the position of Supervisory Special Agent and Chief Division Counsel for the Boston Division of the FBI.

After his FBI career, Mr. Callahan was hired by the Massachusetts Office of the Inspector General and served for several years as a Deputy Inspector General in charge of the Investigations Division before retiring in July 2012. During his tenure as Deputy Inspector General, he conducted and supervised numerous investigations concerning corrupt state and local government officials. While serving as Deputy Inspector General, Mr. Callahan gave numerous presentations on the topic of law enforcement use of deadly force for the New England State Police Information Network (NESPIN), and in 2008 he was selected as the NESPIN Trainer of the Year. Mr. Callahan is the author of *Deadly Force, Constitutional Standards, Federal Guidelines, and Officer Survival*, which was published by Looseleaf Law Publications.

Mr. Callahan is a graduate of Boston College and Boston College Law School and is licensed to practice law in Massachusetts. While in law school, he served as a Suffolk County Corrections Officer at the Deer Island House of Correction, Winthrop, Massachusetts.

Foreword

This book is dedicated as a memorial to all of the brave and dedicated law enforcement officers in America who left their homes and families to protect and serve their communities and never returned. It is dedicated to those brave and dedicated officers who did return home but were never the same due to severe injuries received in the line of duty. It is also dedicated to the families of those officers who have been killed and wounded for the great loss that they have suffered and the sacrifices they have made. These brave officers deserve our profound praise and thanks for their professionalism, courage, dedication, and sacrifice on our behalf. Many of them gave us all they had. They had nothing more to give. May God richly bless them all.

It is my intention through this book to assist law enforcement officers who are currently protecting us and those that will serve in the future by offering them the knowledge and guidance that they need to protect themselves from physical, mental, emotional, and financial harm. It is my hope to share with these dedicated public servants what I have learned through experience and training in my 44 years in law enforcement, and what I have learned through my research in writing this book. The purpose of this book is to save the lives of those who work diligently to protect all of us and to help those officers to protect themselves from inappropriate departmental discipline, criminal prosecution, and civil liability.

This book is designed to provide federal, state, and local law enforcement officers with the legal foundation and the legal knowledge that they need to meet the deadly force challenges they may face with supreme confidence. Officers who are confident in their legal knowledge on the subject of use of deadly force are much more likely to respond without hesitation when confronting a life-threatening situation. As we shall see in the book, hesitation in such circumstances is a contributing factor to bad outcomes for officers in violent encounters.

The constitutional parameters for law enforcement use of deadly force will be set forth in clearly defined terms. Officers will learn that the legality of their use of deadly force is governed by the Fourth Amendment and its "objective reasonableness" standard. The involved officer's conduct will be judged on the basis of what an "objectively reasonable" officer would have done in the same or similar circumstances.

Likewise, officers will learn that the United States Supreme Court has exhibited a profound understanding of what it means to become involved in a deadly encounter with a violent offender. Moreover, they will see how the Court has carefully instructed the lower courts across America to place themselves in the shoes of the "objectively reasonable" officer at the scene of the deadly force incident. Officers will learn that the Court has directed the lower courts to focus on the fact that officers in these violent encounters are forced to make instant split-second decisions in circumstances that are tense, uncertain, and dynamic in nature.

Finally, officers will learn that the Court has instructed the lower courts to refrain from second guessing the actions/decisions of officers in shooting incidents through the 20/20 vision of hindsight. The only question of relevance is whether the involved officer acted with "objective reasonableness." To act correctly within the parameters of the law, the officer need not make the best possible decision that is available to him/her as long as the decision that he/she made is "objectively reasonable."

The impact that the Supreme Court's use of force decisions has had on the federal circuit courts across America will also be examined. Similarly, the book will review and analyze the legal doctrines pertaining to the Fourth Amendment "seizure" in a deadly force context; the scope of the "totality of circumstances" test in deadly force incidents; and the qualified immunity doctrine/defense in connection with the use of deadly force by law enforcement officers.

The analysis of the qualified immunity defense will focus on the Supreme Court's development of the defense and its favorable impact on the outcome of civil litigation for defendant law enforcement officers. In summary, the Supreme Court has emphatically made clear that the qualified immunity defense is available to protect officers from frivolous lawsuits by operating to permit early dismissal of litigation.

The makeup and identity of the "objectively reasonable" law enforcement officer will be defined. It will point out how essential it is for law enforcement to create and define the identity of the "objectively reasonable" officer. It will demonstrate the negative consequences that will flow from abdicating that responsibility and permitting plaintiff's lawyers and their expert witnesses to define who the "objectively reasonable" officer is.

This book will reveal that the "objectively reasonable" officer is one who comprehends the inherent dangers that are connected with the profession. The "objectively reasonable" officer is one who is well trained in use of deadly force law and departmental policy. He/she will understand the need to be physically fit, proficient in the skill of using a firearm, and regularly exposed to shoot/don't shoot situations through interactive video and force on force training.

It will stress the fact that the "objectively reasonable" officer is one who understands the concept and parameters of "action versus reaction"/"the deadly reactionary gap" and take all precautionary steps to keep from being placed at the wrong end of the "gap." This book will demonstrate that the "objectively reasonable" officer must know the meaning and scope of the concept of "wound ballistics" and the fact that shooting a violent offender one or more times does not mean that the fight is over.

Officers will also learn that the "objectively reasonable" officer is one who knows that he/she is likely to be shot and wounded during a violent encounter and that the officer will still be able to not only survive but prevail in the encounter by continuing to fight. The motto of the "objectively reasonable" officer is "No Surrender."

In this book, officers will learn how dangerous it is to pursue an adversary armed with a firearm because of the "deadly reactionary gap" and the concept of "hide and ambush." Several examples of horrific outcomes from such chases will be analyzed and examined. Moreover, the latest U.S. Supreme Court cases on use of deadly force by officers during high speed vehicle pursuits will be reviewed and explained.

Finally, what the "objectively reasonable" officer needs to know about the human body's physiological reaction to the release of adrenaline that will occur in every deadly force encounter will be examined. The "objectively reasonable" officer will never be surprised when he/she experiences tunnel vision, auditory exclusion, vasoconstriction and loss of fine and complex motor skills during a violent encounter. He/she will also learn methods of limiting the negative consequences of these factors. The significance and importance of physically fit law enforcement officers will also be discussed and emphasized.

Introduction

Statistics establish that the law enforcement profession in America is an inherently dangerous occupation. The Federal Bureau of Investigation (FBI) issues an annual report entitled "Law Enforcement Officers Killed and Assaulted" (LEOKA). The LEOKA reports for 1994 (covering a 10-year period) and 2004 (covering a separate 10-year period) combined disclose that for the twenty-year period between 1985 and 2004, 1302 law enforcement officers in America were the victims of murder. Almost 1200 (1195) of the murdered officers were killed by felons using firearms during that time period. According to the 2011 LEOKA report[1] an additional 378 officers were feloniously murdered between 2005 and 2011.

LEOKA figures for 2011 disclose that 72 officers were murdered and 63 of them were killed by firearms.[2] According to the December 29, 2011 issue of the *Boston Globe* newspaper, the number of officers killed by firearms in 2011 involved a substantial increase from the previous year. The *Globe* reported that the number of officer fatalities in 2011 caused by firearms made it one of the deadliest years for US law enforcement in recent history.

These statistics reveal one consistent message. The job of law enforcement in America is an extremely dangerous one. These statistics don't lie. They tell the often sad and tragic story of the danger that law enforcement officers face in America on a daily basis. I have served in the law enforcement profession for 44 years. During my 30-year FBI career, I was personally involved in two officer-involved shootings. I have seen and, by the grace of God, have lived through the danger that confronts law enforcement officers in this country on a regular basis.

The first incident involved a bank robbery that occurred in Richmond, Virginia in February 1972. During the robbery, a lone gunman entered the bank, brandished a sawed-off shotgun loaded with rifle slugs and demanded money. He left the bank with over

---

[1] The latest available LEOKA report was issued on October 28, 2013. The 2013 report pertains to law enforcement officers feloniously killed in the United States for 2012. The LEOKA report disclosed that 48 officers were murdered in 2012, 44 by means of firearms. In addition, 52,901 officers were criminally assaulted and 27.7% of those received various injuries from the attacks.

[2] 50 of the officers were murdered by means of handguns and 3 were killed with their own weapons.

$35,000 in cash and entered a waiting getaway car driven by a second individual. A bank customer observed the suspect leave the bank and followed the getaway car to a nearby motel. He observed the robbers exit the getaway car and enter the motel. The customer returned to the bank and alerted responding police officers and FBI agents to what he had witnessed.

Another FBI agent and I were in an FBI vehicle responding to the bank robbery when an FBI radio report indicated that the robbers were located at a local motel. By coincidence, we were passing this motel at that very moment. We immediately turned the car around and entered the motel parking lot. We observed the getaway car, which was parked and empty in the motel lot. Three Richmond police officers were standing next to the getaway car. Everything appeared to be under control.

My partner decided to enter the motel to check on the room number of the bank robbers. I exited the FBI vehicle and began to walk in the direction of the getaway car. I was approximately 90 feet from joining the Richmond officers at the getaway car when I received the surprise of my life. Suddenly, without any warning, one of the bank robbers appeared from around the corner of the motel.[3] He held a sawed-off shotgun in one hand and had his other arm wrapped tightly around the neck of a woman. There had been no mention of a woman being involved in the bank robbery and she appeared to be a bona fide hostage.

I immediately took cover behind a nearby vehicle and drew my service weapon, a 4-inch barrel Smith & Wesson .357 magnum revolver. The robber stood very close to the woman and threatened to kill her. He ordered the nearby officers to back away from the getaway vehicle. The officers raised their hands in the air and slowly backed up against the motel wall. This provided the robber with the chance to enter the getaway car with the hostage and attempt to escape. I took aim at the robber but did not fire because of the close proximity of the robber to the woman hostage and a concern for the lives of the nearby officers.[4]

---

[3] Law enforcement officers learned later on during a search of the bank robbers' room that they had a police scanner and had overheard Richmond Police radio broadcasts indicating the location of the robbers and their vehicle. Alerted to the potential for police presence, they made an attempt to reach their vehicle and escape.

[4] I was concerned that if I fired a shot that hit the suspect, he might fire the shotgun reflexively, thereby causing death or injury to the officers nearby. I also believed that a head shot was necessary and such a shot from 90 feet with a handgun and an apparent hostage standing next to the subject was not something I felt comfortable making.

The bank robber now had his shotgun pointed directly at the three officers with their backs pressed up against the motel wall.

Instead of entering the getaway car with the hostage as I expected him to do, the robber suddenly, without warning, fired the shotgun at the three police officers from a distance of about 15 – 20 feet. This action was not rational and took me completely by surprise. After all, the officers had followed his orders and provided him with a chance to initiate his getaway. I saw the three officers' drop to their knees and I thought he shot them all. I later learned that the rifle slug fired by the bank robber went over their heads and into the wall of the motel. The officers immediately drew their firearms and fired multiple rounds at the bank robber. He was hit several times and died of his wounds on the spot.

During this exchange of gunfire, the female "hostage" inexplicably pulled a revolver from her purse and fired six shots at the officers. All of her shots missed. This action by an apparent crime victim initially caused confusion among the officers on the scene, including me. Again, I was surprised by the actions of a "hostage" suddenly turning into a deadly threat. My surprise caused me to hesitate in responding. Before I could shoot, another Richmond officer (not part of the original three) was able to fire and hit her with two shots. She fell to the ground wounded but survived.

Fortunately no law enforcement officers were killed or wounded in this bizarre shooting incident. I learned later that the male bank robber had just been released from a federal prison where he had served a long sentence for bank robbery. He and his girlfriend were just passing through Richmond on their way to Alabama, needed money and decided to rob another bank.

At the time of this incident I had been in law enforcement for over four years and had been involved in making numerous arrests of potentially dangerous individuals, some of whom were armed at the time of arrest. None of them resisted and all gave up without a struggle. Because of this, I was lulled into a sense of false security. I came to believe that in the face of sufficient law enforcement numbers and firepower, all rational subjects would simply surrender.[5] This erroneous belief nearly got me killed. In

---

[5] Superior numbers and firepower in making arrests is a luxury often available to FBI agents who frequently have the time to carefully plan for the arrest of violent offenders. This luxury is not often available to local and state police officers who frequently confront violent offenders by themselves on the roads and highways of America without knowing the violent history of the individuals they are stopping for minor traffic violations.

another few seconds, I would have been standing next to the getaway car with the three Richmond officers when the bank robber and his "hostage" appeared out of nowhere. I have already documented my initial reaction to the sudden appearance of the armed bank robber, that is, complete surprise.

This state of mind, although understandable, is totally unacceptable when confronting a life-threatening situation. After the initial volley of shots, my reaction to the "hostage" pulling out a gun and firing it was once again a complete surprise. My state of mind in both situations was not what it should have been. This unprepared state of mind is what results in officers being killed. I learned a valuable lesson that day in the school of street reality. When danger is possible, an officer must be totally ready and prepared mentally for a deadly confrontation. Officers must learn to expect the unexpected. Failure to be mentally prepared for a deadly encounter will likely cost you your very life. From that day forward, I was never unprepared mentally to face deadly threats on the job.

Three years later, the lessons learned in Richmond were valuable in confronting a new deadly challenge. I had been transferred from Richmond to Phoenix, Arizona in 1975. I was assigned to work on an FBI squad that, among other criminal matters, handled the apprehension of dangerous federal fugitives. My partner and I went out to interview a relative of the subject of one of my partner's cases.

This particular subject was a fugitive who was wanted for failing to appear in court on a relatively minor felony in another state. It appeared to be no big deal. We found the relative to be cooperative. He told us that the fugitive was staying in a local motel in Tempe, Arizona. He also told us that he was armed with a pistol and would not be taken alive. After my Richmond experience I took what the relative said quite seriously.

We requested back-up from three additional FBI agents. We met them in the vicinity of the motel and approached the hotel manager. He looked at a photograph of the fugitive and confirmed that he was staying at the motel. He told us what room the fugitive was staying in. He provided us with a key to the fugitive's room. We entered the room with drawn weapons but the fugitive was not inside. While searching the room for the fugitive, we found a loaded pistol. We seized the pistol and staked out the room waiting for him to return.

Several hours passed and darkness set in. Sometime around 11 p.m., the fugitive came back to his room. He did not arrive in a vehicle as we imagined he would. Instead, he appeared suddenly on foot, walking through the trees in the rear of the motel. He was able to enter his room and lock the door before we could arrest him.

There was no rear door or rear windows in his room and only one window on the left side of the room. The right side of his room was connected to the side of the adjacent room. Three agents were behind cover about 40 feet from the front door. Another agent and I were covering the window on the left side of the room. The agents at the front of the fugitive's room identified themselves as FBI agents and ordered the fugitive to come out with his hands up and surrender.

The fugitive opened the front door; claimed that the agents were mistaken and denied that he was the wanted fugitive. While this dialogue was going on, the agent with me was able to reach the edge of the building near the front door in a clandestine fashion. The fugitive was not able to see him and did not realize how close the agent was to him. The agent suddenly moved around the corner and confronted the fugitive with a Remington 870 shotgun pointed right at his face. Instead of giving up, as any rational person would, the fugitive glared defiantly at the agent and said, "Go ahead and shoot me." The fugitive did not appear to have a weapon and the agent did not shoot him. The fugitive slammed the door shut and locked it.

We quickly decided to gain entry by force. The agent at the door handed his shotgun back to me and proceeded to kick the front door off its hinges. The other agents and I moved up behind and to each side of the agent who kicked in the door. The agent was standing in the middle of the now open doorway. We all had firearms in our hands. The room was dark inside and the only light came from the lighting in the motel parking area. The fugitive was standing at the back of the darkened room with his hands behind his back.

The agent in the doorway instructed the fugitive to show his hands but he refused to comply. This was an ominous development. Instead, he began to move slowly forward in our direction with his hands still positioned behind his back. When he reached the middle of the room he showed his hands. In one hand was a large hunting style knife. This was the kind of knife that could instantly kill a human victim.

The agent in the doorway screamed at the fugitive to drop the knife. Instead he took more slow steps toward the door. Again the agent commanded him to drop the knife but to no avail. The agent fired one shot from his .357 magnum revolver and hit the fugitive in the head just below one of his eyes. Because it was a head shot, the subject immediately and dramatically fell backward onto the motel room floor. The imminent threat to our lives was brought to an abrupt end. The fugitive died a short time later in a local hospital.

Because of what I had learned in the Richmond shooting incident described earlier, I was ready and prepared mentally for everything that happened in the Tempe incident. One lifesaving decision that we made in the Tempe incident was to take the relative's warning that the fugitive was armed and would not be taken alive seriously. A second positive decision was to obtain sufficient back-up before attempting the arrest. A third positive lifesaving decision involved the decision to take the fugitive's handgun with us when we initially left his room. When he first returned to the room, he looked for that gun everywhere but could not find it. There is no doubt that he would have used that weapon against us if he was able to. Another positive decision was to bring a shotgun to the arrest location in case it was needed.

These two shooting incidents have a common denominator. That common denominator is one that must be recognized, appreciated, and respected by all law enforcement officers. That common denominator is found in the state of mind of some dangerous criminals. The two male subjects of the above described incidents, the bank robber and the fugitive, clearly had made up their minds long before being confronted by law enforcement that they were not going back to jail under any circumstances. They had decided at some point that if confronted by law enforcement, even when manpower and firepower was overwhelmingly against them, they were not going to surrender. They had decided to fight and get away or fight and die. This type of individual is extremely dangerous and will not hesitate to kill police officers. They will kill, maim, and injure anyone who stands in the way of their freedom.

Law enforcement officers must understand that these kinds of profoundly dangerous people are out there. Rational thinking is not part of their mental anatomy. Because they don't care whether they live or die, they are willing to take extraordinary risks and act with reckless abandon if it will help them to get away. This makes them extraordinarily dangerous and deadly adversaries.

Law enforcement officers must develop the proper mindset to confront these violence prone adversaries before the day when it happens. The decision to use deadly force under circumstance where it is justified should never be made at the moment when it is required. It must be made by officers long before that day happens. Mental and physical preparation before such an incident is an absolute necessity if an officer is to survive and win a deadly confrontation with this kind of criminal.

Officers must prepare themselves mentally by deciding well in advance of a deadly confrontation that they will be ready for any deadly situation that may arise. They must convince themselves that they will not only survive but win these deadly confrontations before they happen. This kind of mental preparation is absolutely essential if officers are to match the mindset of the type of dangerous felons described above.

This winning state of mind is only the beginning of proper preparation. Officers must also prepare for the likelihood that they will face these deadly situations by proper repetitive and recurrent training, involving basic firearms marksmanship, force on force, and firearms simulator training. Regular physical fitness and defensive tactics training must also be provided. In a deadly confrontation, officers will not rise to the level of the situation but rather fall to the level of their training.

Officers must carry with them (preferably on their person) all of the appropriate equipment to be successful in a deadly confrontation. This equipment should include but not be limited to, firearms that they are intimately familiar with and regularly train with; several reserve ammunition magazines to sustain them in a protracted gun battle; body armor worn on their body; radio and electronic communication gear to call for help and communicate with other officers quickly and with precision; and first aid equipment designed to control bleeding (e.g., iT clamps). Anything less will likely result in a wake, eulogy, and burial service for another fallen officer.

Chapter 1

DEADLY FORCE AND CONSTITUTIONAL LAW

Legal Knowledge — An Absolute Necessity

This book was written to provide all federal, state, and local law enforcement officers in the United States with the best information available to win deadly force encounters on the street and defend themselves from adverse administrative action, civil liability, and criminal prosecution in the aftermath of an officer involved shooting incident. The best way for officers involved in shooting incidents to protect themselves from adverse administrative action, civil liability, and criminal prosecution is to know, understand, and follow established law and departmental policy before, during, and after a shooting incident occurs. The ability of law enforcement officers to defend themselves from negative consequences flowing out of a deadly force incident is likely to be substantially diminished by their failure to know, understand and follow established law and departmental policy.

Accordingly, this section of the book is dedicated to educating law enforcement officers concerning the clearly established constitutional standards created by the United States Supreme Court in law enforcement use of deadly force situations. Moreover, this section of the book will identify related legal issues that will be present in most police use of force cases. It has been the observation of the author that government lawyers assigned to defend police officers against excessive force allegations often experience their own learning curve in mounting an aggressive defense on behalf of their clients. Officers accused of using excessive force must be in a position to assist their defense attorneys in crafting exceptional defense strategies that are designed to defeat such accusations. This book will prove valuable to defense attorneys and accused officers in preparing a well-reasoned and productive defense for those officers.

Chapter 1

The Constitutional Standard for the Use of Deadly Force

The first decision of the United States Supreme Court that addressed law enforcement use of deadly force is *Tennessee v. Garner*.[1] This decision involved the use of deadly force by police officers in the "fleeing felon" context. The particular facts of the *Garner* decision will be examined at length later on in this book. For now, the most important aspect of the *Garner* decision, that is, the Supreme Court's initial recitation of a constitutional standard for law enforcement use of deadly force, will be identified and examined. The Court set forth that standard as follows, "We conclude that such [deadly] force may not be used unless ... **the officer has probable cause to believe that the suspect poses a significant threat of death or serious physical injury to the officer or others.**"[2] Later in its opinion, the Court reiterated the constitutional standard by stating, "Where the officer has **probable cause to believe that the suspect poses a threat of serious physical harm, either to the officers or others, it is not constitutionally unreasonable ... [to use] deadly force.**"[3]

The Supreme Court made it clear in *Garner* that law enforcement officers must have **probable cause** to believe that their lives or the lives of other persons are threatened before using deadly force against an adversary. Probable cause is a legal term of art that means a "reasonable belief" on the part of a law enforcement officer based upon articulable facts and circumstances that are present in a particular case.[4]

---

[1] 471 U.S. 1 (1985).

[2] Is. at 3.

[3] Id. at 11.

[4] See, Wayne R. LaFave, "Search and Seizure, A Treatise on the Fourth Amendment," Second Edition, page 556. LaFave quotes from *United States v. Davis*, 458 F.2d 819 (D.C. Cir. 1972). "Probable cause exists when known facts and circumstances are sufficient to warrant a man of reasonable prudence in the belief that an offense has been or is being committed. *** A significantly lower quanta of proof is required to establish probable cause [for an arrest] than guilt [Conviction for a crime requires proof of guilt beyond a reasonable doubt]. *** [Probable Cause] is to be viewed from the vantage point of a prudent, reasonable, cautious police officer on the scene at the time ... guided by his experience and training."

Deadly Force and Constitutional Law

Following *Garner,* the Supreme Court further explicated the constitutional standard for police use of deadly force in its *Graham v. Connor* decision.[5] Graham involved allegations against police officers regarding the use of excessive force rather than deadly force. Nonetheless, the Court ruled that, "all claims that law enforcement officers have used excessive force—**deadly or not**—in the course of an arrest, investigatory stop, or other seizure of a free citizen should be analyzed under the **Fourth Amendment and its 'reasonableness' standard** rather than under a 'substantive due process' approach."[6] The Court rejected the "substantive due process" standard advocated by Officer Connor that would have required alleged victims of police brutality to prove **malice** on the part of offending officers.

By rejecting the "substantive due process" standard, the Court made it easier for alleged victims of police brutality to successfully sue police officers for alleged violations of constitutional rights. If the Court had adopted the "substantive due process" standard, the alleged victims of police use of excessive force would have been required to prove that the defendant officers had acted **with a malicious purpose and a sadistic intent for the very purpose of causing harm.**

This standard would have been very difficult for the alleged victims of police brutality to meet and overcome. Instead, the Court adopted the more lenient constitutional standard found in the Fourth Amendment[7], which the Court identified as its **"reasonableness"** standard. The Fourth Amendment "reasonableness" standard is more favorable to plaintiffs' lawyers and easier for them to meet because it requires no proof of malicious purpose or sadistic intent on the part of the defendant police officers in order to prevail.

---

[5] 490 U.S. 386 (1989).

[6] Id. at 395. The "substantive due process" legal theory rejected by the Supreme Court in *Graham* has its origins in the due process clause of the Fourteenth Amendment to the U.S. Constitution.

[7] The Fourth Amendment to the United States Constitution reads in pertinent part as follows: "The right of the people to be secure in their persons, houses, papers, and effects, against **unreasonable** searches and **seizures**, shall not be violated, and no warrants shall issue, but upon **probable cause,** supported by oath or affirmation, and particularly describing the place to be searched, and the persons or things to be seized."

Chapter 1

The Court's decision to choose the Fourth Amendment's "reasonableness" standard comes as no surprise and is entirely consistent with its earlier law enforcement use of the deadly force decision in *Tennessee v. Garner*[8] described earlier. In fact, the "reasonableness" standard found in *Graham* is simply another way of articulating the "probable cause" standard set forth by the Supreme Court in *Garner*.

The Court in *Graham* took great pains to explain the use of force "reasonableness" standard. First, the Court recognized that the right of law enforcement officers to make arrests and investigatory seizures "carries with it the right to use some degree of physical coercion or the threat thereof to affect it."[9] Second, the Court stated that the question of whether a police officer's use of force meets the Fourth Amendment "reasonableness" standard is to be determined by the facts and circumstances found in each particular case.

The Court explained that among the facts and circumstances to be considered by a reviewing court are the severity of the crime committed by the subject to be arrested; whether the subject posed an immediate threat to the safety of the officers or others; and whether the subject was actively resisting arrest or attempting to flee.[10] This kind of analysis is generally known as a "totality of circumstances" test.[11]

The Court explained further that the Fourth Amendment "reasonableness" standard "is an **objective** one: the question is whether the officers' actions are **'objectively reasonable'** in light of the facts and circumstances confronting them, without regard to their underlying intent or motivation."[12] Put another way, the Court is simply instructing the lower courts (judges and jurors) to focus on the actual facts and circumstances of each case in determining whether the officers acted within the boundaries of the law. The subjective state of mind of the defendant officers is deemed irrelevant. The Court's description of its "reasonable-

---

[8] 471 U.S. 1 (1985).

[9] 490 U.S. 386, 396.

[10] Id.

[11] See e.g., *Tennessee v. Garner*, 471 U.S. 1, 8-9 (1985).

[12] 490 U.S. 386,397 (emphasis added).

ness" standard as an "objective" standard has come to be known as the *Graham* **"Objective Reasonableness"** standard.

Summary of the Constitutional Standard

Through examining the Supreme Court's decisions in *Garner* and *Graham*, we reach the inescapable conclusion that the **"probable cause"** standard articulated by the Court in *Garner* for police use of deadly force and the **"objective reasonableness"** standard for police use of deadly force articulated by the Court in *Graham* are identical. They are in fact one and the same.

The constitutional standard for law enforcement use of deadly force in the United States simply put is as follows: **Law enforcement officers may use deadly force when they have "probable cause," that is, an "objectively reasonable belief," that a suspect poses a significant threat of death or serious bodily harm to the officer or others.**

Graham v. Connor — the "Objectively Reasonable" Officer

Despite the decision of the Court in *Graham* to jettison the "substantive due process" standard, which was more beneficial to law enforcement, the Court used language quite favorable to law enforcement to explain the newly created "Objective Reasonableness" standard. For example, the Court stated that "The reasonableness of a particular use of force must be judged from the perspective of a reasonable officer **on the scene, rather than with the 20/20 vision of hindsight.**"[13] Moreover, the Court explained that, "The calculus of reasonableness must embody allowance for the fact that police officers are often forced to make **split second judgments—in circumstances that are tense, uncertain, and rapidly evolving—about the amount of force that is necessary in a particular situation.**"[14]

Language of this nature makes clear that the Supreme Court understood the unique and potentially lethal challenges that officers face daily on the streets of America. The Court was not simply content with creating a new standard and leaving it to the

---

[13] Id. at 396 (emphasis added).

[14] Id. (emphasis added).

lower courts to analyze and interpret. Instead, the Court provided clear and unambiguous direction to the lower courts on how to understand and apply the deadly force standard. The Court directed the courts below to consider the facts and circumstances in each shooting incident from the perspective of the reasonable officer **on the scene of the event as it happened** and not from the secure confines of the courtroom or the judge's chambers.

The Court instructed future courts to strongly consider the fact that police officers face deadly adversaries in situations where instantaneous decision making is required; situations where time for careful planning is nonexistent; situations that evolve so rapidly that a moment of hesitation will result in death or serious bodily injury to officers and other innocent bystanders. The Court counseled future judges and jurors to place themselves in the very shoes of officers responding to dangerous adversarial confrontations without the benefit of the careful thought and analysis that is available to all of us once a deadly incident is over, that is, 20/20 hindsight. In fact, the Court made this approach abundantly clear when it said, "Not every push or shove, even if it may later seem unnecessary **in the peace of a judge's chambers,**"[15] is a violation of the Fourth Amendment. Because of the Court's erudite analysis, a case that was a loser for law enforcement ultimately became a winner. Make no mistake about it, countless law enforcement officers involved in shooting incidents have been saved from civil and criminal liability because of the Supreme Court's scholarly opinion in Graham.

Meaning and Importance of the Graham Decision

The Supreme Court's decision in *Graham* is the most favorable opinion for law enforcement officers in the history of American jurisprudence. No other case even comes close and its importance cannot be understated. The Court not only set forth in clear and unambiguous terms its Fourth Amendment "objective reasonableness" standard for governing alleged excessive use of force matters but also furnished clear instructions to future judges and jurors in how to apply that standard.

---

[15] Id. at 396 (emphasis added).

After *Graham,* future use of force cases, including those involving use of deadly force, must be examined and analyzed from the perspective of the "objectively reasonable" officer on the scene of the incident. Use of 20/20 hindsight is verboten. Judges and jurors are to consider the fact that deadly force incidents involve split-second decisions under highly volatile, dynamic, and deadly circumstances. Officers are not required to make perfect decisions in such pressure-filled, fast-moving, and dangerous situations. It will be sufficient if their conduct is found to be reasonable. This is all that the law requires.

The Fourth Amendment "Seizure" Requirement

The Supreme Court in *Tennessee v. Garner,*[16] ruled that apprehension of a suspect by means of deadly force is a "seizure" that is subject to the reasonableness requirement found in the Fourth Amendment to the United States Constitution. The Court in *Garner* made clear that for alleged victims of police use of excessive force to prevail, they must first establish that a Fourth Amendment "seizure" of their person was made by the defendant officers. Failure to do so will result in dismissal of the legal action. Once the plaintiffs in deadly force lawsuits establish that the Fourth Amendment "seizure" of their person occurred, they must prove that the conduct of the defendant police officers was not "objectively reasonable."

Following the Court's decision in *Garner,* other law enforcement cases arose that involved the issue of whether a law enforcement "seizure" of the alleged victim of a police shooting had occurred. Some of these cases involved police shooting innocent hostages during armed confrontations with suspects and others involved police shooting fleeing suspects who, though wounded, were not apprehended at the scene of the shooting and managed to escape. In each of these cases, the question of whether there was a "seizure" of the alleged shooting victim was critical to the outcome of the case. In order to understand the reasoning behind the outcome of these cases, other Supreme Court decisions that came after *Garner* must be reviewed and analyzed.

---

[16] 471 U. S. 1 (1985).

Chapter 1

Following *Garner*, the Supreme Court was once again confronted with the issue of whether and when a Fourth Amendment "seizure" of an individual occurred. The case, *Brower v. County of Inyo*,[17] involved a high-speed police pursuit of a stolen car suspect. At the conclusion of the twenty-mile pursuit, Brower was killed when he crashed the stolen vehicle into a police-ordered roadblock. The issue before the Court was whether the police-initiated roadblock amounted to a Fourth Amendment "seizure" of his person. The Court ruled in the affirmative and held that a seizure occurs when there is "a **governmental termination** of [a suspect's] freedom of movement through means **intentionally** applied."[18] Thus, in *Brower*, the Court established the two requirements for a seizure: government initiated **termination** of movement and governmental **intent** to seize the person stopped.[19]

A few years later, the Supreme Court ruled in *California v. Hodari D.*,[20] that no seizure of a drug suspect fleeing on foot occurred until police officers were able to tackle him. In *Hodari D.*, the Defendant argued that the **police chase** amounted to a governmental "show of authority" that constituted a Fourth Amendment "seizure" of his person. The Court framed the issue by stating, "The narrow question before us is whether, with respect to a show of authority as with respect to application of physical force, a seizure occurs even though the subject does not yield. **We hold that it does not.**"[21]

In *Hodari D.*, the Defendant discarded drugs before he was tackled by police. The Court ruled that the Fourth Amendment was implicated at the time he was physically restrained at the conclusion of the chase (not during the chase) and therefore his abandonment of the drugs prior to being tackled was not protected by the Fourth Amendment.

The bottom line rationale of *Hodari D.* is clear: a Fourth Amendment seizure can occur in two ways, an **intentional physical seizure** of the suspect that results in his capture or a

---

[17] 489 U. S. 593 (1989).

[18] Id. at 596 – 97 (emphasis added).

[19] See Wyman, 48 Am. Crim. L. Rev. 1485, 1488 (2011).

[20] 499 U. S. 621 (1991).

[21] Id. at 627 (emphasis added).

show of authority by police that results in submission (i.e., surrender) by the suspect. The Court concluded its opinion by stating, "In sum, assuming that [the officer's] pursuit ... constituted a 'show of authority' enjoining Hodari to halt, since Hodari did not comply ..., he was not seized until he was tackled."[22]

Summary of the Fourth Amendment "Seizure"

By combining the Court's rationale and holding in both *Brower* and *Hodari D.*, we are brought to the inescapable conclusion that a Fourth Amendment "seizure" of a person will occur when: (1) Law enforcement officers **specifically intend** to seize a particular person **and** (2) the person **acquiesces to a police "show of authority"** (i.e., surrenders) **or the police use physical force, including shooting the suspect, to bring him under physical control.**

The "Seizure" Issue—Shooting Innocent Hostages

Following the Supreme Court decisions in *Garner, Brower,* and *Hodari D.*, federal courts of appeals across America[23] began to decide officer involved shooting cases brought by innocent victims by focusing on whether the unintended victims (e.g., hostages) of police shootings were "seized" in violation of the

---

[22] Id. at 629.

[23] See, Wikipedia, "United States courts of appeals." There are 13 Federal Circuit Courts of Appeals strategically located across the United States. These Circuit Courts of Appeals are the intermediate appellate courts of the United States federal court system. A court of appeals decides appeals from the federal district courts (trial courts) located within the geographical area of each federal circuit. Twelve of the thirteen Federal Circuit Courts of Appeals have jurisdiction over appeals from a designated geographical area of the United States. For example, the First Circuit Court of Appeals is located in Boston, MA. and covers the states of Massachusetts, Maine, New Hampshire, Rhode Island and the Commonwealth of Puerto Rico. The Second Circuit Court of Appeals is located in New York City and covers the states of Connecticut, New York, and Vermont. The federal court of Appeals for the District of Columbia handles appeals from the federal district courts within the District of Columbia. All of the 50 states fall within the geographical jurisdiction of one of the federal circuit courts. The other federal circuit courts are located in Philadelphia, Penn. (Third Circuit); Richmond, Va. (Fourth Circuit); New Orleans, La. (Fifth Circuit); Cincinnati, Ohio (Sixth Circuit); Chicago, Ill. (Seventh Circuit); St. Louis, Mo. (Eighth Circuit); San Francisco, CA. (Ninth Circuit); Denver, Co. (Tenth Circuit); Atlanta, Ga. (Eleventh Circuit). The Thirteenth Circuit is also known as the United States Court of Appeals for the Federal Circuit which has nationwide appellate jurisdiction over certain appeals based on subject matter.

Chapter 1

Fourth Amendment. The absence of a "seizure" meant dismissal of the lawsuit because the Fourth Amendment requires a "seizure" before the question of whether the officers involved acted with "objective reasonableness" is examined. Simply put, if there is no seizure, there is no case.

On this point, *Childress v. City of Arapaho Oklahoma*,[24] is instructive. This case began with the escape of two inmates from the Oklahoma State Reformatory. After escaping, they stole a car, two shotguns and a pistol. They subsequently invaded a private home; kidnapped the owner and her two-year-old baby; and stole the family's minivan. Police officials put out a lookout for the stolen vehicle and a truck driver spotted it. He notified the police and the chase was on. During the chase, one escapee fired at a deputy but missed.

The escapees refused to surrender and proceeded with the owner and her child as hostages. The police set up ten roadblocks in an effort to apprehend them and rescue the hostages. At some of the roadblocks, officers shot at the tires and engine block of the minivan to stop it. At the second to last roadblock, an escapee held the baby outside the window of the minivan as the vehicle cleared the roadblock.

As the minivan reached the final roadblock, police officers fired 21 shots at the minivan as the suspect driver attempted to navigate through. The minivan was disabled and the escapees were arrested. However, the female hostage and her child were both shot and wounded by police bullets.

The wounded hostages sued the police officers who shot them in federal court pursuant to 42 U.S.C. § 1983[25] and alleged that they were unreasonably "seized" by police bullets in violation of their Fourth Amendment rights. The Federal District Court dismissed the lawsuit and the plaintiff hostages appealed. The Tenth Circuit Court of Appeals affirmed the decision of the lower court and ruled in favor of the defendant police officers.

The Court of Appeals held that a violation of the Fourth Amendment requires both a "seizure" of the plaintiffs by police

---

[24] 210 F.3d 1154, 1156-57 (10th Cir. 2000).

[25] This federal statute is the vehicle through which lawsuits are brought against police officers in federal court for alleged violations of constitutional rights, including Fourth Amendment claims of excessive force involving police use of deadly force.

officers and a finding of unreasonable or excessive force by the officers. The Court explained that a "seizure" pursuant to the Fourth Amendment requires "an **intentional** acquisition of physical control"[26] of the plaintiffs by police. The plaintiffs' argued that they were intentionally seized by police bullets because the officers deliberately fired at the minivan at the final roadblock with knowledge that the hostages were inside. The Court rejected this argument and stated that, "The police officers ... did not 'seize' plaintiffs within the meaning of the Fourth Amendment but made every effort to deliver them from unlawful abduction. The officers intended to restrain the minivan and the fugitives, not [the mother and baby]."[27] Because the court ruled that no "seizure" had occurred, it found it unnecessary to resolve the question of whether the use of force by the officers was "objectively reasonable."

In reaching its decision, the Tenth Circuit observed that several other federal courts of appeals had reached identical conclusions. For example, the court pointed to the First Circuit Court of Appeals decision in *Landol-Rivera v. Cosme*.[28] In *Landol* the police responded to an armed robbery of a fast food restaurant in Puerto Rico. During the robbery, the assailant took an employee hostage and attempted to escape in a vehicle. The police fired at the vehicle and shot the hostage in the process. The hostage subsequently filed suit against the police who shot him and alleged that he was the victim of a police use of excessive force in violation of the Fourth Amendment.

The First Circuit ruled in favor of the police and concluded that a police officer's deliberate decision to shoot at a car containing a robber and a hostage for the purpose of stopping the robber's flight does not result in the sort of willful detention [i.e., "seizure"] of the hostage that the Fourth Amendment was designed to govern. In effect, the court said the shooting was an unintentional consequence of lawful police action.

---

[26] 210 F.3d 1154, 1156 (quoting *Brower v. County of Inyo*, 489 U.S. 593, 596 (1989)).

[27] Id. at 1157.

[28] 906 F.2d 791 (1st Cir. 1990).

Chapter 1

The "Seizure" Issue—Suspects Who Escape After Being Shot

Several federal appellate courts have examined the Fourth Amendment "seizure" issue in the context of shooting incidents in which officers' shot and wounded a suspect who managed to escape and evade capture. In these cases, the suspects were captured sometime after the shooting and subsequently sued the officers who shot them. The question before the courts was whether the intentional shooting of these suspects by the police amounted to a Fourth Amendment "seizure" when they were able to escape from the scene and evade arrest until sometime after the shooting. The answer is critical to the outcome of these cases because, as mentioned earlier, the failure to establish a Fourth Amendment "seizure" by the alleged shooting victim will result in dismissal of the lawsuit and victory for the defendant law enforcement officers.

Research on this issue reveals a split/disagreement among the Federal Circuit Courts of Appeals that have directly considered this question. For example, the Federal Court of Appeals for the Tenth Circuit decided *Brooks v. Gaenzle*[29] and ruled that no "seizure" occurred when police officers deliberately shot a fleeing suspect in the back during his successful attempt to evade capture.

In this case, Brooks and Acevedo broke into a residential garage in El Paso County, Colorado. Police officers responded to a neighbor's call, entered the garage, and confronted Acevedo. Acevedo ran into the attached home, shut the door and blocked it with his body. As officers tried to break through the blocked door, someone inside fired a shot through the door that barely missed the officers' heads.

The officers retreated to the backyard and observed Brooks flee from the house and attempt to climb over a nearby fence. An officer yelled "stop" as Brooks began to climb the fence. Brooks ignored the officer and continued climbing. The officer shot at Brooks and hit him. Despite being shot, Brooks got over the fence and escaped. Brooks was apprehended three days later after a chase by police.

---

[29] 614 F.3d 1213 (10th Cir. 2010).

At the time of the original burglary attempt, the police focus on Brooks enabled Acevedo to escape from the scene. Thirteen days later, Acevedo was shot to death by police officers. In the shootout, Acevedo used the gun that was previously used to shoot at the officers who tried to arrest him at the scene of the original burglary.

Brooks later sued the officer who shot him at the scene of the burglary attempt for using excessive force in violation of his Fourth Amendment rights. A Federal District Court Judge dismissed the lawsuit and the Tenth Circuit Court of Appeals affirmed.

The Court of Appeals relied heavily on the Supreme Court's decision in *Brower v. County of Inyo*[30] in affirming dismissal of the suit. The court observed that in *Brower*, the Supreme Court ruled that a Fourth Amendment "seizure" of a person occurs, "only when there is a **governmental termination** of freedom of movement through means intentionally applied."[31] The court also noted that the *Brower* opinion states that a "violation of the Fourth Amendment requires an intentional acquisition [by the police] of **physical control**"[32] of the suspect.

The Court of Appeals agreed that the defendant officer intentionally shot Brooks in an attempt to stop him. However, Brooks continued to flee and elude authorities for several days. The court ruled that "[u]nder these circumstances, we cannot say authorities gained intentional acquisition of physical control over Mr. Brooks."[33] The court concluded that in the Tenth Circuit, a Fourth Amendment "seizure" of an alleged police shooting victim will only occur when police bullets result in the actual apprehension of the suspect at the time of the shooting. **Escape of the suspect after being intentionally shot by the police does not constitute a "seizure."**

In reaching its decision in *Brooks,* the Tenth Circuit dismissed certain language used by the Supreme Court in its *Hodari D.*[34]

---

[30] 489 U.S. 593 (1989).

[31] Id. at 596 – 97 (emphasis added).

[32] Id. at 596 (emphasis added).

[33] 614 F.3d 1213,1220.

[34] 499 U.S. 621 (1991).

Chapter 1

decision as nonessential Dicta.[35] The language labeled as Dicta in *Hodari D.* by the Tenth Circuit involved a statement by the Supreme Court that reads as follows: "[A]pplication of physical force [by the police] to restrain movement [of a suspect], even when it is **ultimately unsuccessful,** is a seizure."[36]

Perhaps the Tenth Circuit in *Brooks* so readily declared the above cited language from the Supreme Court's opinion in *Hodari D.* to be Dicta because it appears to be directly contradicted by another statement made by the Supreme Court in the same decision. In the latter statement, the Supreme Court said, "The narrow question before us is whether, with respect to a show of authority as with respect to application of physical force, **a seizure occurs even though the subject does not yield. We hold that it does not.**"[37]

As mentioned earlier, there is a difference of opinion between the federal circuits that have confronted the issue of whether a "seizure" occurs when a suspect is shot by police officers but evades capture and escapes from the location of the shooting. The Eleventh Circuit Court of Appeals decision in *Carr v. Tatangelo*,[38] is illustrative of the disagreement.

In *Carr,* Monroe, Georgia police officers hid in the woods during the early morning hours near Carr's residence in an effort to arrest him on outstanding warrants. Carr and some of his associates detected the police surveillance and approached the officers' location. Officer Fortson heard the sound of a bullet being chambered by Carr and saw him pointing a gun at Officer Tatangelo. Officer Fortson fired at Carr who was shot and wounded. Officer Tatangelo also fired at Carr but missed. Carr was not captured at that time. Instead, Carr ran away from the shooting scene and returned to the nearby house. He was subsequently captured inside the house and taken to the hospital.

---

[35] Dicta is language used by a court in a decision that is not essential to the court's holding in the particular matter. Dicta in a legal opinion is not considered binding legal precedent for future cases. Instead, it is viewed as editorial opinion on the part of the decision rendering court.

[36] *California v. Hodari D.*, 499 U. S. 621, 626 (1991) (emphasis added).

[37] Id. (emphasis added).

[38] 338 F.3d 1259 (11th Cir. 2003). See also, *Moore v. Indehar,* 514 F.3d 756 (8th Cir. 2008).

Carr later sued the officers pursuant to 42 U.S.C. § 1983 for alleged violation of his constitutional rights.

The Eleventh Circuit Court of Appeals ruled that a Fourth Amendment "seizure" of Carr took place at the time he was shot by police, even though he was not apprehended at the scene of the shooting. The court explained that an intentional seizure of a person occurs when police apply physical force to restrain movement, **even when the application of physical force is ultimately unsuccessful.** In reaching this conclusion, the court pointed to similar language found in the Supreme Court's *Hodari D.*[39] decision. The Eleventh Circuit obviously failed to agree with the Tenth Circuit's view in Brooks that such language was merely Dicta that was not essential to the Supreme Court's holding in *Hodari D.*

Once the Eleventh Circuit found that a "seizure" occurred, the court moved on to examine whether the defendant officers' actions were "objectively reasonable" as required by the Supreme Court in *Graham*.[40] The court observed that Officer Fortson did not fire until he saw Carr point what he believed to be a gun toward the woods in the direction of Officer Tatangelo. He also heard the sound of the racking of the slide on a semi-automatic pistol that he recognized as the chambering of a bullet into the barrel of that pistol.

The court observed that Officer Fortson acted in a split-second to a rapidly escalating situation involving perceived deadly force directed against a fellow officer. The court ruled that Officer Fortson acted in an "objectively reasonable" manner to save a fellow officer's life. Likewise, the court held that Officer Tatangelo's gunfire (all shots missed) directed at Carr was also objectively reasonable as well for the same reasons.

The United States Supreme Court had the opportunity to resolve this clear split between the Federal Courts of Appeals as described above but chose not to do so. Instead, the Court in the Tenth Circuit case denied Plaintiff Brooks' Petition for a Writ of

---

[39] 499 U. S. 621, 626 (1991).

[40] 490 U.S. 386 (1989).

Certiorari, which effectively ended the lawsuit.[41] Unless and until the Supreme Court decides to review this issue directly, there will be uncertainty in many federal appellate circuit courts concerning the question of whether a fleeing suspect, shot by police, who escapes capture after being shot, is "seized" at the time of the shooting for Fourth Amendment purposes. In the meantime, law enforcement officers involved in similar situations should bring the *Brooks* decision to the attention of their defense attorneys. Remember no "seizure" equals no case.

The "Totality of Circumstances" Test

As previously discussed, once an alleged victim of police use of excessive force has established that a "seizure" of his/her person pursuant to the Fourth Amendment has occurred, the focus of the case shifts to the question of whether the officers' actions were "objectively reasonable."[42] The determination of whether an officer's conduct in a particular matter was "objectively reasonable" must be made from a review of the **"totality of circumstances"** present in the matter at hand.[43]

The next issue for consideration by the reviewing courts is the question of the **scope** or parameters of the **"totality of circumstances" test**. In other words, what factors should reviewing courts take into consideration in deciding whether the involved officers' acted with "objective reasonableness"? Put another way, should the scope of the "totality of circumstances" test for determining the "objective reasonableness" of an officer's conduct be **narrow** [i.e., limited to the moment when deadly force was used] or **expansive** [i.e., covering the time leading up to as well as the moment when deadly force was used]?

The answer to the scope issue should have been easy for the federal circuit courts following the Supreme Court's decision in *Graham*. As mentioned earlier, the Court, in discussing the kind of factors to be considered in the "totality of circumstances" test,

---

[41] *Brooks v. Gaenzle*, 614 F.3d 1213 (10th Cir. 2010), cert. denied, 31 S. Ct. 1045 (2011). The denial of a petition for certiorari means that at least four Justices of the Supreme Court could not agree to consider the case. When that happens, the appellate court ruling stands.

[42] *Graham v. Connor*, 490 U.S. 386, at 397 (1989).

[43] Id. at 396. See also, *Tennessee v. Garner*, 471 U.S. 1, 8 – 9 (1985).

highlighted certain critical factors. These include the severity of the crime committed by the suspect; the immediacy of the threat of physical harm directed toward the police and others; and whether the suspect attempted to escape and/or resist arrest. All of these factors focus **on the moment of direct confrontation between the police and the suspect.**

Likewise, the Court in *Graham* declared that when lower courts examine police use of excessive force allegations, "[t]he 'reasonableness' of a particular use of force **must be judged** from the perspective of a reasonable officer **on the scene, rather than with the 20/20 vision of hindsight.**"[44] Further, the Court explained that, "[t]he calculus of reasonableness must embody allowance for the fact that police officers are often **forced to make split-second judgments—in circumstances that are tense, uncertain and rapidly evolving—about the amount of force that is necessary in a particular situation.**"[45] Finally, the Court unequivocally stated that, "[w]ith respect to a claim of excessive force, the same standard of reasonableness at the moment [of the use of force by police officers] applies."[46]

As shown by the quoted language, the Supreme Court in *Graham* provided clear and definitive direction to the lower federal appellate courts in deciding future police use of excessive force cases. The Court directed the lower courts to focus on the facts and circumstances confronting the law enforcement officer **at the moment** the decision to use deadly force was made. The Court's use of phrases such as **"on the scene," "20/20 vision of hindsight," "split second judgments," "tense, uncertain, and rapidly evolving,"** and **"at the moment"** could not be more clear in directing lower courts to adopt a **narrow view** of the facts and circumstances that should be included in the "totality of circumstances" analysis.

This guidance and direction was designed by the Supreme Court to preclude endless judicial second-guessing (i.e., 20/20 hindsight) of an officer's actions and decisions that lead up to but are separated from the moment when deadly force was used. It is

---

[44] 490 U.S. 386, 396 (1989) (emphasis added).

[45] Id. (emphasis added).

[46] Id. (emphasis added).

Chapter 1

clear that the Court intended to prevent future lower courts from including in the "totality of circumstances" test the litany of things officers might have done in the hours/ minutes leading up to a deadly confrontation but for whatever reason did not do or even think to do.

Once a deadly confrontation is over, it is easy to imagine how it could have been handled better or even prevented. The concept of "20/20 hindsight" has its genesis in such imaginative thinking. Plaintiffs' lawyers will normally hire a "police expert" to explain how the defendant officer could have done something differently to keep the matter from escalating to the point where deadly force was necessary.

The "expert" will often testify that the defendant officer placed himself in harm's way [i.e., created the situation wherein deadly force became necessary]; or that he should have backed off and called for a Special Weapons and Tactics Team (SWAT); or a mental health expert; or a Supervisor or a police negotiator; or that he should have used less aggressive means to control the situation. When we analyze this line of Monday morning quarterbacking, one can only wonder if the so-called "experts" believe that the best course of action for the police is to leave the scene and return another day.

Thankfully, law enforcement officers courageously respond to confront those situations that we are not capable of handling. They take their oath to protect and serve seriously and walk into danger while the general public is running away. The people who seek monetary damages from the courts in the aftermath of an officer involved shooting are often the intended targets of violence about to be foisted upon them by the individual thwarted only by police intervention. It is ironic that the very persons rescued by police intervention turn on those same officers once their own safety is assured.

In these cases, Plaintiffs' attorneys are determined to move the spotlight away from their clients' own reprehensible conduct **at the moment** when a deadly confrontation was unfolding. Their immediate goal is to shift the blame to officers for creating or exacerbating the situation.

The reason for this is simple to comprehend; in the vast majority of cases, their clients' conduct embraces the horrific.

These so-called victims of police brutality are unmasked when the spotlight is focused squarely on their conduct. The spotlight reveals individuals determined to kill and main the very people we rely on to protect us. When the spotlight shines upon these "victims," they are seen to have picked up a firearm, a knife, a hatchet or a club with a purpose of severely injuring or killing officers or other innocent persons.

The Supreme Court in *Graham* instructed future lower courts to avoid the kind second guessing engaged in by plaintiffs' lawyers and their "expert" witnesses. Nonetheless, several federal circuit courts have failed to follow the Court's direction. This refusal to follow the Supreme Court's instruction has resulted in a split/disagreement among several federal circuit courts regarding the scope of the "totality of circumstances" test to determine whether police officers acted with "objective reasonableness" in deadly force cases.

Federal Circuits Split on Scope of "Totality of Circumstances" Test

Many federal circuit courts have closely adhered to the Supreme Court's directive to consider only those facts and circumstances that are directly related **to the moment** when the defendant officer decided to use deadly force.[47] These courts believe that the scope of the "totality of circumstances" test should be narrowly construed and applied. Others have inexplicably eschewed the Supreme Court's instruction and taken a broad and expansive view of the "totality of circumstances" test.[48]

---

[47] *Salim v. Proulx*, 93 F.3d 86 (2d Cir. 1996); *Waterman v. Batton*, 393 F.3d 471 (4th Cir. 2005); *Rockwell v. Brown*, 664 F.3d 985 (5th Cir. 2011); *Livermore v. Ellsworth*, 476 F.3d 397 (6th Cir. 2007); *Marion v. City of Corydon*, 559 F. 3d 700 (7th Cir. 2009); *Schulz v. Long*, 44 F.3d 643 (8th Cir. 1995); *Jean Baptiste v. Gutierrez*, 627 F.3d 816 (11th Cir. 2010).

[48] *Young v. City of Providence Napolitano*, 404 F.3d 4 (1st Cir. 2005) (Officers' actions need not be examined solely at the moment of the shooting. Actions of officers leading up to the shooting should also be reviewed.); *Abraham v. Raso*, 183 F.3d 279 (3d Cir. 1999); *Rivas v. City of Passaic*, 365 F.3d 181, 198 (3d Cir. 2004) (some courts consider only facts and circumstances at the precise moment that excessive force was used by the police. Others consider all relevant facts and circumstances leading up to the alleged use of excessive force); *Billington v. Smith*, 292 F.3d 1177,1190-1191 (9th Cir. 2002); *Espinosa v. City of San Francisco*, 598 F.3d 528, 547 – 549 (9th Cir. 2010); *Glenn v. Washington County*, 661 F.3d 460 (9th Cir. 2011) (prior police intentional or reckless misconduct that results in an independent Fourth Amendment violation may render

Chapter 1

A case that clearly illustrates the position of those federal circuit courts that follow the **narrow** approach to the scope of the "totality of circumstances" test is the Seventh Circuit's opinion in *Plakas v. Drinski.*[49] Plakas was involved in a motor vehicle accident and was suspected of driving under the influence (DUI). He was in the process of being voluntarily transported to the police station for DUI testing. During the ride, Plakas jumped out of the rear of the police vehicle at about 10 p.m. and ran through nearby woods into a residential neighborhood. He went directly to the home of a friend and was allowed to enter. Police officers tracked him to the home and the owner permitted them to enter. Upon entry, the officers observed Plakas pick up a fireplace poker. He became loud, combative and charged at the nearest officer. Plakas took a full swing at the officer with the poker and hit him on the wrist.

Plakas ran outside and into the nearby woods. Three officers followed him into the woods and caught up to him in a nearby clearing. The officers stood about ten feet from Plakas. Officer Drinski attempted to convince Plakas to surrender for between 15 and 30 minutes but to no avail. Plakas pointed the poker at Drinski and said, "Either you're going to die here or I'm going to die here. Go ahead and shoot, my life isn't worth anything."[50] Plakas then raised the poker over his head and charged at Officer Drinski. Drinski retreated but Plakas aggressively pursued. When Plakas had almost reached Drinski, he fired once, hitting Plakas in the chest. Plakas died and his wife sued Drinski pursuant to 42 U.S.C. §1983 (the federal civil rights statute). The

---

an officer's otherwise reasonable use of force unreasonable as a matter of law); *Sheehan v. City & County of San Francisco*, 743 F.3d 1211 (9th Cir. 2014) (police officers shot and seriously wounded woman who advanced on them with a knife after the officers forced entry into her room. In ruling for the victim of the shooting, the court observed, "The shooting was lawful when viewed from the moment of the shooting because at that point Sheehan presented an immediate danger to the officers' safety. [H]owever, officers may be held liable for otherwise lawful defensive use of force when they intentionally or recklessly provoke a violent confrontation by actions that rise to the level of an independent Fourth Amendment violation."); *Medina v. Cram*, 252 F.3d 1124, 1132 (10th Cir. 2001); *Thomas v. Durastanti*, 607 F.3d 655, 667 (10th Cir. 2010) (prior police reckless or deliberate conduct leading up to a shooting that creates the need for the shooting can be considered in deciding whether the shooting was reasonable).

[49] 19 F.3d 1143 (7th Cir. 1994).

[50] Id. at 1146.

Federal District Court dismissed the lawsuit and the plaintiff filed an appeal with the Seventh Circuit Court of Appeals.

The Seventh Circuit affirmed the judgment of the lower court and ruled in favor of the defendant police officer. The plaintiff's lawyer claimed that Drinski should not have shot Plakas because he had other alternatives to the use of his firearm. For example, he argued that Drinski could have elected to keep some sort of barrier between himself and Plakas (e.g., hedges or bushes); or he could have used a disabling spray (e.g., mace or CS gas); or bring a police attack dog to the scene. (Arguments of this nature involve the kind of second guessing that the Supreme Court in Graham instructed future federal appellate courts to avoid.)

The court ruled that the Fourth Amendment "does not require officers to use the least intrusive or even less intrusive alternatives ... **The only test is whether what the police officers actually did was reasonable.**"[51] The court explained, "As Plakas moved toward Drinski, was he supposed to think of an attack dog, of ... CS gas, of how fast he could run backwards? Our answer is ... no, because there is too little time for the officer to do so and too much opportunity to **second guess** that officer."[52]

The court explained that it did not intend to evaluate the conduct of the officer by examining segments of the event that occurred prior to the time deadly force became necessary. The court stated: "All of this means Drinski was properly standing in a clearing, gun in hand, several feet away from Plakas, **who charged him with a poker raised. It is from that point on we judge the reasonableness of the use of deadly force in light of all the officer knew. We do not return to the prior segments of the event and, in light of hindsight, reconsider whether prior police decisions were correct.**"[53]

The court concluded by stating, "Reconsideration will nearly always reveal that something different could have been done if the officer knew the future before it occurred. This is what we mean when we say we refuse to second guess the officer."[54]

---

[51] Id. at 1149.

[52] Id.

[53] Id. at 1150.

[54] Id.

Chapter 1

We can see from the court's opinion in *Plakas* that the Seventh Circuit is among the many federal circuit courts of appeals that adhere to the Supreme Court's admonition in *Graham* that they focus on the circumstances of the use of deadly force by law enforcement that existed "at the moment" deadly force was actually used.

A much more recent opinion from the Fifth Circuit Court of Appeals is also instructive. The case, *Rockwell v. Brown*,[55] involved a 911 call from the parents of Scott Rockwell to the Garland, Texas Police Department. The police were informed that Rockwell was suffering from schizophrenia and bipolar disorder; had been diagnosed as suicidal; had previously attempted suicide more than once; had refused his medication and declined to see his doctor; was hearing voices and may be taking illegal drugs; refused to come out of his room, was hitting the walls and cursing through the door.

The Garland Police had previously responded to this residence and arrested Rockwell for threatening and assaulting his parents. Several officers responded to the call and attempted to communicate with Rockwell through his bedroom door. Rockwell refused to come out, banged on the walls and threatened the officers. The police decided that they had to arrest Rockwell and could not leave without him because he represented a threat to himself and his parents.

The police forcibly breached the bedroom door. Rockwell rushed toward Lieutenant Brown while holding two eight-inch serrated knives. Lt. Brown fired multiple rounds at Rockwell from a pepper ball gun.[56] This failed to stop Rockwell and his momentum pushed Lt. Brown backwards into the nearby bathroom with such force that it broke the toilet.

Rockwell turned toward a second officer, swung his knives at him and cut him in the process. Other officers fired six or seven rounds from their firearms at Rockwell. Rockwell was hit four times and one of the rounds hit an officer. Rockwell died at the scene and his parents subsequently sued the officers for using excessive force.

---

[55] 664 F.3d 985 (5th Cir. 2011), cert. denied 132 S. Ct. 2433 (2012).

[56] A pepper ball gun is a less lethal weapon that may be used by police officers to bring potentially violent and noncompliant persons under control.

Deadly Force and Constitutional Law

The Federal District Court dismissed the lawsuit and the parents appealed. The United States Court of Appeals for the Fifth Circuit affirmed the judgment of the lower court in favor of the defendant police officers. In so doing, the court rejected the parents' argument that the decision of the police to force entry into their son's room created the dangerous situation that followed and was the proximate cause of their son's death. The court refused to consider the prior decision of the police to force entry to Rockwell's bedroom, deeming it to be irrelevant to the scope of the use of force inquiry.

The court stated that "[t]he excessive force inquiry is confined to whether the officer was in danger **at the moment** of the threat that resulted in the officer's use of deadly force. Regardless of what transpired up until the shooting itself, the suspect's movements gave the officer reason to believe, **at that moment,** that there was a threat of physical harm."[57] The court ruled that "[u]nder **the totality of the circumstances,** then, it was reasonable for the officers to believe that Scott posed a significant and imminent threat of serious physical harm to one or more officers."[58]

As previously mentioned, not all of the federal circuit courts of appeals adhere to the Supreme Court's admonition that they should take a narrow view of the circumstances surrounding a police use of force and confine them to the **moment when deadly force became necessary.** This refusal to accept the clear guidance offered by the Supreme Court in *Graham* has resulted in some troubling and frankly bizarre decisions directed against police officers who were exposing themselves to significant danger when deadly force was used.

For example, the First Circuit Court of Appeals decided *Young v. City of Providence Napolitano.*[59] In *Young,* two Providence,

---

[57] 664 F.3d 985, 991. See also, *Harris v. Serpas* (No.13-30337) (5th Cir. 3/12/14). Suspect raised knife over his head and threatened officers before being shot and killed. Prior to shooting, the officers aroused suspect from a sound sleep and attempted to control him unsuccessfully with tasers. Court ruled that officers' conduct leading up to the shooting was irrelevant. Court held that excessive force inquiry was limited to the danger that officers confronted at the moment the shooting took place. Officers' actions did not violate the Fourth Amendment.

[58] Id. at 992.

[59] 404 F.3d 4 (1st Cir. 2005).

Chapter 1

Rhode Island police officers in uniform responded to a "females fighting" call at a local restaurant during the early morning hours of January 28, 2000. Officer Solitro was an eight-day rookie on the force and Officer Saraiva was on the job for three years at the time of the incident. Upon arrival at the restaurant, the officers observed a man (Diaz) running toward a Camaro parked in the restaurant parking lot. Diaz entered the Camaro and the officers pulled their marked cruiser up to about eight to twelve feet from the Camaro. The officers observed Diaz point a gun out the window of the Camaro. Both officers exited their cruiser; Saraiva took cover behind some nearby poles and Solitro knelt behind the front wheel and engine block of the cruiser. They ordered Diaz to drop the gun and get out of the Camaro. Diaz dropped the gun and began to exit the Camaro. Officer Solitro left his position of cover and walked into the open directly in front of the Camaro.

Meanwhile, Cornel Young, an off-duty Providence Police Officer, was a customer inside the restaurant. He was dressed in plain clothes. As the marked unit arrived outside, Young ran through the inside of the restaurant and identified himself verbally as a police officer. Young ran through the doors of the restaurant to the outside shortly after the uniformed officers arrived. He was heard by customers to yell "police" and "freeze." Young was apparently following the Providence Police policy of "always armed/always on-duty." At the time Young went outside the restaurant, he was holding his firearm in both hands.

Both uniformed officers testified that they yelled simultaneously for Young to drop his gun more than once. Young did not drop the weapon. Both officers fired their weapons at Young multiple times, killing him.

This case went to trial before a Federal District Court jury. During trial, Dr. James Fyfe,[60] an "expert" on police tactics, testified on behalf of the plaintiff (Young's mother). Fyfe testified that in his opinion, Officer Solitro's abandonment of his position of cover, that is, kneeling behind the engine block of the police cruiser, was a move contrary to accepted police tactics because it substantially raised the likelihood that the officer would be shot

---

[60] Fyfe was the Deputy Commissioner of Training for the New York City Police Department and an authority on police tactics and training with a Doctorate in Criminal Justice from State University of New York at Albany.

Deadly Force and Constitutional Law

or need to shoot others. In other words, the officer's own conduct, in effect, created the subsequent need to protect himself and his partner from harm. At the conclusion of the trial, the jury returned a verdict against Officer Solitro, finding that he shot Officer Young in violation of his Fourth Amendment rights.[61]

On appeal to the First Circuit Court of Appeals, the City and the police supervisors challenged the jury finding that Officer Solitro violated Young's constitutional rights. In particular, the defendants argued that the trial judge erred in permitting Fyfe to testify that Officer Solitro's decision to leave a position of cover and step into the open was a violation of police tactics that made a shooting incident substantially more likely.

The First Circuit rejected this argument, affirmed the jury verdict, and observed, "The rule in this circuit is that once it is clear that a seizure occurred, the court should examine the actions of the government officials **leading up to the seizure. Thus, police officers' actions for our purposes need not be examined solely at the 'moment of the shooting.'**"[62] The court explained that "[t]his rule is most consistent with the Supreme Court's mandate that we consider these cases in the 'totality of the circumstances.'"[63]

The court stated that in addition to Officer Solitro abandoning cover, there was evidence that Young identified himself as a police officer, held his weapon in the same way an officer would hold it and was immediately recognized by bystanders as an off-duty police officer. The court concluded, "We think ... that an objectively reasonable officer would have recognized [Young] as an officer, and thus would have recognized that he was not a threat and would not have shot him."[64]

---

[61] Before trial commenced, by agreement of the parties, Officer Solitro and Officer Saraiva were dropped as actual defendants. However, it was stipulated that if the jury found that either or both were guilty of violating Young's constitutional rights, then a second proceeding would follow to determine whether the City of Providence and the Officers' supervisors had also violated Young's constitutional rights. It is established law that there can be no violation of constitutional rights by a City and police supervisory officials, in the absence of a violation of constitutional rights by officers on the scene of an incident. See, *Young v. City of Providence*, 404 F.3d 4 (1st Cir. 2005).

[62] 404 F.3d 4, 22.

[63] Id.

[64] Id. at 23.

Chapter 1

The First Circuit's decision in *Young* is a prime example of why the Supreme Court in *Graham* attempted to limit the scope of the "totality of circumstances" test to facts immediately connected to the shooting of suspects by police officers. The Young shooting was a tragic accident, no more and no less. Cornel Young was doing his duty as an off-duty police officer. Officers' Solitro and Saraiva were likewise doing their duty. The shooting of Young was the result of "friendly fire." None of the officers present that night intended the horrific events that arose from their accidental convergence. The court's ruling forever labels Officer Solitro as one who unconstitutionally (i.e., deliberately) took the life of a fellow officer. Officer Solitro not only has to live with the fact that he shot a fellow officer to death but also that he acted unconstitutionally in the process.

The region's highest court's decision is unconscionable in this regard. The court's "stretch" to consider such things as Solitro's movement from one place to another during an attempt to disarm a dangerous felon with a gun; the manner in which Young held his weapon (i.e., pointed upright and directly forward as police officers are trained to do vs. sideways and forward like street criminals sometimes do) as though the uniformed officers would certainly focus on this in the dark with the barrel of the gun pointing in their direction; the testimony of bystanders (who said they thought Young was a police officer) who were not confronted with a drawn gun; and the fact that Young yelled "police" after leaving the restaurant is beyond ludicrous.

After all, the uniformed officers responded late at night to a disturbance call and upon arrival observed a man run, enter a parked car, draw a firearm and point it out the window of the car. This was a dynamic, fast moving, highly volatile, and dangerous situation. The officers were completely focused on disarming this bad actor without getting shot in the process.

They quickly exited their vehicle, took cover and attempted to bring the dangerous situation under control. While focused on the man with a gun, suddenly without warning, a second man in plain clothes appeared holding a firearm in both hands pointed in their direction. This shocking unforeseen development took the uniformed officers by complete surprise. The uniformed officers reacted to the threat by instructing him to drop the gun but he did not do so. Confronted by a man with a gun pointed at them, the officers both fired. The fact that Young yelled "police" could easily have gone unheard in the **"tense, uncertain and rapidly evolving circumstances"**[65] that confronted the uniformed officers at that moment.

This was the moment that the First Circuit should have focused on. This was the time when the **"objective reasonableness"** of the officers' conduct should have been scrutinized. The First Circuit turned an unavoidable tragedy into an unconstitutional action by doing precisely what the Supreme Court counseled against. Through 20/20 hindsight, the court adopted the testimony of a paid police "expert" and second guessed the officers present at the scene who were risking their lives in the public interest.

This inappropriate result follows the deliberate decision of the First Circuit to reject the Supreme Court's instruction in *Graham v. Connor*. To pave the way for Officer Young's mother to have a case against the City of Providence and police supervisory officials, the court sacrificed Officer Solitro's reputation in the process.[66] Put more bluntly, in the court's view, the end justified the means.

The unfair result in *Young* is highlighted by a recent study reported by Chuck Remsburg, Editor in Chief, Force Science Institute Ltd, in October 2012. Remsburg reported that the Kansas City Missouri Police Department (KCPD) conducted a training study in an effort to determine the likelihood of uniformed police officers shooting undercover officers during a police operation. Over 900 uniformed officers participated in the study.

Prior to the exercise, the participating officers were informed that they were to assist undercover and plain clothes officers in an arrest situation. The training set up included turning targets containing life sized images of armed and unarmed felons. The targets also included an image of an undercover plain clothes police officer who was armed and holding a firearm. The image of

---

[65] Language used by the United States Supreme Court in *Graham v. Connor*.

[66] Officer Young's mother's case against the City and police supervisory officials hinged upon a finding of unconstitutional conduct on the part of at least one of the officers present at the shooting scene.

Chapter 1

the undercover officer also had a silver KCPD badge displayed either on the belt or on a chain located at chest level around the neck of the officer. One half of the officers went through the training in a reduced light situation.

One finding of the study was that 65% of the 920 participating officers fired at the target of the plain clothes, badge displaying officer from a distance of 24 feet. This means that approximately 600 officers fired at their plain clothes counterpart, notwithstanding the fact that they were told that they were there to assist an undercover officer in making an arrest and the undercover officer was prominently displaying a badge.

Not surprising was the fact that six times more uniformed officers fired at the undercover officer target when the police badge was on the target's belt vs. on the chain at chest level. In fact, in full light conditions, the belt badge target contained 1272 hits and the chest level badge target had 196 hits. When the lighting was reduced, the belt level badge target had 5288 hits and the chest level target had 843 hits. Obviously from a training standpoint, plain clothes officers should be instructed to prominently display their badges in the most visible of positions to reduce the probability of an accidental "blue on blue" shooting.

The First Circuit's decision in *Young* was incorrect and misguided. Instead of recognizing the impossible situation in which the uniformed Providence officers found themselves, the court weaved together a set of opinions offered by a so-called "expert" and uninvolved bystanders in order to obtain their desired result. This is what can happen when courts deviate from the clear direction offered by the Supreme Court.

Chapter 2

IMPACT OF GRAHAM AND GARNER DECISIONS ON THE FEDERAL CIRCUIT COURTS

A review of federal appellate decisions pertaining to officer involved shootings in the aftermath of the Supreme Court's decisions in *Graham v. Connor* and *Tennessee v. Garner* reveals that in federal circuit after federal circuit, decisions very favorable to law enforcement officers were issued. In fact, notwithstanding the various disagreements on certain issues between some federal appellate courts described in earlier sections of this book, there are countless opinions issued in almost all of the federal circuit courts of America that are highly positive from a law enforcement perspective. The impact of *Graham* and *Garner* on the vast majority of these legal opinions from coast to coast in the United States cannot be understated.

This section of the book is devoted to an examination of some of these law enforcement opinions in all of the federal circuit courts that have relied on *Graham* and *Garner* to guide them. After reading summaries of the majority of these opinions, law enforcement officers across America should feel secure and confident that if they act with reasonable prudence in a deadly force confrontation, they will prevail in the litigation likely to follow. The case summaries that follow will begin with the First Circuit Court of Appeals in Boston, Massachusetts. and conclude with the Eleventh Circuit Court of Appeals in Atlanta, Georgia. Cases from the vast majority of the federal circuits across the United States are included.[1]

The First Circuit (Boston, MA)[2] —
Bennett v. Wainwright[3]

On January 21, 2000, Oxford County, Maine Deputies and Maine State Police (MSP) Officers were called to a residence in

---

[1] For information concerning the location of each of the federal circuit courts of appeals, See, Supra, note 23.

[2] The First Circuit Court of Appeals covers the States of Massachusetts, Rhode Island, Maine, New Hampshire, and the Commonwealth of Puerto Rico.

[3] 548 F.3d 155 (1st Cir. 2008).

Chapter 2

Sumner, Maine at approximately 2:00 p.m. Their response was predicated upon a 911 call from a relative of Daniel Bennett who informed the Oxford County Sheriff's Department (OCSD) that Bennett had threatened to kill her; had killed a dog with a baseball bat; had stopped taking necessary medication; and that there were firearms in the residence where he was located. Upon arrival, a Deputy was informed that the residence contained a rifle and a shotgun. Responding officers evacuated all other persons from the residence and three officers entered the kitchen and took up defensive positions while waiting for the arrival of a SWAT team. Bennett was believed to be located in a back room in the house.

While the SWAT team was assembling outside, Bennett twice entered the living room of the residence. During one of these forays, an officer pointed a rifle at him and ordered him to put his hands up. Bennett raised his hands but retreated to the back room. Shortly thereafter, Bennett entered the living room again and aimed a single-shot, breach-loader shotgun at an officer. The officer yelled, "Danny, drop the gun, drop the gun." Bennett fired the shotgun at the officer but missed. The officer fired 5 rounds from his AR-15 semi-automatic assault rifle at Bennett causing non-deadly wounds. A second officer fired 13 rounds from his .40 caliber pistol at Bennett but all of these shots missed. This officer then entered the living room and fired 2 or 3 more shots at Bennett who had fallen behind a sofa. One of these shots hit Bennett in the head and a second entered his chest. Bennett was killed by these shots.

Bennett's Estate sued the involved officers pursuant to 42 U.S.C. § 1983 for alleged use of excessive force in violation of the Fourth Amendment. The Federal District Court dismissed the suit and the Estate appealed. The First Circuit affirmed the dismissal of the suit by the lower court and observed that "the use of deadly force is not excessive if an **objectively reasonable officer** in the same circumstances would have believed that an individual **'posed a threat of serious physical harm either to the officer or others.'"** [4]

---

[4] Id. at 175.

Impact of Graham and Garner Decisions

The court additionally observed that "[w]e must remember that the reasonableness of an officer's use of force must be judged from the perspective of a reasonable officer on the scene, rather than with the 20/20 vision of hindsight."[5] The quoted language comes from the Supreme Court's opinions in *Garner* and *Graham* and demonstrates beyond doubt that the First Circuit is carefully following these opinions in deciding the outcome of this case.

The First Circuit concluded its opinion by stating, "reasonable officers ... faced with an armed mentally ill man, who had already shot at them once, could reasonably believe that they were faced with imminent and grave physical harm that justified resort to deadly force. The fact that officers ... fired multiple shots at Bennett, and might even have reloaded their weapons, does not change our assessment."[6]

Additionally, the court found it within reasonable bounds that one officer fired 2 or 3 additional rounds at Bennett after he fell to the ground behind a sofa in the living room of the residence. The court observed, "in the context of this tense and dangerous situation, [the officer] could have reasonably believed that Bennett posed a continuing threat, and that his own safety and the safety of the other officers required him to keep firing."[7]

The Second Circuit (New York, NY)[8] — *Salim v. Proulx*[9]

East Hartford, Connecticut Police Officer Proulx, dressed in plain clothes, attempted to locate and arrest Reyes, a 14-year-old juvenile, who had recently escaped from a juvenile detention center. Reyes had twice before eluded capture by East Hartford officers after his initial escape. Officer Proulx was armed only

---

[5] Id.

[6] Id.

[7] Id. at 176. The First Circuit has decided multiple officer involved shooting cases that are favorable to law enforcement. Included among them are *Berube v. Conley*, 506 F.3d 79 (1st Cir. 2007); *Napier v. Windham*, 187 F.3d 177 (1st Cir. 1999); *Hegarty v. Somerset County*, 53 F.3d 1367 (1st Cir. 1995); *St. Hilaire v. City of Laconia*, 71 F.3d 20 (1st Cir. 1995); and *Roy v. Inhabitants of the City of Lewiston*, 42 F.3d 691 (1st Cir. 1994).

[8] The Second Circuit Court of Appeals covers the States of New York, Connecticut, and Vermont.

[9] 93 F.3d 86 (2d Cir. 1996).

Chapter 2

with a .22 caliber pistol that he kept in his pocket. He had no handcuffs or any other disabling devices.

Proulx located Reyes near his home and a foot chase ensued. Reyes threw a rock at Proulx, which hit him in the arm and bounced off his forehead. During the chase, Proulx fired a warning shot because he believed that Reyes was armed with a knife. In fact, Reyes was unarmed. Proulx caught Reyes, and they both fell to the ground in a struggle. Proulx pinned Reyes to the ground and suddenly a group of six children between the ages of 8 and 12 arrived on the scene. The children proceeded to attack Proulx, hitting and kicking him, in an attempt to free Reyes.

One child beat Proulx with a stick and others attempted to remove his gun from his pocket. Somehow, Proulx's gun was removed from his pocket and ended up in Reyes' hand. Reyes held the gun by the barrel and Proulx grabbed the handle and pulled the trigger. The gun fired and the bullet killed Reyes.

Reyes' mother subsequently sued Proulx pursuant to the federal civil rights statute and alleged that Officer Proulx used excessive force in violation of the Fourth Amendment. The Federal District Court refused to dismiss the lawsuit and Proulx filed an appeal with the Second Circuit Court of Appeals.

The Second Circuit reversed and decided the case in favor of Officer Proulx. The court ruled that when Officer Proulx used deadly force against Reyes, it was objectively reasonable for the officer to view the use of deadly force as not excessive in the circumstances presented to him. The court observed that the "Supreme Court has made it clear that an officer's actions are not to be assessed with **20/20 hindsight**. Rather [police are protected] from liability and suit when they are required to make **on the spot judgments in tense circumstances**."[10]

The court stated that the threat against the officer in this case was **immediate** and he acted in self-defense. The court opined that the officer acted instinctively in reaction to seeing the barrel of his weapon in Reyes' hand while the two were locked in a physical struggle.

The court rejected as irrelevant the Plaintiff's claim that Proulx created the need to use deadly force through his own

---

[10] Id. at 91.

Impact of Graham and Garner Decisions

failures, e.g. the failure to carry a police radio; the failure to call for back-up; the failure to retreat when Reyes' friends began to attack him. The court explained that, "[t]he reasonableness inquiry depends only upon the officer's knowledge of circumstances immediately prior to and **at the moment** that he made the **split-second decision** to employ deadly force."[11]

The highlighted language comes directly from the Supreme Court's decision in *Graham*. As mentioned earlier in this section, the impact of *Graham* on these deadly force cases is significant and in most cases forecasts an outcome favorable to the defendant law enforcement officers.

The Third Circuit (Philadelphia, PA)[12]—
Lamont Estate of Quick v. New Jersey[13]

New Jersey State Troopers responded to a wooded area adjacent to an Interstate Highway to provide assistance to local police officers who had been involved in a pursuit of a stolen car suspect. The suspect had abandoned the stolen car and fled into the nearby woods. The Troopers entered the woods shortly after 10 p.m. on July 21, 2003. The troopers needed flashlights to see where they were going. One of the Troopers stumbled upon the suspect who was hiding under some brush. The Trooper ordered him to surrender but he ran away.

Two Troopers pursued him and caught up to him when he got tangled up in a thicket. The suspect turned and faced the Troopers who drew their pistols. Three additional Troopers arrived at that time to assist. Two of the officers told the suspect to freeze and show his hands. The suspect was standing at an angle from the officers who were between five and eight feet away. The suspect's right hand was tucked into his waist band and appeared to be clutching an object. Suddenly, without warning, the suspect pulled his hand from his waistband quickly as though he were drawing a pistol. Three of the officers fired their guns and one of

---

[11] Id. at 92.

[12] The Third Circuit Court of Appeals covers the States of Pennsylvania, Delaware, New Jersey, and the U.S. Virgin Islands.

[13] 637 F.3d 177 (2011).

Chapter 2

the officer's flashlights was hit by a ricochet bullet and he fell to the ground.

According to the court's opinion, the Troopers' fired continuously at the suspect for roughly ten seconds. They fired a total of 39 shots in his direction. Eighteen bullets hit the suspect. During the shooting, the suspect turned away from the officers and eleven rounds entered his body from behind. Two of the rounds that hit the suspect were identified by the Medical Examiner as likely fatal. The two fatal rounds entered his chest from the front. The suspect finally fell to the ground and landed on his stomach, facing away from the Troopers. The suspect, later identified as Eric Quick, did not have a gun in his hand but held a crack pipe instead. Two of the Troopers fired 14 rounds and a third fired 11 rounds.

Quick's estate sued the Troopers for allegedly using excessive force in violation of the Fourth Amendment. The Federal District Court dismissed the lawsuit and the estate appealed. The Third Circuit Court of Appeals affirmed in part and reversed in part. The court initially observed that when the troopers confronted Quick in the thicket, they told him to show his hands and freeze. Instead, he suddenly withdrew his hand from his waist band as though he was drawing a gun. The court ruled that at that moment, the Troopers were justified in opening fire. The court explained that, "[a]n **officer is not constitutionally required to wait until he sets his eyes upon a weapon before employing deadly force to protect himself against a fleeing suspect who moves as though to draw a gun. Waiting in such circumstances could well prove fatal. Police officers do not enter into a suicide pact when they take an oath to uphold the constitution.**"[14]

In reaching this conclusion, the court noted that the Supreme Court's opinion in *Graham* requires it to view the situation in light of the fact that officers are **often forced to make split second judgments in circumstances that are tense, uncertain and rapidly evolving.** The court explained that the Supreme Court mandated that it review the matter from the **perspective of a reasonable officer on the scene and**

---

[14] Id. at 183.

Impact of Graham and Garner Decisions

observed that Monday morning quarterbacking is not allowed.

The court next examined the number of shots fired by the officers; the time it took to fire them; and the fact that 11 rounds entered Quick's body from the rear. The court observed that "[e]ven where an officer is initially justified in using force, he may not continue to use such force after it has become evident that the threat justifying the force has vanished."[15] The court observed that once Quick's right hand was visible to the troopers; from a distance of between five and eight feet away; with their flashlights pointed at him; they fired at Quick for a total of roughly ten seconds and fired 39 rounds in his direction.

The court took into account the fact that as the shooting began, a trooper's flashlight was hit by a ricochet, which caused the trooper to fall to the ground. The court opined that this would have caused the other troopers to reasonably believe that the flashlight was hit by fire from Quick, thus justifying further use of deadly force. However, the court also noted that the flashlight was hit as the first shots were being fired.

The court also observed that 11 of the 18 bullets that struck Quick hit him from behind. The court noted that the Troopers stated that Quick spun around during the shooting and offered that as the reason why bullets entered his back. The court stated that this explanation seemed far-fetched because over half the bullets that hit Quick entered his body from behind.

The court ruled that a jury could find that the continuous firing of 39 rounds for roughly 10 seconds, with 11 bullets entering Quick's body from the rear, was excessive. The court remanded the case back to the lower court so that a jury could decide whether the continuous firing after Quick's hand became visible; the number of shots fired; the time taken to fire them; and the number of bullets entering from the rear, constituted an unreasonable use of deadly force.

The outcome of this case is troubling because, in the opinion of the author, it demonstrates that the court applied uneducated logic to reach an erroneous conclusion. Cases of this nature require, that is, mandate, that the attorneys' for the defendant

---

[15] Id. at 184.

Chapter 2

police officers obtain the services of an "expert" witness of their own. Only law enforcement "experts" with the appropriate background, credentials and experience will have the ability to educate jurists and jurors on little known but absolutely essential facts that are often present in officer involved shooting incidents.

For example, a law enforcement study conducted by William Lewinski Ph.D., Force Science Institute Ltd., which will be examined in great depth later in this book, has established that police officers, with drawn weapons and the decision to shoot already made, can fire bullets from semi-automatic handguns at a rate of nearly 4 rounds per second.[16] With this in mind, an officer can empty a semi-automatic pistol containing 16 rounds pointed at an adversary in between 4 and 5 seconds.

Given this fact, a law enforcement expert, like Doctor Lewinski would be able to testify that firing 39 rounds at a suspect by three officers who all simultaneously and reasonably believed that their lives were in danger is not unreasonable. In this case, two of the Troopers fired 14 shots and the other fired 11. These shots were likely fired in less than 4 seconds, once the officers concluded that their lives were in danger; for example, three officers would be able to fire 12 shots each in approximately 3.06 seconds. Firing for less than 4 seconds toward a man who defied officers' commands and recklessly simulated drawing a gun, is not unreasonable or excessive. This is especially true, when one of the officers falls to the ground as though he has been shot.

The court's opinion makes no mention of how it was known that the shooting of Quick took roughly 10 seconds to complete. The author believes that it is highly unlikely that anyone timed or filmed the actual shooting. The 10-second time frame was probably based on a **guess** from one or more of the Troopers involved. The actual duration of the shooting was probably well under 10 seconds.

---

[16] See, William J. Lewinski, Ph.D., Force Science Institute Ltd., Mankato, MN, and Dr. Bill Hudson, "Time to Start Shooting?—Time to Stop Shooting?—The Tempe Study." This study established that when a light was activated, it took officers involved in the study an average of .31 of a second to pull the trigger on a Glock semi-auto pistol the first time in a multiple pull sequence. Subsequent trigger pulls were executed at .25 of a second intervals. Thus, the average officer is able to fire 4 rounds in 1.06 seconds in response to an external stimulus, i.e. a light being turned on.

Impact of Graham and Garner Decisions

A law enforcement "expert" would be able to explain that the time sequence of a shooting incident will always include a **reaction time interval, that is, a reactionary gap** between the time a deadly threat directed toward an officer is first recognized by the officer and the time it takes for an officer to respond to the threat. The shooting time period begins to run when the officers first saw that Quick suddenly pulled his right hand from his waistband to simulate drawing a gun. Law enforcement studies have carefully examined this **reaction time interval/reactionary gap** between the time when a life threatening action by a suspect presents itself to an officer and the officer is able to respond by firing his weapon at the suspect.

This reactionary time interval/gap is sometimes referred to by law enforcement experts as the concept of **action v. reaction.** The rule of thumb to remember is simple. When all other things are equal, **action always beats reaction.** There will always be a **time lag** between a hostile action taken against an officer; the officer's recognition of that action; and the decision by the officer to counter it.

In a book involving a discussion of the reactionary gap, two retired FBI deadly force experts, former Supervisory Special Agents John Hall and Urey Patrick state that the generally accepted rule of thumb is that it "takes 0.7 to 1.0 seconds for an individual to first recognize another's action, identify the nature of the action, then formulate and initiate a response."[17] This reactionary gap **decision making time** must be added to the total length of any shooting incident involving police officers. Thus, if it takes an officer approximately 4 to 5 seconds to empty his semi-automatic pistol of 16 rounds, that is, 16 rounds in approximately 4.06 seconds, about 1 additional second must be added to the shooting duration because of the decision time involved in the reactionary gap. If no other factors were involved in the shooting involving the New Jersey Troopers, one could reasonably conclude that the shooting would have been over in approximately 5 seconds.

---

[17] See, John C. Hall and Urey W. Patrick, "In Defense of Self and Others," 2005, page 108. The authors are both retired FBI Supervisory Special Agents who are experts in the law enforcement officer use of deadly force.

Chapter 2

A deadly force "expert" also knows that there is a "lag time" for officers involved in a shooting between the time the officer realizes that his/her adversary is no longer a threat (the critical time here is not when the suspect is no longer an actual threat, but rather when the officer first reasonably comprehends that he is not a threat), makes the decision to stop firing, communicates his decision to his trigger finger, and the trigger finger stops pulling the trigger. Studies have shown that this "lag time" under nonthreatening laboratory conditions will be an average of 0.35 of a second. In fact, the Force Science Institute study mentioned above disclosed that some of the officers involved in the study, took as long as 0.6 seconds to stop shooting when responding to a light being turned off.

We know from the Force Science Institute Study that an officer can fire at least 2 and possibly 3 rounds in 0.6 seconds. Thus, if the decision to stop firing takes the officer 0.35 seconds to make, he/she would likely fire 2 additional rounds before the shooting is terminated. In other words, the trigger finger will continue to function for an additional .035 of a second, sending 2 more rounds toward the suspect. This could explain why at least some of the 11 shots that hit Quick in the back after he turned away from the Troopers were fired. After all, three Troopers were threatened with what each perceived as great bodily harm by his sudden hand withdrawal movement. Three fired at him and all three would have experienced the "lag time" decision making process, once they individually determined that Quick was no longer a threat.

This real life shooting did not happen in the pristine conditions of a laboratory setting. It happened in a dense forest, in the dark, with only artificial light available. The suspect suddenly and without warning simulated drawing a firearm. In addition, after one trooper fell, it appeared to the other troopers that a fellow trooper had been shot by Quick at the outset of the encounter.

Under these conditions, the decision for each officer concerning the continued existence of the threat (i.e., when did each officer determine that Quick was no longer a threat?), combined with the separate "lag time" for ending the shooting action, was probably in the order of between 1 and 2 seconds for each trooper. This time frame can easily account for the 11 rounds fired into

Impact of Graham and Garner Decisions

the back of the suspect. As mentioned earlier, in one second, each officer can fire approximately 4 rounds.

A defense "expert" would also testify concerning the concept of **"wound ballistics"** and emphasize that 39 rounds fired by three Troopers was not excessive, especially when the facts show that Quick remained upright during the shooting. He would explain that **"wound ballistics"** science demonstrates that only a **direct shot into Quick's brain or upper spinal column would immediately cause** him to fall to the ground dead or severely injured and end the threat. He would testify that Quick continued to be a threat as long as he remained on his feet, even if he began to turn away. Moreover, Quick could still remain a threat on the ground as long as he was alive and able to use his hands.

The "expert" would inform the court and the jury that even a direct hit to the heart of an adversary will allow him to continue deadly mayhem for between 10 to 15 seconds after receiving the fatal bullet. Scientific studies, examined later in this book, have shown that blood will continue to flow to the brain for this time period, enabling the perpetrator to continue his deadly threat to police officers, even if mortally wounded and on the ground. As long as the suspect is conscious and his hands are still operational, he remains a threat, unless he clearly is no longer in possession of a firearm.

The Hollywood-generated myth that, once a person is shot, he falls to the ground dead is simply false and over the years has probably resulted in the tragic deaths of many law enforcement officers. In the tragic FBI shootout in Miami, Florida on April 11, 1986, one of the suspects involved in the shooting killed two FBI agents and seriously wounded three more, after receiving a nonsurvivable gunshot wound to the right upper arm and chest at the beginning of the shootout.

The failure of police counsel to enlist the assistance of a qualified police deadly force "expert" in a case of this nature would amount to professional malpractice. If the case involved criminal charges, it would amount to ineffective assistance of counsel in violation of the Sixth Amendment.

Chapter 2

The Fourth Circuit (Richmond, VA) [18]—
Noel v. Artson [19]

Baltimore County police officers obtained a search warrant for the Noel residence to search for illegal controlled substances. The Baltimore County Police decided that the search warrant should be executed without knocking and announcing prior to entry because they believed that it was too dangerous for them to do so. The decision to enter without knocking and announcing was based upon the belief that the residence contained firearms that were legally registered to Mrs. Noel and one of her sons; that Mr. Noel had a 30-year old conviction for second-degree murder; and that another son had recently been charged with attempted first degree murder for shooting another man.

During the early morning hours of January 21, 2005, several Baltimore County officers executed the search warrant at the Noel residence. They forced entry into the residence with a battering ram and used a so-called "flash-bang" explosive device at the time of entry to distract the home's occupants. Once inside, an officer announced "Police-Search Warrant" and continued to do so when officers went to the upstairs portion of the home.

Officer Artson entered the Noel bedroom and was immediately confronted by Mrs. Noel who was spinning toward him with a pistol in her hand. Artson immediately fired two shots at Mrs. Noel, hitting her in the left shoulder and the right chest. She slumped to the floor but continued to hold onto the gun. Artson ordered her to drop it several times. She finally released it but it remained only 8 inches from her hand. Artson ordered her to move her hand away from the gun. The parties disputed what happened next. Artson stated that he saw Mrs. Noel move her hand toward the firearm and he shot her in the chest. The third shot was lethal, striking her in the heart.

The Noel family sued Officer Artson and other Baltimore County officers pursuant to 42 U.S.C. § 1983 and alleged that they violated Mrs. Noel's Fourth Amendment rights by using excessive force. The case eventually went to trial in the Federal

---

[18] The Fourth Circuit Court of Appeals covers the states of Maryland, North Carolina, South Carolina, Virginia, and West Virginia.

[19] 605 F.3d 580 (4th Cir. 2011), cert. denied, 132 S. Ct. 516 (10/31/2011).

Impact of Graham and Garner Decisions

District Court and after a nine-day trial, the jury returned a verdict in favor of the defendant police officers. The plaintiffs filed an appeal with the Fourth Circuit Court of Appeals, which affirmed the jury's verdict.

On appeal, the plaintiffs challenged the validity of the jury instructions given to the jury by the trial court judge. They argued that the jury instructions were erroneous because the trial judge refused to include an instruction that would require the jury to specifically consider the reasonableness of the third shot fired by Officer Artson. The plaintiffs requested the trial judge to add the following instruction: "Even if you decide that the initial use of force was reasonable ... you must consider whether the third shot was a reasonable use of force. The force used at the beginning of an encounter may not be justified even seconds later if the justification for the initial use of force has abated."[20]

The Fourth Circuit rejected the plaintiffs' argument by examining the actual language of the jury charge. The jury charge included the following language:

"[Y]ou must determine whether the amount of force ... exceeded that which a reasonable officer would have employed ... under similar circumstances. In this regard, you consider all of the attending and surrounding circumstances including **the nature and severity of the crime ... whether Mrs. Noel posed an immediate threat to the safety of any of the officers or others, and whether she was actively resisting or attempting to interfere with the lawful execution of the search warrant.**"[21] "Reasonableness of an officer's conduct ... must be judged from **the perspective of a reasonable officer on the scene,** and not with the **20/20 vision of hindsight.** The test of reasonableness must allow for the fact that police officers are **often forced to make split-second judgments in circumstances that are tense, uncertain and rapidly evolving ...** "[22]

---

[20] Id. at 587.

[21] Id. at 586.

[22] Id.

The court ruled that this jury charge covered the appropriate legal standard and left counsel more than enough room to argue the facts in light of that standard. The court observed that under this jury instruction, plaintiffs' counsel was able to offer a spirited closing argument that the third shot that killed Mrs. Noel was unreasonable because in his view she was already incapacitated and no longer a threat. The jury was able to consider this claim and reject it. The court explained that this is what good jury instructions do—"let counsel argue factually in terms of a legal standard, rather than having the judge make counsel's particularized arguments for them."[23]

By this time, readers of this book should be able to recognize the highlighted language in the trial judge's charge to the jury. The highlighted language was taken straight from the Supreme Court's opinion in *Graham v. Connor*. One can readily observe that this language had a direct, substantial, and significant bearing on the outcome of the case. The judge was obviously directed by this language from *Graham* to instruct the jury in a certain manner and the jury was directed by the judge to follow the Graham language in determining the outcome of the case. As mentioned earlier in this section of the book, the importance of the Graham decision in this area of legal jurisprudence to law enforcement officers cannot be understated.[24]

The Fifth Circuit (New Orleans, LA)[25]— *Elizondo v. Green*[26]

On March 18, 2009, Elizondo, a 17 year old, returned to his home in Garland, Texas around midnight. He had been drinking and was emotionally upset. His mother heard him crying in his bedroom, entered the room, and found him holding a knife to his stomach. Elizondo had previously attempted suicide by stabbing himself a month earlier. Another family member called 911

---

[23] Id. at 587.

[24] For other Fourth Circuit cases regarding police use of deadly force see, *Waterman v. Batton*, 393 F.3d 471 (4th Cir. 2005) and *Brockington v. Boykins*, 637 F.3d 503 (4th Cir. 2011).

[25] The Fifth Circuit Court of Appeals covers the states of Louisiana, Mississippi, and Texas.

[26] 671 F.3d 506 (5th Cir. 2012).

Impact of Graham and Garner Decisions

because she was afraid that he would try to hurt his mother with the knife. A Garland police officer responded to the call, was admitted to the residence, and was directed to Elizondo's room. Officer Green found Elizondo still holding the knife to his stomach. He drew his sidearm, backed out of the bedroom and repeatedly ordered Elizondo to put the knife down. Elizondo refused and tried to close the bedroom door. Green blocked him from closing the door. Elizondo responded by cursing Green and baited him to shoot him.

Officer Green responded by telling Elizondo that he did not want to shoot him but would do so if he came any closer with the knife. Elizondo ignored the warning and moved toward Green with his knife raised in a threatening manner. Green fired his weapon three times and Elizondo was killed. Elizondo's estate filed suit against Officer Green and the City of Garland, Texas pursuant to 42 U.S.C. §1983, alleging use of excessive force in violation of Elizondo's Fourth Amendment rights. The Federal District Court dismissed the lawsuit and the Fifth Circuit affirmed.

The Fifth Circuit examined Supreme Court precedent and observed that the Court held in *Graham v. Connor* that excessive force claims must be analyzed under the reasonableness standard of the Fourth Amendment. Moreover, the Fifth Circuit noted that the Supreme Court ruled in *Tennessee v. Garner* that law enforcement use of deadly force is constitutional when the suspect poses a threat of serious physical harm to the officer or others.

Guided by these precedents, the court observed that Elizondo ignored repeated orders to put his knife down. The court noted that at the time Green fired his weapon; Elizondo was hostile, armed with a knife, and moving closer to him. The court ruled that in these circumstances, it was reasonable for Officer Green to conclude that Elizondo posed a threat of serious harm toward him. The court also ruled that in the absence of a constitutional violation on the part of Officer Green, there could be no municipal liability for the City of Garland.

Chapter 2

Once again in this case, it is clear that the Supreme Court opinions highlighted earlier, directed the lower courts to a favorable outcome for the involved police officer and the City he represented.[27]

The Sixth Circuit (Cincinnati, OH)[28]— Simmonds v. Genesee County[29]

On November 23, 2007, Genesee County police received multiple 911 calls regarding Kevin Simmonds threatening behavior. Simmonds had threatened to kill his ex-girlfriend's parents. Several Genesee officers responded to the call and met with Simmonds's father. The father met with them outside the family residence. It was now dark and the residence was located on a heavily wooded property. The father told the officers that his son was possibly suicidal, wasn't acting right and had been drinking. He told the officers that Kevin owned a pistol and a rifle. Shortly after the officers completed their conversation with the father, Kevin drove his pick-up truck toward the officers.

The police officers activated the overhead lights on their patrol vehicles and ordered Kevin to stop, raise his hands, and exit from his vehicle. Instead, he shifted the vehicle into reverse and backed away from the officers into a heavily wooded area. The officers pursued him in their patrol cars. Kevin's pick-up became stuck in the snow. The officers exited their vehicles and approached the pick-up on foot. They repeatedly ordered Kevin to show his hands. He refused to do so. One officer opened the pick-up's door, yelled "taser" and deployed a taser in Kevin's direction. The taser failed to penetrate Kevin's jacket and was not effective in bringing the situation under control.

Kevin suddenly turned toward the officer with his arms extended forward in a firing position. He yelled that he had a gun. The officer turned around and moved in the direction of his patrol vehicle.

---

[27] See also, the Fifth Circuit's opinion in *Carnaby v. City of Houston*, 636 F.3d 183 (5th Cir. 2011).

[28] The Sixth Circuit Court of Appeals covers the states of Ohio, Michigan, Kentucky, and Tennessee.

[29] 682 F.3d 438 (6th Cir. 2012).

Impact of Graham and Garner Decisions

Two other officers immediately fired their handguns at Kevin. Kevin died from his wounds. Police searched the pick-up and the area nearby. They discovered a rifle in the snow outside the truck and a cell phone with its antenna extended on the front seat. No firearm was found in Kevin's possession or proximate to his body. Kevin's estate sued the involved officers pursuant to 42 U.S.C. § 1983 and alleged that they used excessive force in attempting to arrest Kevin in violation of the Fourth Amendment. The Federal District Judge dismissed the suit and the estate filed an appeal.

The Sixth Circuit Court of Appeals affirmed the judgment of the lower court and ruled in favor of the involved officers. In reaching its decision, the court relied heavily upon the Supreme Court opinions in *Graham* and *Garner*. The court observed that the standard for an officer's use of deadly force is whether the officers' actions were "objectively reasonable." The factors to be considered include the severity of the crime; and the immediacy of the threat to the officers or others. The court explained that "we must be sure to view the facts from the perspective of a reasonable officer on the scene, rather than with the 20/20 vision of hindsight."[30] This language was taken from the Supreme Court's opinion in *Graham*.

The court also quoted directly from the Supreme Court's opinion in *Garner* and stated, "[w]here the officer has probable cause to believe that the suspect poses a threat of serious physical harm, either to the officer or to others, it is not constitutionally unreasonable ... [to use] deadly force."[31]

The court observed that Kevin threatened to kill his ex-girlfriend's parents; was drinking, and reportedly mentally unstable and suicidal; reportedly was the owner of a pistol and shotgun; refused to exit his truck and attempted to escape; refused to surrender when contacted again; refused to show his hands and yelled that he had a gun; and pointed a silver object at the officers as though it was a firearm. Even though in fact, he was unarmed, the court ruled that the officers had probable cause

---

[30] Id. at 444.

[31] Id. at 445.

Chapter 2

to believe that Kevin posed a threat of serious physical harm toward them at the time of the shooting.[32]

The Seventh Circuit (Chicago, IL)[33]— *Marion v. City of Corydon, Indiana*[34]

On January 20, 2006, Marion was stopped by Louisville, Kentucky police officers who suspected him of shoplifting from a supermarket. Marion was carrying his baby in an infant seat at the time. He ran from the market, tossed the baby into his 1993 Ford Explorer while still in the infant seat, and attempted to enter the vehicle to escape. A police officer tried to stop him and a scuffle ensued. During the scuffle, the baby was removed from the vehicle by a store employee. Marion was able to break away from the officer, enter his Explorer, and back it up with the door still open. He quickly collided with another car and fled the parking lot. A dangerous high speed chase followed through the streets of Louisville to Interstate 64.

The chase continued from Kentucky into Indiana on I-64 west bound. Corydon County, Indiana officers joined the pursuit. Louisville officers eventually dropped out of the pursuit altogether. Marion was traveling at speeds in excess of 80 mph.

A Deputy Sheriff from Harrison County, Indiana, deployed "stop sticks" on I-64, which deflated three of Marion's tires. Marion's speed decreased to about 40 mph but he refused to stop, swerving from one side of the highway to the other. The pursuing officers attempted to stop him with a rolling roadblock. Marion resisted and swung his vehicle toward an officer's police car, making contact with it. Marion attempted to pull around the police car in front of him without success.

Suddenly, Marion made a hard left turn onto the grass median between the west and east bound traffic lanes. He attempted to drive through the median toward the eastbound traffic lanes on I-64. The grass in the median was wet and muddy. Marion's vehicle slowed as he attempted to maneuver

---

[32] The Sixth Circuit decided another case that is also instructive on the police use of deadly force. See, *Smith v. Freeland*, 954 F.2d 343 (6th Cir. 1992).

[33] The Seventh Circuit Court of Appeals covers the states of Illinois, Indiana, and Wisconsin.

[34] 559 F.3d 700 (7th Cir. 2009).

Impact of Graham and Garner Decisions

through the slippery median. Police officers exited their vehicles and moved on foot to surround the Explorer. Marion refused to stop and some of the officers fired their weapons. Marion responded by putting his vehicle in reverse and revved the engine, causing the tires to spin and spray mud. The Explorer was able to move in a backward direction.

The officers approaching from the rear had to scatter to avoid being hit. One of these officers yelled for Marion to stop. When he continued, the officer fired six shots into the vehicle. Other officers demanded that Marion stop and raise his hands. Undaunted, Marion shifted the vehicle into forward gear and attempted to move forward toward the east bound traffic lanes. Officers, who were now standing in front of the vehicle, fearing lethal danger to themselves and others, fired their weapons at Marion. Marion was hit by some of these rounds and suffered the loss of sight in his right eye and severe damage to his left hand.

Marion subsequently sued the involved officers pursuant to 42 U.S.C. §1983 and alleged that his Fourth Amendment rights were violated because the officers used excessive force to arrest him. The Federal District Court dismissed the lawsuit and Marion filed an appeal.

The Seventh Circuit Court of Appeals affirmed the dismissal of the lawsuit. In doing so, the court relied heavily upon prior United States Supreme Court opinions regarding excessive force claims. In particular, the court observed that the Supreme Court in *Graham v. Connor* ruled that in cases of this nature, the standard for review is whether the involved officers acted with "objective reasonableness." The court also stated, "The Supreme Court further has counseled [in *Tennessee v. Garner*] that it is reasonable for a law enforcement officer to use deadly force if an objectively reasonable officer in the same circumstances would conclude that the suspect posed a threat of death or serious injury to the officer or others."[35]

The court observed that in this case, Marion, once in the median, attempted to regain traction and drive toward the eastbound lanes of I-64. The court noted that if Marion reached his goal, several additional innocent drivers would have been

---

[35] Id. at 705.

exposed to serious injury or death. Moreover, the court opined that if the officers did not fire at Marion, he would have run over the police officers in front of his vehicle. The court concluded, "under the totality of circumstances, it was reasonable for the officers to think that Marion seriously endangered officers and innocent bystanders, and it was reasonable for the officers to discharge their firearms ... to stop him." [36]

In this case, the suspect had consistently and repeatedly resisted all law enforcement efforts to arrest him over a sustained and protracted period of time. In the process, he put innumerable persons and police officers in multiple life-threatening situations. He acted with reckless abandon, and no doubt would have done so with his infant child in the car, if the child had not been luckily removed before the chase began.

Critics of this opinion are likely to say that the court sanctioned the shooting of an unarmed man since no weapon was found on Marion or in his vehicle. To them, I would respond that Marion was indeed armed; armed with several thousand pounds of motor vehicle; quite capable of literally crushing the bodies of police officers and innocent bystanders alike.[37]

The Eighth Circuit (Saint Louis, MO)[38]—
Lee v. Anderson[39]

On July 22, 2006, Lee, age 19, and his friends were riding bikes in the vicinity of an elementary school in North, Minneapolis. Anderson, a Minneapolis Police Officer, and a Minnesota State Trooper were on routine patrol when they observed Lee and his friends. They approached Lee and friends in their patrol car. Lee and another bike rider jumped the curb with their bikes and rode away from the cruiser. Anderson activated his overhead lights and pursued Lee and the other bike rider onto a grassy area on school property. The officers observed the two bike riders

---

[36] Id. at 706.

[37] For other Seventh Circuit Court of Appeals cases involving police use of deadly force, see, *Carter v. Buscher*, 972 F.2d 1328 (7th Cir. 1992) and *Plakas v. Drinski*, 19 F.3d 1143 (7th Cir. 1994).

[38] The Eighth Circuit Court of Appeals covers the states of Arkansas, Iowa, Minnesota, Missouri, Nebraska, North Dakota, and South Dakota.

[39] 616 F.3d 803 (8th Cir. 2010).

Impact of Graham and Garner Decisions

come together and one handed a gun to Lee. Lee jumped off his bike and began to run away.

Both officers exited their vehicle, drew their firearms, and chased Lee. Anderson took the lead and while in pursuit, repeatedly yelled, "Police. Drop the gun." Anderson chased Lee around a corner of the school and Lee turned back to see where Anderson was. At this time, Anderson could see that Lee had a gun in his right hand. Anderson felt threatened when Lee turned toward him and fired one shot that missed. Lee continued to run and again turned back to see where Anderson was. The gun was still in his hand.

Although Lee did not point the gun at him, Anderson believed that he was in mortal danger and fired three more shots. The bullets hit Lee and he fell to the ground. Anderson yelled for Lee to drop his gun. Instead, Lee tried to rise from a seated position. Anderson fired five more shots; Lee fell backward and the gun fell from his hands. Lee was shot eight times and succumbed from his wounds. A semi-automatic pistol was located close to his body, near one of his hands.

In February 2007, Lee's Estate sued Officer Anderson and the City of Minneapolis pursuant to 42 U.S.C. §1983, alleging a violation of Lee's constitutional rights. The lawsuit ultimately went to trial in Federal District Court before a jury. The jury returned a verdict favorable to Officer Anderson and the City and Lee's Estate filed an appeal with the Eighth Circuit Court of Appeals. The Eighth Circuit denied the appeal and affirmed the jury's verdict.

The Estate's appeal, among other things, challenged the language of the trial judge's charge to the jury. The jury charge instructed the jury that they could return a verdict in favor of the Estate, if they found that Anderson's use of deadly force was excessive because it was not **reasonably necessary to protect Anderson or others from apparent death or great bodily harm.** Moreover, the jury charge instructed the jury to consider **"whether a reasonable officer on the scene, without the benefit of 20/20 hindsight, would have used such force under similar circumstances."**[40]

---

[40] Id. at 811.

Chapter 2

The Eighth Circuit approved the language used by the Trial judge in the jury charge. This language comes directly from the Supreme Court's opinions in *Graham v. Connor* and *Tennessee v. Garner*. The court observed that Anderson testified that Lee made threatening movements in the moments leading up to the shooting. He testified that Lee turned his body, with gun still in hand, toward Anderson. This action caused Anderson to reasonably believe that his life was in danger and that Lee was going to shoot him.

Once again, this case illustrates the significant impact that the Supreme Court decisions in *Graham* and *Garner* have on the final outcome of civil rights excessive force lawsuits directed at police officers for allegedly violating the Fourth Amendment. The trial judge used language right from these cases to instruct the jury in how to apply the law to the facts.

During the author's tenure in the FBI, the FBI deadly force policy made it abundantly clear that agents were permitted to use deadly force against suspects carrying firearms, when they were running away from the agents and believed to be seeking the tactical advantage of cover or concealment. Later in this book, considerable time will be spent on the issue of shooting armed and unarmed fleeing suspects. The extremely dangerous concepts of "hide and ambush" and "action v. reaction" in foot chase situations will be analyzed and examined.

For now, suffice it to say that the author's expert opinion is that shooting armed fleeing felons from behind is justified to avoid "hide and ambush" situations and the negative consequences flowing from the "action v. reaction" concept. The latter concept will allow the felon to turn and fire several shots at a pursuing officer before the officer can respond in kind. Pursuing an armed suspect is extremely dangerous and the risk of serious bodily harm or death to the officer is greatly magnified.[41]

---

[41] For other Eighth Circuit cases involving police use of deadly force, see, *Kolski v. City of Brooklyn Park, Minn.* (No.13-1640) (8th Cir.7/3/14). City police officers shot and killed Kolski after entering his home in response to an armed domestic violence complaint. Upon entry, Kolski pointed a 20 gauge shotgun at the officers who responded by firing 27 shots at Kolski, hitting him 16 or 17 times. The Eighth Circuit determined that officers' use of deadly force was reasonable and not a violation of the Fourth Amendment; *Loch v. City of Litchfield*, 689 F.3d 961 (8th Cir. 2012); *Hayek v. City of St. Paul*, 488 F.3d 1049 (8th Cir. 2007); *Cole v. Bone*, 993 F.2d 1328 (8th Cir. 1993); *Krueger v. Fuhr*, 933 F.2d 1358 (8th Cir. 1993).

Impact of Graham and Garner Decisions

The Ninth Circuit (San Francisco, CA)[42]—
Glenn v. Washington County[43]

On September 15, 2006, Lukas Glenn, 18 years old, returned to his home during the early morning hours. He was agitated and intoxicated. He told his parents that he wanted to drive his motorcycle and was told that he could not do so. He became angry and began to inflict damage on his parents' property, including home windows, the front door, and car windows. He subsequently held a pocket knife with a three inch blade to his own throat and threatened to kill himself.

Glenn's mother called 911 and told the police dispatcher that her son was out of control, busting out windows, holding a knife and threatening them. She informed the dispatcher that her son was drunk and threatening to kill himself. She also said that her son stated that he would not leave until the cops come to shoot and kill him.

The police dispatcher informed responding Washington County, Oregon Deputies that they were to go to the caller's home to handle a domestic disturbance involving a fight with a weapon. Further, they were told that the caller's son had a pocket knife, was suicidal and drunk. They were informed that the son had broken windows, busted through the front door and was standing in the driveway of the residence. The officers were told that hunting rifles were in the house but that the son could not get to them.

Upon arrival, the first Deputy walked up the driveway and positioned himself between 8 to 12 feet from Lukas Glenn. Lukas was holding a pocketknife to his own throat. His parents and two friends were standing near him in the driveway. Lukas's grandmother was inside the house. Lukas was not threatening anyone else. The Deputy drew his firearm and ordered Lukas to drop the knife and threatened to shoot him if he refused.

A second Deputy arrived and joined the first Deputy in confronting Lukas. The second Deputy stood between 6 and 12 feet away from Lukas. He likewise drew his firearm and ordered Lukas to drop the knife or be shot. Lukas refused to obey the

---

[42] The Ninth Circuit covers the states of Alaska, Arizona, California, Hawaii, Idaho, Montana, Nevada, Oregon, Washington and the U.S. Territories of Guam and the Northern Mariana Islands.

[43] 673 F.3d 864 (9th Cir. 2011).

officers' commands and kept the knife at his own throat. The officers' ordered the parents to go inside the house and the friends to leave the area. They all complied.

Neither of the Deputies had a beanbag shotgun or a Taser[44] in their possession. Shortly thereafter an officer from another Department arrived in possession of a beanbag shotgun. This weapon is capable of firing "less lethal" beanbag projectiles at a suspect who is resisting arrest. This officer was also in possession of a Taser but did not inform the other officers that he had one.

The officer with the beanbag shotgun was ordered by one of the Deputies to fire the beanbag gun at Lukas. The officer yelled "beanbag, beanbag" and fired six beanbag projectiles at Lukas. Lukas was hit by the projectiles and took one or two steps toward the direction of the house. The two Deputies on the scene had made independent subjective determinations that if Lukas moved toward the house, they would use deadly force to protect the parents and grandmother from possible harm.

As Lukas moved toward the house, both Deputies fired their handguns at Lukas. A total of eleven shots were fired and eight hit Lukas who died moments later. Lukas Glenn's family sued the involved Deputies in Federal District Court pursuant to 42 U.S.C. §1983, alleging excessive force in violation of the Fourth Amendment. The Federal District Court Judge dismissed the lawsuit and the family appealed.

The Ninth Circuit Court of Appeals reversed and remanded the case to the District Court for a jury trial. In so doing, the court initially examined the constitutional propriety of the police use of the beanbag shotgun against Glenn. The court observed that the beanbag shotgun is considered a "less lethal" weapon because it is capable of causing serious injury or death if fired from within 50 feet of a suspect and if the projectile hits the suspect in the head or left chest.

The Ninth Circuit noted that the lower court determined that the use of the beanbag shotgun was justified. The lower court found that Lukas Glenn was an immediate threat to the officers and others because he was in possession of a deadly weapon. The Ninth Circuit disagreed and observed that when the first Deputy

---

[44] A Taser is an electroshock weapon that uses electric current to disrupt the voluntary control of muscles in a human being causing temporary incapacitation.

Impact of Graham and Garner Decisions

arrived, Lukas was holding the knife to his throat but also simply talking with his parents and friends. He was not threatening anyone else with his knife and no one was trying to get away from him. Moreover, although Lukas refused to drop the knife upon being ordered to do so, he never attacked the Deputies or threatened to do so. Further, the parents and friends were ordered out of the immediate area when the Deputies arrived. The court concluded that in these circumstances, a jury could determine that the use of the beanbag shotgun was not appropriate because there was little evidence that he posed an immediate threat to anybody.

The court also noted that Lukas had not committed any serious crime and that the officers, based upon what they were told and what they saw, should have recognized him to be an emotionally disturbed individual. The court opined that the government's justification for using potential lethal force, that is, the beanbag shotgun, is diminished when the person is mentally ill instead of a felon who has committed a serious crime against others.

The court also gave weight to the family's argument that the officers' had less than lethal options available to them. First, the family argued that the officers should not have drawn their handguns and forcefully shouted commands at Lukas, which in their opinion simply escalated the situation. Second, the family opined that the officers should have used time as a tool to de-escalate the situation by waiting for back-up to arrive, instead of trying to end the situation quickly as they did.

Finally, the court examined the family's claim that the police should have employed a Taser against Lukas, instead of the beanbag shotgun and their handguns. The court did not rule that the officers were mandated by existing law to adopt any or all of these less than lethal options and in fact stated that it is well settled law that officers are not required to employ the least intrusive means available so long as they act reasonably in what they actually chose to do. The court nonetheless ruled that, "[t]he available lesser alternatives are, however, relevant to ascertaining that reasonable range of conduct."[45]

---

[45] 673 F.3d 864, 878.

Chapter 2

The Ninth Circuit ruled that if the jury later finds that the use of the beanbag shotgun amounted to excessive force; it would justify a finding of liability for the use of firearms that followed as well. The court explained, "where an officer **intentionally or recklessly provokes a violent confrontation,** if the provocation is an independent Fourth Amendment violation, he may be liable for his otherwise defensive use of force."[46] Thus, a jury finding of unreasonable conduct relative to the use of the beanbag shotgun, would also support a finding of liability for killing Glenn. This would be true, even if the jury determined that the use of firearms was otherwise justified as a reasonable measure to protect the people in the house from harm when Lukas began to move in that direction.

The court also ruled that even if a jury later determines that the use of the beanbag shotgun was reasonable, it still could find that the use of firearms by the Deputies was itself an unreasonable and excessive use of force. The court observed that the two involved Deputies commenced firing at Lukas before the final beanbag round was fired. Moreover, Lukas was not running toward the front door of the house. Instead, he took one or two steps in that direction, which could be interpreted as an involuntary reaction to being hit by beanbag rounds.

The court noted that Lukas had not threatened to harm his family in the officers' presence and had not attempted to attack anyone. The court opined that if the officers were so concerned with the parents' safety they could have positioned themselves between Lukas and the front door. The court remanded the case back to the District Court for trial.

At the outset of this opinion, the Ninth Circuit quoted extensively from the Supreme Court decisions in *Graham* and *Garner*. For example, the court observed that in Graham, the Supreme Court ruled that, "reasonableness ... must be judged from the **perspective of a reasonable officer on the scene rather than with the 20/20 vision of hindsight.**"[47]

Notwithstanding the Supreme Court's clear directive, **the Ninth Circuit proceeded to analyze and examine this case**

---

[46] Id. at 879.

[47] Id. at 871.

Impact of Graham and Garner Decisions

with its own 20/20 vision of hindsight. The Ninth Circuit's opinion adopts an approach that is the polar opposite of the Supreme Court's instruction in cases of this nature. Instead of recognizing that officers are forced to confront life threatening situations in circumstances that are, "tense, uncertain and rapidly evolving," the Circuit judges, with the aid of their law clerks; in the secure and safe location of their US Marshal protected judicial chambers; pour over lengthy depositions for protracted time periods; to reach their own conclusions about what the officers did right and what they did wrong.

It comes as no surprise. The Ninth Circuit is one of four federal circuits that have chosen to ignore the Supreme Court's instructions to the lower federal courts on the handling of deadly force cases. These circuits all pay lip service to the Supreme Court's mandate but invariably wander off to reach their own version of justice.

The application of judicial second guessing in the *Glenn case* is quite startling and amazing. The Ninth Circuit, with perfect 20/20 hindsight, was critical of so many things the officers said and did upon their arrival on the scene. For example, although this incident lasted only four minutes from start to finish, the court raised questions concerning whether it was appropriate for the officers to draw their firearms; order the suspect with commanding language to drop his knife; order the parents to enter their home knowing that the front door had been damaged; stand too close to the subject with a knife; fail to stand between the suspect and the front door of the house; fail to bring with them their own beanbag shotgun and Taser; order the use of the beanbag shotgun when the suspect had not moved directly toward them or other innocent bystanders with his knife; fail to treat the suspect more kindly because he was an emotionally distressed person; fail to recognize that the suspect's movement toward the house after being hit by beanbag projectiles might be involuntary; fail to wait for back-up to arrive; fail to wait to observe the effect of the beanbag rounds hitting the suspect before shooting at him with firearms, and so on. The judicial second guessing abounded without limitation.

In *Glenn,* officers were dispatched to a private residence during night time hours based upon an emergency call placed by the suspect's mother. Prior to the call, the suspect had exhibited

Chapter 2

potentially violent behavior involving breaking windows in the family home and vehicle and damaging the front door of the residence. Moreover, the parents tried to calm him down without success and called two of his friends to the scene for help. They were likewise unsuccessful in bringing him under control. Instead of reacting positively to the pleas of the parents and the friends, the suspect pulled out a three-inch knife, held it to his neck, and threatened to kill himself.

During the 911 call, the suspect's mother informed the dispatcher that her son was "out of control, busting out our windows, has a knife and is threatening us."[48] She also said that her son was intoxicated and stated that "he was not leaving until the cops shoot him and kill him."[49] The dispatcher told responding officers that they needed to handle a domestic disturbance involving a **fight with a weapon. He also told them that there were hunting rifles inside the house but Lukas could not get to them.**

Upon arrival, two Deputies (who did not know Glenn and who never went to the home with the intention of killing him) found themselves confronting an angry, emotionally upset young man holding a knife to his own throat. They moved closer and positioned themselves between 6 and 12 feet from the suspect. They drew their firearms for their own protection and the protection of the four people standing close to Lukas. The officers confronted with a dangerous person, had the presence of mind to order the suspect's parents to enter their own home for safety purposes. Likewise, concerned for the safety of Lukas' friends, they ordered the friends to move behind them for protection.

The officers forcefully and repeatedly ordered the suspect to drop his knife. He ignored the orders and defiantly held on to his knife. A knife in the hands of a resisting, recalcitrant suspect is a deadly weapon and both officers were clearly within the knife **"kill zone"** range. Cases of this nature require defense lawyers to utilize the services of an expert witness of their own to explain to the judges, and if required, the jury, the inherent dangers faced by officers when confronting a knife-wielding suspect.

---

[48] Id. at 867.

[49] Id.

Impact of Graham and Garner Decisions

An expert witness could testify about a law enforcement study conducted at the FBI Academy[50] (along with other similar studies) that established that a suspect can kill or seriously injure an officer with a knife if he suddenly attacks the officer who is standing less than 21 feet away from the suspect at the beginning of the assault. Inside 21 feet is the **kill zone.** In the FBI study, one agent held a pistol firing non-lethal rounds in his hand. A second agent (the "suspect"), holding a rubber knife and standing **just inside 21 feet,** would without any warning, rush the agent holding the gun. The agent with the knife was able to "stab" the agent with the gun **every time.** The agent with the gun was able in most cases to get off one shot as he was being stabbed. At closer distances, the agent with the gun was **unable to fire a shot before being stabbed by the charging "suspect."**

It should also be noted here that the science of "wound ballistics" must be considered in all cases of this nature. A law enforcement expert would be able to testify that the science of "wound ballistics," which will be examined at length later in this book, teaches us that the only way to bring an **immediate halt** to a knife/gun wielding suspect's deadly use of a knife/gun, is to shoot him in the brain or the upper spinal column. This will cause an **instantaneous end** to a deadly situation. Anything else, for example, shooting the knife-wielding suspect in the arm, leg, stomach, or even the chest, will allow that suspect to continue to threaten the officer with the knife or repeatedly stab him until the suspect has lost sufficient blood to deprive his brain of oxygen. This could take several seconds up to several minutes or even longer to happen. In the meantime, the suspect, even if mortally wounded, can continue to stab an officer over and over again.

In *Glenn,* the officers confronted a suspect who has resisted all reasonable efforts by his parents and friends to calm down; destroyed property in and around his own home; threatened his parents before the police arrived; pulled out a knife and held it to his throat; **told his parents that he wanted the police to shoot and kill him;** and refused repeated orders from uniformed police officers to drop the knife; continued to hold on to the knife after being hit by beanbag projectiles; and moved in the direction

---

[50] See, Urey W. Patrick and John C. Hall, "In Defense Of Self And Others ..." 2005, page 109.

Chapter 2

of a home containing firearms and occupied by innocent bystanders, before the officers used their own firearms.

In judging the reasonableness of the officers' conduct in *Glenn,* the judges need to ask themselves what they would expect the "objectively reasonable" police officer to do in the same circumstances. For example, is it reasonable to expect the officers to move closer to the suspect and attempt to disarm him before ordering the use of the beanbag shotgun? This would require the officers to move even more directly into the **knife "kill zone"** and subject themselves to serious bodily harm or death. No one can reasonably expect an officer to exhibit such "tombstone courage."

Once the suspect had been hit by the beanbag projectiles, is it reasonable to expect the officers to intercept the knife-wielding suspect and block him from moving toward the house containing firearms and innocent bystanders? Once again this would require the officers to move directly into the knife "kill zone" and place their lives in direct and serious jeopardy. It is unreasonable to expect police officers to act with such reckless disregard for their own safety.

Should the officers be expected to permit this mentally unstable suspect to move further in the direction of the nearby home with a knife? After all, the officers knew that the home contained innocent persons and firearms. Would the situation have become more or less dangerous if the officers allowed the suspect to enter the home?

Should the officers have simply left the scene altogether and allow the situation to resolve itself? Tragically, without police intervention, these situations often result in the suicide of the suspect, but only **after** he has killed numerous innocent victims. Should we expect officers to shrink from their duty to protect and serve whenever the going gets rough and return another day?

When the involved officers answered the call for help, it was never their intention to kill Lukas Glenn. They attempted to do their duty to protect and serve the people of their jurisdiction. Tragically, an emotionally disturbed person, whose expressed intent was to be shot and killed by police, precipitated his own demise. A peaceful result was possible, if only Lukas Glenn would have acquiesced and dropped his deadly weapon. To suggest that these officers acted unconstitutionally is the equivalent of suggesting that they deliberately took the life of another person. This was never true in the *Glenn* case.

The Ninth Circuit did all it could do to avoid the clear directives from the Supreme Court. Instead of placing themselves in the shoes of the officers **on the scene,** facing a **tense, uncertain, and rapidly evolving situation,** they second-guessed the officers' every move from beginning to end. The court even intimated that the officers' acted recklessly, thereby causing the tragic result that followed. In the process, the court clearly and deliberately understated the danger to the officers and the others present at the scene and the prominent role played by the suspect in precipitating his own shooting.

The court also failed to give the officers any credit for protecting the innocent bystanders and attempting to resolve the situation by verbal commands to drop the knife and the use of the beanbag gun. The court's decision does a great disservice to the men and women of law enforcement who put their lives on the line every day to protect the rights and lives of the innocent. This case provides another example of an unjust result that flows from the failure of a subordinate court to follow the directions mandated by the highest court in the land.[51]

The Tenth Circuit (Denver, CO)[52]—
Thomas v. Durastanti[53]

On January 13, 2006, two special agents of the Federal Alcohol, Tobacco, and Firearms Department (ATF) were tracking a fugitive in Wichita, Kansas. They were driving an unmarked ATF vehicle and observed a white Lincoln Town car drive past them at a high rate of speed. The Lincoln was proceeding away from a known high crime area of the city.

The vehicle did not appear to have a rear license plate and was occupied by three adult males. The agents turned around and followed the Lincoln. They saw the Lincoln stop in front of a

---

[51] For a recent Ninth Circuit Court of Appeals case with a favorable result to law enforcement, see, *Wilkinson v. Torres,* 610 F.3d 546 (9th Cir. 2010). See also, *Scott v. Henrich,* 39 F.2d 912 (9th Cir. 1994).

[52] The Tenth Circuit Court of Appeals covers the states of Colorado, Kansas, New Mexico, Oklahoma, Utah, and Wyoming.

[53] 607 F.3d 655 (10th Cir. 2010).

Chapter 2

residence. One of the occupants made a brief entry into the residence and returned to the vehicle. At this point the agents observed a dealer plate in the back window of the Lincoln. The plate was later determined to be valid but a computer check at the time of the incident showed that the plate was "not in file."

The Lincoln left the residence and the agents continued to follow. They contacted the Kansas State Police and requested a Trooper to assist them in stopping the vehicle. In the meantime, the Lincoln pulled into a gas station/convenience store parking lot and stopped in front of the store. The agents pulled their vehicle in front of the Lincoln and stopped. A Kansas State Trooper, presumably in full uniform, pulled up behind the Lincoln and turned on his marked unit's overhead flashing lights.

The ATF agents exited their vehicle with drawn guns and started to walk toward the Lincoln. One passenger of the Lincoln was starting to exit his vehicle when he saw the agents approaching. The agents, who were dressed in plain clothes, told the passenger to get back in the car and he complied. One of the agents yelled "police" and the Trooper partially exited his patrol car and yelled for the Lincoln's occupants to have a seat in their vehicle. He then ordered them to all put their hands where he could see them.

The Lincoln's occupants later claimed that they thought the ATF agents were trying to rob them. The passenger that attempted to exit the Lincoln claimed that he saw the Trooper and his vehicle but did not tell the Lincoln's driver and other passenger what he saw. This was an obvious attempt to justify their failure to obey the Trooper's commands.

The driver of the Lincoln suddenly tried to drive around the ATF vehicle in front of him to leave the parking lot. In so doing, he drove directly at ATF Agent Durastanti. Durastanti responded by firing two shots into the Lincoln at the driver. The driver of the Lincoln continued to drive at Durastanti and hit him with the car. Durastanti rolled off the hood of the Lincoln, spun around, and somehow landed on his feet. He was able to fire two more shots at the rear of the Lincoln as it left the parking lot of the gas station.

The other ATF agent and the Trooper gave chase and stopped the Lincoln a few blocks away. The driver of the Lincoln and the

Impact of Graham and Garner Decisions

front seat passenger were both shot and wounded by Agent Durastanti. Thomas, the front seat passenger, later became the plaintiff in this lawsuit. It was subsequently determined that the Lincoln's occupants were transporting crack cocaine for a planned sale.

As mentioned previously, Thomas filed a lawsuit against the two ATF agents and the Kansas State Trooper in federal court. The suit was dismissed against one ATF agent and the Trooper. Durastanti, the remaining ATF Agent, moved for dismissal of the suit with the Federal District Court Judge. The Judge denied the motion and ruled that it was a "close question" whether a jury could find that the Agent had used excessive force. Agent Durastanti filed an appeal with the Tenth Circuit Court of Appeals. The Tenth Circuit reversed and ordered dismissal of the lawsuit.

In reaching its conclusion favorable to the ATF Agent, the court observed that the use of deadly force is not unlawful if a reasonable officer has probable cause to believe that he faces a threat of serious physical harm to himself or others. The court noted that if threatened with a weapon, including a vehicle attempting to run him over, an officer may use deadly force. The court also cited the Supreme Court in *Graham v. Connor* for the proposition that the reasonableness of a particular use of force must be judged from the perspective of a reasonable officer on the scene, rather than with the 20/20 vision of hindsight. The court also stated that, "[w]e must consider whether Agent Durastanti could have reasonably perceived he was in danger at the precise moment that he used force and **whether his own reckless or deliberate conduct ... unreasonably created the need to use force.**"[54]

Initially, the court concluded that Agent Durastanti acted with objective reasonableness in firing at the Lincoln as it proceeded toward him in the parking lot. The court observed that an officer in such close quarters is no match for a two-ton vehicle. The court noted that the driver of the Lincoln (who was not the plaintiff in this lawsuit) plead guilty to assaulting two federal agents, thereby admitting that he was driving directly at both of them. The court

---

[54] Id. at 664.

stated that Durastanti had mere seconds to react and fired his first two shots with a reasonable belief that he was justified.

With regard to the two additional shots fired by Durastanti after the Lincoln hit him, the court observed that Durastanti was disoriented after being hit and believed that the vehicle was still approaching him when he fired the second two shots. The court concluded that given the disorienting experience of being hit by the car, Durastanti had no assurance that the threat posed by the Lincoln had passed. The court stated that this was a split-second decision concerning the use of deadly force under hardly ideal circumstances. The court concluded that, "[e]ven if Agent Durastanti was mistaken, it was a reasonable mistake."[55]

The court next confronted the issue of whether Agent Durastanti **recklessly and deliberately created the need to use deadly force through his own inappropriate conduct. It should be noted here that the Tenth Circuit has added this element to the "objective reasonableness" equation. This added dimension was never part of or even discussed by the Supreme Court in its *Graham* or *Garner* decisions.**

The Tenth Circuit attempted to justify its creation/addition of a new element to the "objective reasonableness" analysis by stating that it is part of the "totality of circumstances" inquiry required by the Supreme Court. This added element, that is, whether the officer recklessly and deliberately created the situation that required the use of deadly force, was never contemplated by the Supreme Court or considered to be part of the "objective reasonableness" analysis. The Supreme Court in *Graham* particularly was focused solely **on the moment when deadly force was used** and not on whether the officer did or failed to do something which created the need to use deadly force.

The Plaintiff argued that Agent Durastanti created the situation that caused him to use deadly force. He stated that Durastanti failed to identify himself to the Lincoln's occupants and drew his weapon upon exiting the ATF vehicle. The court examined the failure to identify claim and stated that it was not reckless that Durastanti failed to identify himself. After all, the Trooper activated his marked cruiser's overhead lights and gave

---

[55] Id. at 666.

Impact of Graham and Garner Decisions

the occupants orders, including telling one occupant to get back in the vehicle. The court found that this display of police presence was sufficient to provide the Lincoln's occupants with notice that the persons surrounding them were law enforcement officers.

With respect to approaching the Lincoln with his weapon drawn, Agent Durastanti knew that the operator of the vehicle had driven erratically at a high rate of speed, left a known high crime area, and was possibly driving a stolen car. He knew that the vehicle contained three young men who may represent a threat to his life and safety. His perception proved to be correct. The court agreed and ruled that an objectively reasonable officer could believe that in this situation drawing a firearm was permissible.

This case demonstrates how quickly a situation can change from a simple traffic stop into a deadly confrontation. The involved law enforcement personnel had no way of knowing that the occupants were involved in a drug-trafficking situation. However, their "street" instincts were ultimately correct. These guys were up to no good.

The driver of the Lincoln, despite the presence of three armed law enforcement officers, one in uniform in a marked unit with lights flashing, chose to roll the dice and attempt to escape. In so doing, he drove directly at an ATF Agent and hit him with a two thousand pound deadly weapon, that is, a Lincoln Town car. The shooting that followed was caused directly by this action on the part of the driver. The law enforcement officers were not reckless and did not cause the situation that resulted in the shooting. The shooting was the direct result of the deliberate and reckless conduct of the driver of the Lincoln. No one else is to blame.

As mentioned previously, this part of the court's examination was not required by the Supreme Court and was created by the Tenth Circuit as an added, and in the opinion of the author, unnecessary element of the "objective reasonableness" analysis.

Chapter 2

The Eleventh Circuit (Atlanta, GA) [56]—
Penley v. Eslinger [57]

On January 13, 2006, Penley, a 15-year-old middle school student in Seminole County, Florida, displayed what appeared to be a semi-automatic pistol in his classroom inside the school. Penley's classmates and teacher fled from the classroom. Penley briefly took one student hostage but the student was able to escape. Seminole County Sheriff's Deputies responded to the school. Penley was quickly confronted by Seminole County Deputy Maiorano, who commanded Penley to drop his weapon. Penley refused, held the gun under his chin, and told the Deputy that he (Penley) was going to die one way or another. He "slithered" into a nearby school bathroom that had an open entranceway.

Deputy Maiorano positioned himself outside the bathroom and tried to speak with Penley. Penley declined to speak with the Deputy and began to walk back and forth across the open entrance to the bathroom. He alternately pointed his weapon at the Deputy and then back under his chin. Maiorano holstered his own weapon in an effort to convince Penley to drop his gun. Instead of dropping the gun, Penley pointed his weapon directly at Maiorano. The Deputy feared for his life and hugged the wall. He drew his gun and never holstered again during the remainder of the incident.

Shortly thereafter, a police hostage negotiator and Lieutenant Weippert, a SWAT team member, arrived on scene. Weippert was armed with a semi-automatic rifle. The hostage negotiator attempted to convince Penley to drop his weapon and surrender without success. Penley never threatened the hostage negotiator with his weapon.

While Weippert was present, Penley moved across the bathroom entrance three times. Each time, Penley pointed the weapon at Weippert and Maiorano. Weippert concluded that Penley was a danger to himself and others, including students in the vicinity. At that moment, Penley began to cross the open doorway once again. He pointed his weapon at the officers nearby.

---

[56] The Eleventh Circuit Court of Appeals covers the states of Alabama, Florida, and Georgia.

[57] 605 F.3d 843 (11th Cir. 2010).

Impact of Graham and Garner Decisions

Without a warning, Weippert fired a single shot at Penley with his rifle. The bullet struck Penley in the head. He died two days later. When police entered the bathroom, they discovered that Penley's handgun was a plastic replica of a semi-automatic pistol.

Penley's parents sued Lieutenant Weippert and the Seminole County Sheriff Eslinger pursuant to Title 42 U.S.C. §1983 and alleged that Deputy Weippert used excessive force and violated their son's Fourth Amendment rights. The Federal District Court Judge dismissed the lawsuit and the Penleys' appealed to the Eleventh Circuit Court of Appeals. The Eleventh Circuit affirmed the dismissal of the lawsuit and began its opinion by stating, "The loss of such a young life is an undeniable tragedy. However, with their suit, the Penley's ask us to conduct precisely the sort of **20/20 hindsight inquiry against which the Supreme Court ... [has] repeatedly cautioned."** [58]

In affirming the dismissal of the lawsuit, the court relied heavily on the United States Supreme Court precedent found in its *Graham* and *Garner* decisions. In particular, the Eleventh Circuit focused on language from Graham that called for examination of the "objective reasonableness" of an involved officer's conduct from the perspective of a reasonable officer on the scene of the incident rather than with a 20/20 vision of hindsight. The court also observed that in *Graham,* the Supreme Court instructed that the "objective reasonableness" analysis must include consideration of the fact that police officers are often forced to make split second decisions under circumstances that are tense, uncertain, and rapidly evolving about the amount of force to use in a particular situation.

The court also noted that the reasonableness of Lieutenant Weippert's conduct depends primarily on whether Penley presented an imminent threat to Weippert and others in the vicinity. The court quoted from the Supreme Court's opinion in *Garner* and stated, "'where the officer has probable cause to believe that the suspect poses a threat of serious physical harm, either to the officer or to others,' use of deadly force does not violate the constitution." [59]

---

[58] Id. at 846.

[59] Id. at 851.

Chapter 2

The court observed that Weippert had reason to believe that Penley was armed with a real semi-automatic pistol, which he deliberately brought with him to school. After all, he had already threatened his teacher and fellow students with it and even took one of them hostage. Penley refused repeated commands for him to drop the weapon and surrender. Moreover, he continually pointed the weapon at two deputies, including Weippert. Lt. Weippert had a reasonable belief that other students were still in the vicinity of the location of the stand-off. Furthermore, although not mentioned by the court, Penley had informed a Deputy that he intended to die that day. Statements of this nature are bright signals of a perpetrator's state of mind and demonstrate that officers are confronted with a highly dangerous individual.

The court concluded that Penley represented an imminent threat to Weippert and others nearby. The court ruled that it would not second guess with 20/20 vision of hindsight, the decision of a twenty year law enforcement veteran on the scene of the incident. In this situation the decision to use deadly force was appropriate and constitutional.[60]

---

[60] For another recent Eleventh Circuit case favorable to law enforcement see, *Jean Baptiste v. Gutierrez*, 627 F.3d 816 (11th Cir. 2010).

Chapter 3

THE QUALIFIED IMMUNITY DEFENSE

The Officer's Shield Against Frivolous Constitutional Lawsuits

Readers of this book have already been alerted to the fact that the United States Supreme Court has demonstrated remarkable understanding of and empathy for the very difficult and dangerous challenges that confront law enforcement officers on the streets of America today. The Supreme Court's strong interest in protecting our nation's domestic sentinels is further demonstrated in decisions that recognize and support a "qualified immunity" legal defense for law enforcement officers who must defend themselves in lawsuits arising out of life and death street confrontations.

In fact, the Supreme Court has characterized the "qualified immunity" doctrine as more than a legal defense. The Court has made clear that qualified immunity is a doctrine that involves **immunity from suit** rather than a mere defense to a legal action.[1] Because it involves immunity from suit, the establishment of qualified immunity by a law enforcement officer requires **dismissal of a lawsuit** before protracted discovery and without trial. The contours of this valuable and important defense are examined at length in the following.

The law enforcement community should welcome and appreciate the Supreme Court's support for the extraordinary difficulties that officers confront daily across the United States. It is ironic that in many cases the very people that officers sought to protect from madness and mayhem turn around and sue the officers who risked their lives to save them. A viable defense against these lawsuits, many of them frivolous in nature, is sorely needed.

---

[1] *Mitchell v. Forsyth,* 472 U.S. 511, 526. (1985).

Chapter 3

The Genesis of the Qualified Immunity Defense—*Harlow v. Fitzgerald*

In *Harlow v. Fitzgerald*,[2] the Supreme Court observed that there are two kinds of immunity defenses that are available to public officials who are sued in connection with alleged unconstitutional actions taken as part of their official duties.[3] The first is **absolute immunity** and this defense is reserved for special classes of public officials who require complete protection from suit. The Court cited several examples of public officials who, because of their unique and special positions in our government structure, are entitled to absolute immunity from suit. These officials include **legislators** performing legislative functions, **judges** exercising their judicial functions, **prosecutors** acting in their prosecutorial role, and the **President** of the United States.

The Court also recognized the existence of a second legal defense, **that is, qualified immunity,** which is generally available to all public officials whose duties, although very important, do not rise to the level of those very special classes of officials who are entitled to absolute immunity. This is the defense available to all federal, state, and local law enforcement officers who are accused of acting with excessive force in violation of the Fourth Amendment.

In *Harlow,* the Supreme Court recognized the need for the qualified immunity defense to protect public officials, including law enforcement officers, from the often frivolous lawsuits that flow from their necessary official actions. The Court observed that lawsuits directed at public officials have significant negative societal costs associated with them. For example, lawsuits are costly to defend; have the effect of diverting the defendant's attention away from important public duties; have the potential effect of leading qualified persons to seek employment in other venues; and will likely dampen the will of present public officials to provide their best effort to protect and serve the public interest in the performance of their charged responsibilities.

---

[2] 457 U. S. 800 (1982).

[3] Fitzgerald was a former civilian employee of the United States Air Force and Harlow was a high-level aide to former U.S. President Richard Nixon. Fitzgerald sued Harlow claiming that he was involved in his wrongful discharge from his government employment in violation of his constitutional rights.

The Qualified Immunity Defense

The *Harlow* Court expressed the view that the qualified immunity defense offered the best attainable accommodation between two competing interests. The first involves providing a remedy for legitimate claims of harm by innocent citizens at the hands of rogue public officials. The second involves protection for public officials who act reasonably but still suffer as defendants in frivolous law suits. The Court observed that the goal of the qualified immunity defense was to allow for the **"dismissal of insubstantial lawsuits without trial."** [4]

The Court stated that the qualified immunity defense is an affirmative defense that must be asserted by the defendant in a particular litigation. The Court noted that in its past decisions the qualified immunity defense had two components: a **"subjective"** component and an **"objective"** component. The *subjective component* focused on the **state of mind of the defendant** official and whether or not he acted with **malicious intent** to deprive the plaintiff of his constitutional rights. The *objective component* focused on what the official actually did and whether those actions violated the constitution.

The *Harlow* Court observed that the "subjective" component of the defense often prevents constitutional law suits from being decided by a judge through a summary judgment motion before trial. Instead, extensive deposition taking, concerning the defendant's subjective state of mind and subsequent full-blown jury trials often follow. To prevent needless trials and costly pre-trial discovery, the Court jettisoned the "subjective" component of the qualified immunity defense and stated, "We therefore hold that government officials ... generally are shielded from liability ... **insofar as their [objective] conduct does not violate clearly established ... constitutional rights of which a reasonable person would have known.**" [5]

With this language, the Court preserved the **"objective" component** of the qualified immunity defense and made it the **sole component** of the defense. From this point forward, the qualified immunity defense would involve the question of whether the **officer's actual conduct** violated clearly established consti-

---

[4] 457 U.S. 800, 814.

[5] Id. at 807 (emphasis added).

tutional rights. For future cases, the test for the viability of qualified immunity would be an **objective test only**. From now on, qualified immunity would prevail if the defendant official had an **objectively reasonable belief** that his conduct conformed with **clearly established constitutional rights.**

Although the *Harlow* Court declined to grant lower level public officials' absolute immunity from suit, the Court nonetheless emphasized the value of the qualified immunity defense to these officials and refashioned the defense to make it a more effective and powerful shield in the defense of frivolous lawsuits.

The Development of the Qualified Immunity Defense after Harlow

Mitchell v. Forsyth

In 1985 the Supreme Court decided *Mitchell v. Forsyth*.[6] Mitchell, the Attorney General of the United States in the Nixon Administration, authorized the FBI in November 1970 to install a warrantless wiretap on the phone of a suspected member of a United States–based domestic terrorist group. The group was planning to blow up heating tunnels connected to federal buildings in Washington D.C. and kidnap National Security Advisor Henry Kissinger. Forsyth, the plaintiff in this suit, was overheard on the wiretap. Almost two years later, in 1972, in the so-called "Keith" case, the Supreme Court ruled that wiretaps involving domestic threats to national security were illegal in the absence of a warrant.[7]

Forsyth subsequently sued Mitchell in federal court for violating his rights under the Fourth Amendment and the federal wiretap statute.[8] Mitchell filed a motion for summary judgment on both absolute and qualified immunity grounds. The Federal District Court denied the motion and Mitchell appealed.

---

[6] 472 U.S. 511 (1985).

[7] *United States v. United States District Court,* 407 U.S. 297 (1972). This is the case that has come to be known as the "Keith" case.

[8] 18 U.S.C. §2510-2520.

The Qualified Immunity Defense

The Third Circuit Court of Appeals ruled that Mitchell was not entitled to absolute immunity and that the decision of the trial judge to reject Mitchell's qualified immunity claim could not be appealed before trial because it was not a *final judicial order.*

The Supreme Court accepted the case for review, affirmed in part and reversed in part. The Court affirmed the Third Circuit's ruling that the Attorney General was not entitled to absolute immunity because he was not acting as a prosecutor in this case but rather was exercising a National Security function.

The Court stated that denial of absolute immunity did not render the Attorney General impotent in the defense of possibly frivolous and vexatious lawsuits. The Court observed that the qualified immunity defense was clearly available to the Attorney General. The Court instructed that the **"Attorney General will be entitled to qualified immunity so long as his actions do not violate 'clearly established statutory or constitutional rights of which a reasonable person would have known.'"**[9]

The Court reaffirmed the validity of its decision in *Harlow* and observed that the Harlow Court refashioned the qualified immunity doctrine to allow for resolution of insubstantial law suits without trial and the burdens of protracted discovery. The Court observed further that unless allegations in a lawsuit state a claim of a violation of a clearly established constitutional right, the defendant pleading qualified immunity is entitled to dismissal before the commencement of discovery. The Court made clear that the qualified immunity doctrine is an **"immunity from suit rather than a mere defense to liability;** and ... it is effectively lost if a case is erroneously permitted to go to trial."[10]

The Court also ruled that denial of a defendant public official's qualified immunity claim by a trial court judge, to the extent that "it turns on an issue of law, is an appealable 'final decision'...."[11] In so doing, the Court made clear that when a public official/law enforcement officer's claim of qualified immunity is denied by a trial court judge, that denial is subject to an immediate appeal to

---

[9] 472 U.S. 511, 524 (quoting *Harlow v. Fitzgerald,* 457 U.S. 800, 818 (1982) (emphasis added).

[10] Id. at 526 (emphasis added).

[11] Id. at 530.

the appropriate court of appeals. The defendant law enforcement officer does not have to suffer the burdens of discovery and trial before an appellate court can review the rejection of the qualified immunity defense.

Finally, the Court examined the state of the law relative to wiretaps in domestic national security cases at the time Mitchell authorized the warrantless wiretap and ruled that the state of the law, that is, whether a warrant was necessary, was not clearly established. In fact, the Court observed that it wasn't until over a year after Mitchell approved the wiretap, that the Supreme Court ruled in the "Keith" case that a warrant was required. The Court also examined the state of the law prior to its definitive ruling in "Keith," and found the law to be uncertain. Because Mitchell's actual conduct did not violate clearly established constitutional law, qualified immunity prevailed and Mitchell was victorious.

The *Mitchell* decision was important for several reasons. First, it established beyond question, the Supreme Court's commitment to protecting public officials from unsubstantial lawsuits by enshrining the qualified immunity doctrine. Second, it made clear that denial of the qualified immunity defense at the trial court level is immediately appealable by the defendant law enforcement officer to the appropriate appellate court. Third, the Court demonstrated for future appellate courts how quickly and efficiently a court can dispose of a meritless constitutionally based claim against a public official, thereby avoiding costly protracted discovery and the uncertainty of a trial.

Anderson v. Creighton

Five years after *Harlow* the Supreme Court further clarified the nature and scope of the qualified immunity defense in *Anderson v. Creighton*.[12] Anderson, an FBI Agent, participated in a warrantless search of Creighton's home to look for a suspected bank robber. The search proved fruitless and Anderson was subsequently sued by Creighton for allegedly violating his Fourth Amendment rights to be free from unreasonable search and

---

[12] 483 U.S. 635 (1987).

The Qualified Immunity Defense

seizure. Anderson filed a motion to dismiss on the grounds of qualified immunity.

The Federal District Court Judge ruled that the undisputed facts disclosed that the FBI Agent had probable cause and exigent circumstances that justified the warrantless search. The judge concluded that the suit must be dismissed on qualified immunity grounds without proceeding to further discovery and trial.

On appeal, the Eighth Circuit Court of Appeals reversed and reinstated the suit. The court ruled that Anderson was not entitled to dismissal on qualified immunity grounds because Creighton had alleged (without attempting to describe with particularity how this was so) that Anderson had violated a clearly established constitutional right, i.e. the right to be free from a warrantless search in the absence of probable cause and exigent circumstances.

The Eighth Circuit accepted Creighton's general nonspecific allegation of a violation of a clearly established constitutional right and ruled that this alone was sufficient to trump Anderson's claim of qualified immunity. In the process, the court **refused to consider whether the undisputed facts disclosed that Anderson acted with objective reasonableness based upon a reasonable belief that he had probable cause and exigent circumstances that justified his warrantless search.** In essence, the Court of Appeals ruled that Creighton could overcome the qualified immunity defense by simply claiming without specificity that Anderson violated a clearly established constitutional right. If this holding were to stand, it would result in destroying the efficacy of the qualified immunity defense not only for Special Agent Anderson, but for all future law enforcement defendants.

The qualified immunity defense was created to protect public officials from facing extensive discovery and trial in the many frivolous lawsuits filed against them. The Eighth Circuit's approach, if allowed to stand, would directly contravene the express intent of the Supreme Court in creating the defense in the first place.

Fortunately for law enforcement, the Supreme Court accepted the case for review and reversed. The Court began by once again reaffirming the validity and availability of the qualified immunity defense to protect public officials (including law enforcement officers) from civil lawsuits. The Court observed that, "qualified immunity protects, 'all but the plainly incompetent or those who knowingly violate the law.'"[13]

Next, the Court reiterated the legal standard for asserting the defense and stated, "whether an official protected by qualified immunity may be held personally liable for an allegedly unlawful action ... turns on the **'objective legal reasonableness'** of the [official's] action"[14] in relation to **clearly established constitutional** law.

The Court moved on to examine the scope and meaning of the term **clearly established law.** The Court observed that the Eighth Circuit's analysis of the "clearly established law" principle was much too broad and generalized. The Court noted that the Eighth Circuit was simply content to accept Creighton's allegation that Anderson violated the **general principle of law** that a warrant is needed to search a home unless the police possess both probable cause and exigent circumstances. For the Eighth Circuit, this was enough to demonstrate that Anderson violated clearly established law; defeat the qualified immunity defense and move the suit forward for pre-trial discovery and trial.

The Supreme Court ruled that this approach to examining the **clearly established law** principle lacked the **particularity** that is necessary to preserve the qualified immunity defense for the police officer. The Eighth Circuit erred by refusing to review **the undisputed particular facts known to the FBI Agent which allowed him to conclude that he had both probable cause and exigent circumstances that would justify a warrantless search.**

The Court clarified the meaning and judicial application of the "clearly established law" principle by declaring that the general legal principle at issue must be construed in conjunction with the **known specific facts of the actual incident** in order to decide whether "clearly established law" has been violated by the defendant's conduct.

Post *Anderson,* plaintiffs can no longer summarily defeat assertion of qualified immunity by a law enforcement officer by

---

[13] Id. at 638 (quoting, *Malley v. Briggs,* 475 U. S. 335, 344-345).

[14] Id. at 639 (quoting, *Harlow v. Fitzgerald,* 457 U.S. 800, 819). (emphasis added).

The Qualified Immunity Defense

simply claiming that the officer violated some **generalized constitutional right**. For example, in *Anderson,* Creighton's basic generalized claim was, "They searched my home without a warrant, without probable cause, and without an emergency." Judges are now required to reject such claims when considering the viability of qualified immunity. They are instead required to review such allegations in conjunction with the known facts in order decide whether the officer had an objectively reasonable belief that his conduct conformed with "clearly established law."

Finally, the Court concluded its analysis with a profound and important statement. The Court observed, **"We have recognized that it is inevitable that law enforcement officials will in some cases reasonably but mistakenly conclude that probable cause is present, and we have indicated that, in such cases, those officials ... should not be held personally liable."** [15] This statement is profound because it makes clear that law enforcement officers are entitled to qualified immunity when they reasonably believe that their conduct was constitutional, even if in fact, their actual conduct falls short of the constitutional standard.

After *Anderson,* lower courts deciding constitutional rights lawsuits against police officers are mandated to dismiss them on qualified immunity grounds, not only when the officer's actual conduct conforms with clearly established constitutional rights but also when the officer had a reasonable belief that this was so, even if that belief was mistaken. Put another way, the defendant officer will prevail on qualified immunity grounds, even when his conduct violates a clearly established constitutional right, because he had a reasonable but erroneous belief that his conduct was constitutional.

For example, clearly established law declares that probable cause is necessary to validate a Fourth Amendment search. A court could determine that an officer lacked probable cause but still rule favorably for that officer on qualified immunity grounds as long as the officer had a reasonable belief that he had probable cause, even though that belief was mistaken. The favorable significance of this development in the law for law enforcement officers cannot be understated.

---

[15] Id. at 641. (emphasis added).

Chapter 3

Anderson reveals the true value of the qualified immunity defense. To be safe from debilitating lawsuits, law enforcement officers are not required to act with precise conformity to the clearly established principles of the constitution, as long as they have an **objectively reasonable belief** that they did so.

In the author's experience, countless law enforcement officers have been spared from the burden of defending themselves from the otherwise protracted and costly nature of constitutional rights lawsuits because of qualified immunity. The author has examined voluminous cases involving claims of excessive force in law enforcement shooting situations. Every one of those cases involves the assertion of qualified immunity by the defendant officers. Many of them result in dismissal without trial on qualified immunity grounds.

Pearson v. Callahan[16]

In 2009, the Supreme Court in *Pearson* further clarified the application of the qualified immunity doctrine at the trial court level by modifying its earlier ruling in *Saucier v. Katz*.[17] In *Saucier*, the Court established a rigid two step analysis that trial court judges were mandated to follow in ruling on the applicability of the qualified immunity defense. *Saucier* required the trial judge to first decide whether the facts alleged or shown by the plaintiff *make out a violation of a constitutional right*. Second, if the answer is in the affirmative, the court must decide whether the constitutional right at issue was *clearly established*. If the answer to either question was no, the qualified immunity defense would be established and the lawsuit would be dismissed.

The **Pearson Court** believed that the rigid two part application of the qualified immunity defense that it mandated in *Saucier* was too inflexible and caused undue constraint upon trial court judges. The Court explained that in certain cases, it is more prudent and efficient when examining the viability of the qualified immunity defense, to first consider whether the constitutional right at issue was clearly established. If it was not, there would be no need to determine whether the facts alleged by the

---

[16] 555 U.S. 223 (2009).

[17] 533 U.S. 194 (2001).

plaintiff made out a constitutional violation and the case against the law enforcement officer would be dismissed.

On this basis, the Court proceeded to modify its ruling in Saucier by holding that in future cases, the trial court judges have the choice to juxtapose the order of reviewing the two parts of the qualified immunity test. This would permit but not require the judge to examine whether the constitutional right at issue was "clearly established" first. From now on, the trial judge has the discretion to review the two part qualified immunity doctrine in any order they wish.

Qualified Immunity and Officer Involved Shootings—*Brosseau v. Haugen*[18]

In 2004, prior to the Supreme Court's decision in *Pearson* described previously, the Supreme Court issued its ruling in *Brosseau*. The *Brosseau* decision proved to be a foreshadowing of the Court's later decision in *Pearson*.

In *Brosseau*, the Court jumped over part one of the two-step examination process for the qualified immunity defense required by its earlier decision in *Saucier*. In so doing, the Court declined to consider the Ninth Circuit's ruling on whether the plaintiff's claim made out a violation of the Fourth Amendment. Instead, the Court went immediately to part two of the *Saucier* qualified immunity analysis and focused on the question of whether the law was clearly established in ruling on the defendant's assertion of qualified immunity. By so doing, the Court deliberately ignored the order of the two step process it had previously mandated in *Saucier*.

Brosseau is an important case because it involves the assertion of the qualified immunity defense by a police officer who used deadly force against a suspect. In this case, Brosseau, a Puyallup, Washington police officer, attempted to arrest Haugen on a no-bail warrant for felony drug violations. He was also a suspect in a theft of stolen property. Instead of submitting to arrest, Haugen ran from the driveway at his mother's home and hid somewhere in the neighborhood. During a subsequent search

---

[18] 543 U.S. 194 (2004).

by police officers, Haugen ran back to his mother's home, entered a Jeep parked in the driveway and locked its doors.

The Jeep was facing the street. There were also two vehicles parked in front of the Jeep; each one had two passengers inside. One of these vehicles contained a 3-year-old child. One vehicle was in the driveway and the other was on the nearby street.

Officer Brosseau ran into the driveway and positioned herself next to the Jeep. She pointed her firearm at Haugen and ordered him out of the Jeep. He ignored her and appeared to be searching for the keys. She repeated her commands and hit the driver's side window several times with her pistol. The window shattered and Brosseau hit Haugen in the head with the butt of her sidearm. Undeterred, Haugen started the Jeep and began to move forward. Brosseau jumped back. As the vehicle continued to move forward, Brosseau fired one shot through the rear driver's side window. This shot hit Haugen in the back. She later said that she fired at Haugen because she feared for the safety of other officers in the area, the people in the other two vehicles and other persons who might be in the area.

After being shot, Haugen maneuvered the Jeep out of the driveway and drove down the street for a short distance. After realizing he was shot, he stopped the vehicle. He was treated at a local hospital and later pleaded guilty to felony eluding of a police officer. By so doing, he admitted that he was guilty of driving in a "wanton" and "willful disregard" for the lives of other people.

Haugen later sued Brosseau in federal court pursuant to 42 U.S.C. §1983 and alleged that she used excessive force in arresting him in violation of his Fourth Amendment rights. Brosseau defended herself by asserting the qualified immunity defense. The trial court judge ruled in her favor and dismissed the suit. The Ninth Circuit Court of Appeals reversed and remanded the case for trial.

The Ninth Circuit examined the qualified immunity defense by means of the process mandated by the Supreme Court in Saucier, the controlling precedent at that time. The Ninth Circuit first ruled that the shooting was excessive and violated the Fourth Amendment because in its view, Haugen did not represent a threat of serious bodily harm to Brosseau or others when he

The Qualified Immunity Defense

was shot. The Circuit Court also ruled that the state of the law was **clearly established** at the time and that no reasonable officer could believe that the shooting was lawful.

The Supreme Court accepted the case for review and reversed. The Supreme Court expressed "no view as to the correctness of the Court of Appeals' decision on the constitutional question itself."[19] Instead, the Court jumped immediately to the second part of the qualified immunity test outlined in *Saucier,* that is, was the constitutional right alleged to be violated **"clearly established."**

The Court observed that the Ninth Circuit decided that the right of persons to be free from police use of excessive force was clearly established by the Supreme Court in *Tennessee v. Garner*[20] and *Graham v. Connor.*[21] The Court noted that the Ninth Circuit had focused on the use of force standard set forth by the Supreme Court in *Garner*, which required an officer to have probable cause that the suspect posed a threat of serious physical harm before using deadly force. Based on the *Garner* use of force standard, the Ninth Circuit ruled that Brosseau had indeed violated Haugen's clearly established constitutional rights.

The Supreme Court ruled that the use of force standard it created in *Garner* was not sufficiently **particularized** to serve as the clearly established legal standard by which Brosseau's actions must be judged. The Court explained that "[t]he relevant, dispositive inquiry in determining whether a right is clearly established is whether it would be clear to a reasonable officer that his conduct was unlawful in the **[particular]** situation he confronted."[22]

The Court proceeded to examine existing case law relevant to the particular kind of situation that Brosseau confronted in the Haugen shooting. The Court framed the particular issue by stating, "whether [it is permissible] to shoot a disturbed felon, set

---

[19] Id. at 198. This statement by the Court makes clear that in deciding the applicability of the qualified immunity defense the Court did not believe it was necessary to evaluate the first part of the Saucier test, i.e., whether the facts most favorable to Haugen made out a violation of the Fourth Amendment.

[20] 471 U.S. 1 (1985)

[21] 490 U.S. 386 (1989).

[22] 543 U.S. 194, 199.

Chapter 3

on avoiding capture through vehicular flight, when persons in the immediate area are at risk from that flight."[23] The Court first reviewed the Eighth Circuit's opinion in *Cole v. Bone*.[24]

In *Cole* the driver of an 18-wheel tractor-trailer drove his truck at a high rate of speed through a Kansas Interstate highway toll booth without stopping and proceeded to drive recklessly at 90 mph through Kansas into Missouri. He was pursued by numerous police agencies and attempted to ram several police cars during the chase. He also forced several civilian vehicles off the road during the pursuit. Pursuing police officers attempted several maneuvers to stop the truck, including fixed and rolling roadblocks and shooting at the truck tires but to no avail. Finally a State Trooper fired a shot at the driver and he was killed. The Eighth Circuit ruled that the shooting was justified because of the threat that Cole posed to pursuing police officers and other drivers on the road.

The Court next examined the Sixth Circuit's opinion in *Smith v. Freland*.[25] Smith failed to stop at a stop sign and refused to pull over for a police officer. Instead, he engaged police in a high speed pursuit at speeds in excess of 90 mph. During the pursuit, Smith tried to run a police car off the road. He finally turned into a dead end street and was cornered by officers in the process. An officer drove up next to Smith's temporarily stopped car and exited his patrol car. Smith backed up and then sped forward, ramming the police car. He backed up again, drove around the police car and smashed into a nearby fence and gate.

Smith attempted to drive away but the officer drew his firearm and fired a shot at Smith. Smith was killed. The Sixth Circuit ruled that the shooting was lawful and not excessive. The Circuit Court explained that Smith posed a major threat to other officers on the scene of the incident and observed that although unarmed, he was not harmless because his car could be used as a deadly weapon.

The Supreme Court concluded, based on its review of the cases described earlier, that the law was "by no means clearly

---

[23] Id. at 200.

[24] 993 F.2d 1328 (8th Cir. 1993).

[25] 954 F. 2d 343 (6th Cir. 1992).

The Qualified Immunity Defense

establish[ed]"[26] that Brosseau's conduct in this case was unconstitutional.

The Supreme Court's decision in *Brosseau* is significant for several reasons. First, it once again demonstrates the Court's determination to give police officers the benefit of doubt when reviewing their split-second life-changing decisions from the entirely safe contours of judicial chambers. Second, it reiterates the Court's willingness to use the qualified immunity doctrine to adjudicate police use of deadly force cases at the pre-trial stage of litigation and spare defendant police officers from the monetary and emotional burdens of protracted discovery and trial. Third, it demonstrates the real value of the qualified immunity defense to police officers who use deadly force in the performance of their duty when the need for such force was not clear-cut and obvious.[27]

After all, Haugen was wanted for drug violations, not crimes of violence; although resisting, he had not yet harmed anyone during the arrest attempt; although behind the wheel of a potentially dangerous weapon, that is, a vehicle, he had not driven it recklessly with intent to injure; and he was shot in the back by the officer. This case was by no means a "slam dunk" victory for the defendant police officer. Nonetheless, the Supreme Court evaluated the efficacy of the officer's assertion of qualified immunity and ruled that the officer's conduct did not violate clearly established law.

Based on my review of the relevant case law on officer involved shootings and the application of the qualified immunity doctrine/defense in those cases, I believe that the Supreme Court has, without question, grasped the magnitude of the danger faced ever so suddenly by law enforcement officers on the streets of America. The Supreme Court recognizes that police officers believe that their duty is to protect and serve the public. The Court understands that officers do not begin every shift with the idea that they will kill some innocent citizen before the shift ends.

---

[26] 543 U.S. 194, 201.

[27] For the most recent Supreme Court decisions favorable to law enforcement on the qualified immunity doctrine, see, *Messerschmidt v. Millender,* 132 S. Ct. 1235 (2012); *Ryburn v. Huff,* 132 S. Ct. 987 (2012); and *Reichle v. Howards,* 132 S. Ct. 2088 (2012). These cases do not involve use of deadly force by police officers but all involve successful use of the qualified immunity doctrine by law enforcement officers to defend alleged constitutional rights violations law suits brought against them.

Chapter 3

The Court realizes that police officers use deadly force because they reasonably believe in split-second circumstances that they had no choice. I salute the Supreme Court for its solid choice to support law enforcement officers when they act with objective reasonableness in defense of their own lives and the lives of the public that they serve.

Qualified Immunity—Material Facts in Dispute—*Tolan v. Cotton*

On May 5, 2014, the United States Supreme Court decided *Tolan v. Cotton*.[28] This case involved an allegation that Jeffrey Cotton, a Bellaire Texas Police Sergeant, used excessive force against Robbie Tolan when he shot and seriously wounded him during an encounter at Tolan's home in Bellaire, Texas during the early morning hours of December 31, 2008.

While on routine patrol, Bellaire Officer Edwards observed a black Nissan make an abrupt turn onto a residential street. Because there had been numerous vehicle break-ins in the area on the previous night, Officer Edwards became suspicious and decided to investigate. Edwards obtained the Nissan's license plate number and entered it into a police computer. He entered the wrong plate number by mistake.

In response to Edwards' incorrect entry, the computer disclosed that the black Nissan was stolen. At this time, the Nissan was parked in front of a home which was later determined to be Robbie Tolan's own residence. Officer Edwards exited his patrol car after illuminating Tolan and his passenger Anthony Cooper with his cruiser's spotlight. He drew his service firearm and ordered Tolan and Cooper to approach him. Both men cursed at him and refused to comply. Edwards told the men that he believed the Nissan was stolen and ordered them to get down on the ground. Cooper denied that the car was stolen and Tolan told the officer that the car was his. Tolan went to the ground but Cooper remained on his feet until Tolan's father appeared from inside the home and told Cooper to get down.

Tolan's father informed the officer that his son and nephew were the occupants of the vehicle and that the Nissan belonged to

---

[28] (No. 13-551).

The Qualified Immunity Defense

the Tolan family. Mrs. Tolan came outside and told the officer that this was all a big mistake. She said the car was not stolen and that it belonged to the family. Officer Edwards called for back-up and Sergeant Cotton arrived on the scene. Sgt. Cotton drew his firearm and moved in to assist. Cotton was told by Edwards that the two suspects on the ground had exited from a stolen vehicle. Cotton decided to immediately handcuff and search the prone suspects for the safety of all present.

Sgt. Cotton ordered Mrs. Tolan to stand in front of the garage so that the officers could properly secure the suspects. She refused to comply and said, "Are you kidding me? We've lived here 15 years." The parties dispute what happened next. Mrs. Tolan stated that Cotton grabbed her arm and slammed her into the garage door with such force that she fell on the ground. Tolan's son supported his mother's claim and offered photos of bruises on his mother's back and arms. By way of contrast, Sgt. Cotton stated that he attempted to escort Mrs. Tolan to the garage but she flipped her arm up and told him "get your hands off me."

The parties also dispute what happened next. Tolan's son claimed that upon seeing his mother being pushed, he rose to his knees. The two officers's claimed that he rose to his feet. All parties agree that the son then exclaimed, "Get your fucking hands off my mom." The parties also agree that Sgt. Cotton drew his pistol and fired three shots at Tolan. Tolan was shot once in the chest, seriously wounded but survived. A subsequent search revealed that Tolan was unarmed. Mrs. Tolan and her son both claimed that Cotton offered no verbal warning before shooting Tolan.

In April 2009, Sgt. Cotton was indicted for aggravated assault and was subsequently acquitted after a jury trial in May 2010. The Tolans sued Sgt. Cotton pursuant to 42 U.S.C. §1983, claiming that excessive force was used in violation of the Fourth Amendment. Sgt. Cotton defended against the lawsuit by asserting the qualified immunity defense and moved for dismissal prior to trial in a motion for summary judgment. The United States District Court Judge dismissed the lawsuit on qualified immunity grounds and ruled that there was no excessive use of force in violation of the Fourth Amendment.

Chapter 3

The Tolans filed an appeal and the Fifth Circuit Court of Appeals affirmed the decision of the lower court but on different grounds. The Fifth Circuit declined to rule that Cotton's conduct was reasonable under the Fourth Amendment. Instead, it affirmed the lower court's finding of qualified immunity on the grounds that Cotton's conduct did not violate clearly established law.

The Supreme Court reversed the Fifth Circuit in a Per Curiam opinion (i.e., an opinion from the entire Court instead of being written by one Justice). At the outset, the Court outlined the two-pronged analysis for determining whether a police officer is entitled to qualified immunity for allegedly using excessive force. The Court identified the first prong as involving the question of "**whether the facts taken in the light most favorable to the party asserting injury [Tolan]** ... show the officer's conduct violated a federal right" (i.e., the Fourth Amendment."). The Court identified the second qualified immunity prong by stating, "The second prong ...asks whether the right in question was **clearly established at the time of the violation.**" The Court reiterated what it had decided previously in *Pearson v. Callahan,* 555 U.S. 223, 236 (2009) by stating "Courts have discretion to decide the order in which to engage these two prongs" (i.e., a court may examine them in reverse order if it chooses and possibly avoid deciding prong number one by ruling that the law pursuant to prong number two was not clearly established).

Nevertheless, the Court made it abundantly clear that "**under either prong, courts may not resolve genuine disputes of fact in favor of the party seeking summary judgment**" (i.e., Officer Cotton). The Court stated unequivocally that "Summary Judgment (dismissal by the Judge before trial) is appropriate only if the movant (Officer Cotton) shows **that there is no genuine issue as to any material fact and that the movant is entitled to judgment as a matter of law**" (i.e., by the Judge alone without a jury).

The Court next examined how the Fifth Circuit reached its qualified immunity decision in favor of Officer Cotton. The Court concluded that the Fifth Circuit failed to view the evidence at summary judgment in the light most favorable to Tolan with

The Qualified Immunity Defense

respect to the central facts of the case. First, the Circuit Court appeared to accept Officer Cotton's statement that the area was dimly lit rather than Tolan's view that the area had better lighting. Second, the lower court credited Officer Cotton's claim that Mrs. Tolan was very agitated when she spoke to the Officers, but Mrs. Tolan claimed that she was neither aggravated or agitated. Third, the Court observed that while the parties agreed that Tolan said "get your fucking hands off my mom," there was disagreement between the parties as to the manner in which the statement was made and whether it could reasonably have been construed as a threat of bodily harm. The Court noted, "A jury could well have concluded that a reasonable officer would have heard Tolan's words not as a threat, but as a son's plea not to continue any assault of his mother."

Fourth, the Court determined that the Circuit Court appeared to have adopted Cotton's view that Tolan had risen to his feet in a charging position as if poised to attack. However, Tolan maintained that he was on his knees when Cotton shot him. Given the failure of the Circuit Court to properly assess disputed material facts in favor of Tolan for purposes of deciding the summary judgment motion, the Court reversed and remanded the case back to the trial court for further review consistent with the Court's ruling.

Summary of the Law on the Qualified Immunity Defense

The Qualified Immunity Doctrine/Defense was designed by the United States Supreme Court to be more than a defense for public officials, including law enforcement officers, to use in lawsuits when defending against allegations of a violation of constitutional rights. The Court intended the Doctrine/Defense to serve as immunity from suit rather than a mere defense to be asserted at trial. Accordingly, the Doctrine/Defense should be asserted by defendant law enforcement officers early in a constitutionally based lawsuit before protracted discovery and trial.

The Doctrine/Defense will be asserted in a Motion for Summary Judgment submitted well before trial on behalf of the defendant law enforcement officers. The Doctrine/Defense will be based on a fact-based assertion that the defendant officers acted

Chapter 3

in an "Objectively Reasonable" manner and in accordance with clearly established Fourth Amendment principles. Remember, according to the Supreme Court's decision in *Anderson v. Creighton,* the qualified immunity Doctrine/Defense will be successful as long as the officer had a reasonable belief that his/her conduct was lawful, even when that conduct falls short of the appropriate legal standard.

Upon receiving the Defendant's Motion, supported with appropriate witness (including expert witness) affidavits, the Federal Trial Judge (District Court Judge) will review the Defendant's Motion and the Plaintiff's Opposition Motion. The Judge will determine if there are any disputed **material** facts. If so, for purposes of deciding the Motion, the Judge must normally accept the Plaintiff's version of the disputed facts in deciding the Motion.

However, the Supreme Court ruled in *Scott v. Harris,* 550 U.S. 372 (2007) that this will not always be the case in the future. Instead, the Court ruled that when it appears to an appellate court based on a review of clear and convincing evidence, that is, videotapes of crucial events, that the plaintiff's version of the facts is simply incredible, the reviewing court must reject the plaintiff's version of the facts in deciding the Motion. This of course is of great benefit to future law enforcement defendants and highlights the valuable nature of video/audio based evidence which captures actual events in real time. A full analysis of *Scott* is presented later in this book.

If the Judge rejects the Qualified Immunity Doctrine/Defense, the defendant officers have the right to file an immediate (interlocutory) appeal with the appropriate federal appellate court. Many frivolous Fourth Amendment lawsuits are dismissed before trial by means of the Qualified Immunity Doctrine/Defense. This Doctrine/Defense should be asserted by the defendant in every officer involved shooting constitutionally based lawsuit.

Chapter 4

GRAHAM V. CONNOR/CRIMINAL PROSECUTION FOR USING DEADLY FORCE

Even more to be feared than the threat of departmental discipline and civil liability for using deadly force in the line of duty is the threat of criminal prosecution. After surviving a deadly encounter with violent offenders, nothing could be worse than facing a murder or manslaughter indictment arising out of an officer involved shooting incident. The threat of going to jail for trying to protect one's own life, the lives of fellow officers, innocent bystanders, and crime victims can be overwhelming. Nonetheless, over the years there have been several prosecutions of law enforcement officers who never intended to kill anyone but were forced by suspects they attempted to arrest to make a split-second decision to use deadly force.

An interesting example of this situation is found in the October 2004 edition of *Police Chief Magazine* in an article authored by Karen P. Tandy, Administrator of the US Drug Enforcement Administration (DEA). In the article entitled "Standing Together for the Officer's Right to Self-defense," Administrator Tandy tells the story of DEA Special Agent Jude Tanella. SA Tanella along with two other DEA agents and a New York City Detective attempted to arrest cocaine trafficker Egbert Dewgard on May 1, 2002. The officers attempted to box in Dewgard's car at a Brooklyn, New York intersection. Dewgard refused to yield and rammed the NYPD Detective's vehicle.

Dewgard attempted to escape by driving at high speed up onto the sidewalk and back onto the congested streets of a residential neighborhood. He drove recklessly and at times into oncoming traffic. Because of his erratic driving, only SA Tanella was able to maintain the pursuit. During the pursuit, Dewgard lost control of his vehicle and crashed. He exited his car and took off on foot while carrying a bag full of cocaine.

SA Tanella informed the other officers of his location and took off after Dewgard on foot. During the approximately 400-foot chase, Tanella's badge was displayed around his neck and he repeatedly yelled "Police" and ordered Dewgard to stop. Tanella pursued Dewgard with service weapon in hand. At the conclusion

Chapter 4

of the chase, Dewgard tripped and fell. This allowed Tanella to catch up and the fight was on.

Dewgard was much taller and heavier than Tanella and offered significant resistance. He punched Tanella repeatedly in the face and chest. He swore at Tanella and dared him to shoot. A crowd gathered around but no one stepped in or called for assistance, despite being repeatedly asked to do so by Tanella. Tanella was unable to holster his drawn weapon during Dewgard's attack, and he had to defend himself with one hand. The drawn weapon became a significant liability during the fight.

Eventually, Dewgard knocked Tanella to the ground and reached for Tanella's exposed gun. SA Tanella at that point was in fear of death or great bodily harm and fired one shot at Dewgard. The bullet hit Dewgard in the lower right side of his back. Despite being shot, Dewgard continued to resist the now exhausted agent. Finally, two other DEA agents arrived on the scene and were able to subdue and handcuff the still resisting suspect. Dewgard was taken to a local hospital and died from the single gunshot wound he received.

The Brooklyn, New York District Attorney's Office conducted an investigation of the shooting, which included an interview with one witness who stated that Dewgard was shot after he was handcuffed. This testimony was given to the grand jury. The DA's office later conceded that the testimony was false but it is not known whether the false nature of the testimony was ever brought to the attention of the grand jury.

The grand jury indicted SA Tanella for first degree manslaughter on 10/29/02. Tanella retained private counsel paid for by the U.S. Department of Justice. He entered a not guilty plea and the case was removed pursuant to a federal statute from State to Federal court. Tanella's lawyers asserted that the case should be dismissed. They argued that Tanella was entitled to immunity from state prosecution on federal supremacy grounds because he was a federal agent acting within the scope of his official federal authority when he shot Dewgard.

The Brooklyn DA's Office countered that Tanella shot Dewgard to keep him from escaping and that he was not immune from prosecution. Tanella asserted that he acted solely in self-defense because he had a reasonable fear that Dewgard would take his gun and shoot him. After all, Tanella had been beaten, knocked

Criminal Prosecution for Using Deadly Force

to the ground, and was exhausted from attempting to defend himself from Dewgard's assault. Tanella saw the bigger and stronger man make a move to disarm him and only then fired a shot.

The Federal Trial Court Judge observed that if Tanella had wanted to shoot Dewgard to keep him from escaping he could have done so many times before he actually shot him. He refrained from shooting until Dewgard gave him no other choice. The Federal Court dismissed the manslaughter charge against SA Tanella and the Brooklyn DA's office filed an appeal with the United States Court of Appeals for the Second Circuit. The International Association of Chiefs of Police (IACP) and the group known as "Americans for Effective Law Enforcement" (AELE) filed an amicus (Friend of the Court) brief with the Second Circuit in full support of SA Tanella and the DEA. The amicus brief took note of the fact that Dewgard was shot in the side of the back and that the prosecution argued that this demonstrated that Dewgard was trying to escape when shot.

The amicus brief cited a study by a **law enforcement expert,** Professor William Lewinski, Ph.D., Minnesota State University that determined, "the time it takes for an officer to process visual stimuli and then react to a person's threat, is a longer period than the suspect's turning actions."[1] In other words, Dewgard was facing Tanella when he decided to shoot but began to turn away before Tanella could complete the shooting action. The point is that a person who is facing an officer and engaging in life-threatening conduct can turn away after the officer decides to shoot in self-defense but before the pull of the trigger on the officer's weapon is completed. Thus, making it appear that the officer intended to shoot the suspect in the back.

The Second Circuit affirmed the judgment of the lower court and ruled that Tanella's shooting of Dewgard was "objectively reasonable." The court agreed that Tanella's belief that Dewgard was trying to disarm him was reasonable.[2] The court observed, "Tanella knew Dewgard to be a seasoned drug dealer and ... experienced first-hand his violent efforts to avoid arrest. Tanella saw Dewgard drive recklessly to evade police capture and nearly hit a pedestrian and her child in the process. Dewgard further

---

[1] See, William Lewinski, "Why Is the Suspect Shot in the Back?" The Police Marksman 25 (6) (Nov. – Dec. 2000): 28

[2] *New York v. Tanella,* 374 F.3d 141 (2d Cir. 2004).

Chapter 4

demonstrated his criminal tenacity by fleeing from an armed police officer while carrying a large bag ... containing three kilograms of cocaine rather than submit to arrest."[3]

The court concluded by stating, "It is clear that the close-quarter situation was hardly conducive to detached deliberation; any reaction by Tanella was necessarily made on a split-second basis. Under these tense and perilous circumstances, Tanella's perception that Dewgard was reaching for his (Tanella's) gun was objectively reasonable as a matter of law."[4]

In reaching its favorable conclusion regarding Tanella, the court cited the U.S. Supreme Court's decision in *Graham v. Connor* and its language that requires lower courts to review excessive force allegations from the perspective of a reasonable officer on the scene of the incident and not with the vision of 20/20 hindsight. Moreover, the Second Circuit observed that when deciding cases of this nature *Graham* calls for the reviewing court to "allow for the fact that police officers are often forced to make split-second judgments—in circumstances that are tense, uncertain, and rapidly evolving."[5]

The Tanella case is significant because it demonstrates that the impact of *Graham v. Connor* extends beyond civil litigation into the criminal prosecution arena. Tanella had his criminal prosecution dismissed because his actions were "objectively reasonable" as required by the U.S. Constitution. He did not go to work that day with the intention of killing Dewgard. Tanella was simply doing his job and in the process of defending his life when Dewgard's own actions forced Tanella to shoot him in self-defense.

The Tanella case is also significant because it demonstrates, in a criminal prosecution of an officer, the valuable nature of expert testimony to defend the actions taken by an officer in a life and death encounter. Attorneys who represent police officers charged with murder, manslaughter or excessive force in criminal cases must seek the expertise and input of expert witnesses who can, by experience and science, support the conduct of the defendant officers.

---

[3] Id. at 151.

[4] Id. at 151,152.

[5] Id.

Chapter 5

THE "OBJECTIVELY REASONABLE" OFFICER DEFINED

The United States Supreme Court in *Graham v. Connor*[1] has identified the legal test for determining the validity of an officer's use of deadly force as involving the question of whether the officer's conduct conforms to what an "objectively reasonable" officer would have done in the same circumstances. In *Graham*, the Court instructed the courts below to examine an officer's conduct from the perspective of a reasonable officer on the scene of an incident and not from 20/20 hindsight. Moreover, the fact that officers are required to make split-second decisions in dynamic, dangerous, and rapidly changing circumstances, involving life and death, must be considered in every case.

The Court also instructed the lower courts to examine vitally important circumstances involving the severity of the crime, the magnitude and imminency of the threat to officers and the public, and whether the suspect was resisting arrest or attempting to flee. All of these factors help to define the "objectively reasonable" law enforcement officer. They are all necessary to the equation but they are not sufficient. They are the outline of the body but not the flesh and bones of the "objectively reasonable" officer.

It is the obligation and duty of law enforcement officers everywhere to define the scope and parameters of the "objectively reasonable" law enforcement officer. No one else has the specific training, the years of actual street experience, and the wisdom gained from training and experience to do it better.

Nonetheless, mark my words, if law enforcement fails in its duty to define the "objectively reasonable" officer, others will step in and do it for them. The outcome will not be pretty. Plaintiffs' lawyers and so-called plaintiffs' expert witnesses will gladly fill the vacuum and in doing so will deliberately attempt to skew the result. They will define the "objectively reasonable" officer in ways that are inaccurate, incorrect and favorable only to their monetary agenda.

---

[1] 490 U.S. 386 (1989).

Chapter 5

Judges and jurors deciding officer involved shooting cases are not experts in the law enforcement field. They must be educated in law enforcement techniques and tactics like anyone else. If law enforcement fails to embrace the challenge to define the "objectively reasonable" officer, others will step in and educate them in ways contrary to reality.

Failure to accomplish this obligation is not an option. Failure will likely result in personal liability for involved officers and their departments and possible criminal prosecution as well. Conversely, the probability of negative legal consequences flowing from deadly force incidents for involved officers is greatly reduced when law enforcement defines the "objectively reasonable" officer.

Accordingly, one of my goals in writing this book is to utilize my 44 years of law enforcement training and experience to assist law enforcement officers and their attorneys in defining the "objectively reasonable" law enforcement officer.

The "objectively reasonable" law enforcement officer is a multidimensional. This officer understands that the **law enforcement occupation is inherently dangerous.** The inherently dangerous nature of the job must not only be understood by officers themselves but they in turn must educate the general public, judges, lawyers, jurors and the media to the nature and depth of danger involved.

The "objectively reasonable "law enforcement officer must be **well-equipped to perform his/her duties.** Officers must, to the extent financially feasible, be equipped with the best available equipment to do their jobs safely and correctly. This should include quality handguns, ammunition, extra ammunition magazines, shoulder weapons to include shotguns, rifles and submachine guns, Tasers and other nonlethal or less lethal weapons, batons, night vision equipment, body armor (soft and hard), ballistic shields, communications equipment, and vehicles.

The "objectively reasonable" law enforcement officer must be **well-trained.** Building upon the initial training at the police academy, training must include **regular firearms training** to maintain and enhance the skill of shooting firearms. This in-service training, at a minimum, must meet all state standards and requirements. In addition the "objectively reasonable" officer must receive **regular shoot/don't shoot training** that rein-

The "Objectively Reasonable" Officer Defined

forces the state and federal constitutional standards for use of deadly force. Officers must also be **trained regularly on their own departmental deadly force policy**, which in some instances will be more restrictive than constitutional standards.

To prepare officers for what they may face in real life street encounters, police departments and law enforcement agencies must, to the extent financially feasible, provide officers with regular opportunities to participate in realistic **interactive computer laser/video shoot/don't shoot training and force on force scenarios** involving realistic weapons that fire paint bullets, aka marking cartridges, or airsoft projectiles.

No "objectively reasonable" officer should be able to avoid regularly scheduled training of the nature described above. If unable to attend, officers must be required to attend make-up sessions. Records of attendance, performance, and proficiency must be created and maintained. Proficiency failure must be corrected through effective remedial training.

The "objectively reasonable" officer understands the concept of **action/reaction (aka, the reactionary gap).** This concept means, assuming that all other things are equal, action will always beat reaction. For example, if a person points a gun at another person, the person pointing the gun will always be able to shoot first before the other person can react and shoot back. There will always be a gap in time between the bad guy taking a threatening action against an officer and the officer's ability to defend against that threat. Officers who believe to the contrary are likely to end up in the obituary column of their local newspaper.

The "objectively reasonable" officer understands the concept of **wound ballistics.** This concept, simply put, means that shooting a person once or even several times is highly unlikely to immediately incapacitate the wounded person. The inability to immediately incapacitate the wounded person provides that person with the ability to continue to try and kill police officers and civilians in the course of a deadly confrontation.

Similarly, the "objectively reasonable" officer also knows that if he/she is shot and wounded once or several times, he/she must continue the fight. Failure to do so provides the bad guy with the

Chapter 5

opportunity to continue to shoot the wounded officer and even approach and execute the officer at close range.

The "objectively reasonable" officer understands the concept of **hide and ambush** which allows an armed fleeing felon to hide during a police chase and ambush pursuing officers as they run past him. This makes the practice of chasing armed fleeing individuals extremely dangerous and unsafe. Over the years many police officers have been killed and wounded in pursuits of this nature. Officers, who decide to chase armed fleeing felons instead of shooting at them from behind (after the appropriate warning, if feasible), do so at their own peril.

The "objectively reasonable" officer understands that in the midst of a potentially deadly firefight, his/her body is likely to experience certain **involuntary physiological changes** that will have a negative impact on the officer's ability to respond to the danger at hand. During a gunfight, the heart rate of a participating officer will rise rapidly as adrenaline is released into the body. Unless the heart rate is kept in check, the officer is likely to experience a loss of fine and complex motor skills; extremely high blood pressure; tunnel vision; loss of depth perception; inability to hear; loss of near vision; inability to think properly; observing things in slow motion and more.

My goal here is to discuss each of these concepts in depth to provide law enforcement officers and their trainers with the information they need to save their own lives and the lives of their fellow officers during an actual deadly force confrontation. Moreover, it is my goal to insure that officers and their trainers are capable of explaining these concepts to their superiors, attorneys, judges, jurors, the media and the general public before and after an officer involved shooting. Educating these individuals is the key to winning in the courtroom and the court of public opinion in the aftermath of an officer involved shooting. Each of these concepts will be examined in detail.

The Inherent Danger of the Law Enforcement Job

The Law Enforcement Officers Killed & Assaulted (LEOKA) reports produced annually by the FBI disclose that between 1985 and 2011, 1680 law enforcement officers in the United States were feloniously murdered while in the performance of their

The "Objectively Reasonable" Officer Defined

sworn duties. Although these statistics speak for themselves and tell a tragic tale, it is my goal to examine them in greater depth to determine what lessons can be learned from them to save officers' lives in the future.

Never Underestimate Your Adversary

The "objectively reasonable" officer will never underestimate his/her street adversaries. In 2006, the FBI published a study entitled "Violent Encounters," which included interviews with 43 offenders and 50 officers involved in 40 shooting incidents across America.[2] The study reported that the offenders' weapon of choice in these incidents was predominantly the handgun and all but one was obtained illegally.[3]

More than 40% of the offenders had been involved in actual shooting confrontations before they shot at a police officer.[4] Only 8 of the 50 officers had been involved in a prior shooting.[5] About 60% of the offenders claimed to be instinctive shooters, that is, pointing and shooting their firearms without aligning the sights.[6] The study found that nearly 70% of the offenders were able to shoot officers during the encounters, while only about 40% of the officers were similarly successful.[7] In all but three cases, the offenders fired at the officers first, usually catching the officers by surprise.[8]

Ed Davis, one of the authors of the study for the FBI said, the study team "did not realize how **cold blooded the younger generation of offender is. They have been exposed to killing after killing. They fully expect to get killed and they don't hesitate to shoot anybody, including a police officer.**"[9] The study reveals that **"Offenders typically dis-**

---

[2] Anthony J. Pinizzotto, Ph.D., Edward F. Davis, Charles E. Miller (all employees of the FBI), "Violent Encounters, 2006, Executive Summary," p. iii.

[3] See, Ken Corpus, "Firearmz—Firearms Training And Defense" blog, Feb. 10, 2007.

[4] Id.

[5] Id.

[6] Id.

[7] Id.

[8] Id.

[9] Id.

Chapter 5

played no moral or ethical restraints in using firearms. In fact, the street combat veterans survived by developing a shoot-first mentality."[10]

An example of this kind of mind set is found in an interview with one of the offenders in the Study. After firing an entire magazine full of bullets at a police officer and shooting him numerous times, the offender explained later, "To tell you the truth, I didn't even really think about it.... I didn't think about killing or not killing. It was just a target that I needed to stop chasing me. And, after I emptied my clip ... it was done. Like I said, he was chasing me and he needed to be stopped and so I did. I mean, I didn't think about him as a person or a police officer. He was just an obstacle."[11]

"Objectively reasonable" officers must know their adversary, understand the sociopathic nature of their personalities and appreciate the high degree of danger they face on the street. Underestimating them is a ticket to eternity. The offenders have little or no regard for human life and will not hesitate to shoot a police officer. This lack of human compassion gives them a distinct advantage in a gunfight. Officers must prepare mentally for violent confrontations before they are in one. Anything less will result in their family hearing "Taps" from a trumpet and being handed an American flag at their funeral.

The "Kill Zone"

LEOKA statistics disclose that 543 officers were murdered in the line of duty during the years 2002 – 2011. Five hundred of those officers were killed by firearms. The statistics reveal the distances between the victim officers and their killers during the shooting incidents. Statistics show that 235 officers were located from 0 to 5 feet away from their killers when they were shot. Ninety-two of the victim officers were located between 6 and 10 feet from their killers and 72 officers were between 11 and 20 feet from their adversaries. When combined, the figures disclose that 399 of the 500 officers (approximately 80%) killed by firearms

---

[10] Id.

[11] Anthony J. Pinizzotto, Ph.D., Edward F. Davis, Charles E. Miller (All employees of the FBI), "Violent Encounters, 2006, Executive Summary," p. iii., p. 74.

The "Objectively Reasonable" Officer Defined

during the ten-year period were located between 0 and 20 feet from their killers.

These statistics speak directly to "objectively reasonable" law enforcement firearms trainers and administrators. They tell a story that should resonate with persons responsible for sound firearms training policies. Although the skill of distance marksmanship is important to master, the vast majority of law enforcement firearms training should take place in close quarters.

Given the clear "kill zone" statistics, "objectively reasonable" officers should be required to fire most of their training rounds from the 7 yard line and in toward the target. Officers should be timed in their shooting drills to fire as quickly and accurately as possible under time pressure. **The statistics prove that from 0 to 20 feet is the "kill zone."** Eighty percent of the officers murdered by firearms from 2002 through 2011 were killed in this zone. This is the area where officers live or die and their training must focus on this zone.

A good example of the kind of brutal unexpected events that can transpire in the **"kill zone"** is found in the tragic shooting death of Laurens County, Georgia Deputy Kyle Dinkheller in 1998. Dinkheller was on "routine" road patrol when he observed Andrew Brannan driving his pick-up truck at 98 mph. Dinkheller pulled Brannan over. Brannan exited his vehicle and proceeded to verbally assault the Deputy with a tirade of expletives and called on the Deputy to shoot him. He approached Dinkheller in an aggressive and threatening manner twice and was ordered to retreat. The vast majority of Dinkheller's encounter with Brannan can be seen and heard on Dinkheller's dash-cam video.

During the encounter, Brannan disobeyed Dinkheller's order and returned to the cab of his truck. He obtained an M-1 Carbine from under the front seat. Dinkheller observed him grab the rifle and repeatedly ordered him to put it down. When Brannan continued to hold the rifle, Dinkheller fired a shot at him with his sidearm. The shot missed. Approximately 26 seconds elapsed between the time Dinkheller first ordered Brannan to drop his rifle and when Dinkheller began to fire at Brannan.

Instead of trying to escape or seeking cover, Brannan, a Vietnam War veteran, aggressively approached Dinkheller's position, firing the carbine repeatedly as he moved forward. Brannan

Chapter 5

received a bullet wound to the stomach during his attack but was undeterred. The video dash-cam reveals that Brannan never hesitated in his attack after receiving his bullet wound. In fact, by looking at the video, I saw no evidence that he was shot. He continued to move forward, reloaded and shot Dinkheller at least ten times, including a fatal shot to the head. Dinkheller can be heard on the audio portion of his dash-cam video screaming as he is literally executed by Brannan in the "kill zone" at close range.

Deputy Dinkheller bravely fought for his life and must be recognized as a law enforcement hero. Nonetheless, what happened to him must be closely examined by "objectively reasonable" law enforcement officers, trainers and administrators to minimize or prevent future similar tragedies.

The first of several lessons to be learned from the Dinkheller shooting is to **avoid hesitating to fire** at an adversary who refuses to drop a weapon immediately. This hesitation surely gave Brannan a tactical advantage that contributed to Dinkheller's death. Brannan returned to his truck to grab an M-1 .30 caliber carbine. When the rifle was first observed by Dinkheller, his firing should have commenced. Instead of immediately firing at Brannan while he was still centered in a fixed location, that is, between the driver's side open door and the front seat of the truck, Dinkheller repeatedly ordered Brannan to drop the rifle. The failure to fire multiple rounds at Brannan immediately gave him the chance to leave a fixed area and move aggressively forward toward Dinkheller.

When an apparently unarmed man disobeys a direct order, returns to his truck and grabs a high-powered rifle, his actions speak for themselves. He is bent on performing mayhem. The "objectively reasonable" officer must react immediately to such clear danger signals. **The time for orders and warnings had ended;** the time to shoot him had begun. A warning to drop the weapon is required by the law only if it is feasible to do so.[12]

Second, "objectively reasonable" officers must **expect the "unexpected."** Nothing is ever really "routine." After all, Brannan was not wanted for murder, rape, armed robbery, or some other serious felony. He had been stopped for excessive

---

[12] *Tennessee v. Garner,* 471 U.S. 1 (1985).

The "Objectively Reasonable" Officer Defined

speed. Nonetheless, his verbally combative manner, threatening approaches, and refusal to take orders from the Deputy were red flag warnings of bad things to come. This type of **aggressive verbal and non-verbal behavior must be taken seriously** and carefully evaluated by the officer. When the officer is alone, it calls for **delaying close contact to the extent possible and a request for immediate back-up.** Deputy Dinkheller did call for back-up and tried to avoid close contact with Brannan but it was not enough.

Third, the "unexpected" takes on an additional extremely ominous dimension when the traffic offender obtains a firearm from inside his truck. The "routine" traffic stop has suddenly become mortal combat. Being armed with a shoulder weapon was about to provide Brannan with another distinct tactical advantage in the firefight that followed, that is, rifle vs. pistol. Bringing a pistol to a rifle fight is never a good idea.

The rifle Brannan grabbed was an M-1 .30 caliber carbine (a military assault rifle that fires rounds at approximately 1970 feet per second). Suddenly, the recalcitrant traffic offender morphed into a well-trained and well-armed military style adversary intent on taking a life. Only a shoulder weapon like an AR-15 rifle would have provided Deputy Dinkheller a good chance to survive the deadly confrontation that he faced.

The lesson here is for "objectively reasonable" police administrators to give their officers a fighting chance by placing AR-15 rifles in patrol vehicles. Shame on police administrators and politicians who deprive officers of the immediate ability to defend themselves by denying them the right to have AR-15 rifles in their patrol vehicles. This sort of shameful political correctness has and will continue to result in officers being killed and maimed. (See my discussion on "Politics and the Patrol Rifle," infra.).

Fourth, the "unexpected" continued unabated in this incident. One might expect that when a police officer fires his weapon at a person, that person would likely run or seek cover. This did not happen in the Dinkheller murder. **Instead, Brannan moved rapidly forward, shooting as he moved.** The victim officer was not in the picture of the video during Brannan's attack but one can only wonder whether he looked down to reload as Brannan closed the distance between them.

Changing magazines should be accomplished, to the extent possible, by keeping your eyes focused in the direction of potential adversaries. No more than momentary downward glances should be necessary to complete a magazine change. Magazine changes should be so frequently practiced that they become second nature. Looking down for more than a quick glance while changing magazines will allow an adversary to aggressively attack an officer's position or flank the officer to gain tactical advantage.

Finally, officers should take at least one more thing away from the Dinkheller murder. During the firefight, Dinkheller shot Brannan in the stomach. That wound did not slow Brannan down for one second. He continued forward and fired multiple rounds at Dinkheller. "Objectively reasonable" **officers must understand that shooting an adversary is highly unlikely to incapacitate the person trying to kill them.** The battle is almost never over when your adversary is shot. **Officers must continue to shoot their adversary until the threat is over.**[13]

Pre-Battle Precautions

LEOKA statistics disclose that in 2011, fifty of the sixty-three officers killed by firearms were killed with handguns. These same statistics reveal that only seventeen of these officers returned fire at their killers. Because only seventeen officers fired at their killers, the statistics suggest that the victim officers were likely surprised by their adversaries at the beginning of the gun battle.

There can be little doubt when only 17 of the murdered officers returned fire that the killers quickly pulled firearms from on or near their persons and caught the victim officers by surprise. **In order to avoid surprise, officers must approach**

---

[13] Brannan was convicted of the murder of Deputy Dinkheller in 2000 after a jury trial and sentenced to death. His conviction and sentence was affirmed by the Georgia Supreme Court in 2002. In 2006 Brannan's death sentence and possibly his conviction was overturned because of ineffective assistance of counsel. In 2008, the Georgia Supreme Court reinstated Brannan's murder conviction and death sentence. Brennan was executed by lethal injection at the Jackson, Georgia State Prison at 8:33 p.m., January 13, 2015.

The "Objectively Reasonable" Officer Defined

the "kill zone" of every suspect encounter with great caution. The time honored saying, "stay alert, stay alive" teaches law enforcement officers a lesson for the ages.

Approach Vehicles with Extreme Caution

No suspect encounter is ever "routine." Remember the Deputy Dinkheller murder during every traffic stop. During vehicle stops, to the extent feasible, **officers should approach cautiously and slowly on the passenger side of the vehicle.** It is safer from a traffic safety perspective; it also gives the officer more opportunity to see inside the passenger compartment of the suspect vehicle and move to a safer spot in the event of a threat.

In March 2013, Dr. William J. Lewinski, Force Science Institute, reported on his law enforcement vehicle stop study entitled, "The Influence of Officer Positioning on Movement during a Threatening Traffic Stop Scenario." At the outset, Dr. Lewinski cited FBI statistics for the time period of 2001 – 2010, which disclosed that 60 of the 541 officers murdered in that time frame were killed during traffic stops. Dr. Lewinski's study involved 93 participating police officers.

During the study, officers were instructed to approach a vehicle they had stopped for speeding that was parked in front of their cruiser. They were permitted to approach on either side of the stopped vehicle and were allowed to stand at certain designated positions next to the stopped vehicle that would be normal places for officers to stand while engaging the driver.

One of the positions available for approaching officers to stand was on the driver's side at a 45° angle forward from the B-Pillar of the suspect vehicle. The B-Pillar is the door post of the suspect vehicle just behind the front seat on both sides of the suspect vehicle. Eighteen officers chose to stand at this location. Another option for approaching officers was to stand at a 45° angle forward from the B-Pillar on the passenger side of the suspect vehicle to engage the driver. Seventeen officers chose to stand at this location.

There is a safety zone that is located on each side of a suspect vehicle that is called the Mitigation Zone (MZ). The MZ is located on both sides of the suspect vehicle behind the B-Pillar. The size of the MZ is determined by testing the angle/angles that make it most difficult for a driver of a suspect vehicle to shoot a police

Chapter 5

officer while sitting in the front seat of the suspect vehicle. In the study, the MZ on the passenger side of the suspect vehicle extended to a 45° angle backward and out from the B-Pillar. The MZ on the driver's side of the suspect vehicle extended at approximately a 10° angle backward and out from the B-Pillar.

During the study, the driver of the suspect vehicle, from a sitting position facing forward, was able to aim and fire a marking cartridge/paint bullet at the officers who stood at a 45° degree angle forward from the B-Pillar on the driver's side in .50 of a second. If the driver had not taken time to aim, this shot would have been fired even more quickly.

Conversely, it took the officers starting from the 45° angle described above, an average of 2.46 seconds to place their entire body in the driver's side MZ. Once a suspect fires the first shot from a handgun, subsequent shots will be fired at .25 second intervals. (See action/reaction section of this book, infra.). This would permit the suspect to fire at least 9 shots at the officer before he/she fully reaches the MZ. The average time that officers in this position were able to fire their first shot at the driver was 1.99 seconds.

When the officers approached on the passenger side of the suspect vehicle and stood at a 45° angle forward from the B-Pillar, the results were slightly better, that is, safer, for the responding officers. In this situation, the suspect driver was able to aim and fire a shot at the officers in .52 of a second. Again, the first shot would be faster if no time was taken to aim. The officers on average were able to place their entire body in the passenger side MZ in 1.5 seconds. This would allow the suspect to fire at least 4 and possibly 5 shots at the officer before he/she reached the MZ. In this situation on average, officers fired their first return shot at the driver in 2.15 seconds.

This study involved three approaches of the suspect vehicle by each of the participating officers. The first two approaches resulted only in verbal jousting between the officers and the driver. Only the third approach resulted in a surprise life-threatening situation. Three approaches were chosen to make the third approach more of a surprise to participating officers, that is, more realistic.

The "Objectively Reasonable" Officer Defined

The study makes abundantly clear the real danger involved in officer vehicle approaches. It also demonstrates that although no approach is totally safe, approaching from the passenger side is safer because it takes the officer less time to reach the MZ. This study further demonstrates the deadly nature of the so-called "reactionary gap," that is, the time between when a suspect begins to shoot at an officer and the time it takes the officer to respond in kind.

To avoid becoming victims of the reactionary gap, approaching officers should instruct all passengers to **make both of their hands visible to the officer.** This can be accomplished by instructing occupants to place their hands on the steering wheel, dashboard, and on the top back of the front seats. There can be little doubt that some of the officers killed in 2011 did not see both hands of the subjects who shot them. The hands of adversaries are universally involved in officer murders.

Protect Your Firearm

LEOKA statistics show that between 2002 and 2011, 46 officers were murdered with their own weapons. Tragedies of this nature are largely preventable. Officers in uniform carrying exposed weapons **must use holsters that have built in levels of protection to insure that only the officer has access to his/her handgun.** Anything less is unacceptable. Officers who utilize protective holsters must constantly practice drawing a safe unloaded firearm from these holsters. Drawing from them must become second nature, quick, smooth and easy. Difficulty should be left only for the suspect. Many things that will happen in a firefight are unpredictable. The job of the "objectively reasonable" officer is to take reasonable precautions to prevent those dangerous things that are predictable, for example, being killed with your own gun.

Wear Your Body Armor

LEOKA statistics disclose that between 2002 and 2011, 543 officers were feloniously murdered and only 358 of those officers were wearing body armor. Not all of these police killings would have been prevented if every murdered officer wore a bullet proof vest because 292 officers were shot in the head. Nonetheless, **the failure to wear body armor in the face of police officer**

Chapter 5

murder statistics is unthinkable and defies logic and common sense.

The Associated Press reported a story on May 25, 2006, that provides a good example of the value of wearing body armor. The story reported that Tampa, Florida Officer James Wilkinson stopped Tomas Montesdeoca for a traffic violation at 1: 30 am. The suspect subsequently shot Wilkinson at close range with a .357 caliber pistol directly in the chest. The powerful bullet passed through Wilkinson's uniform shirt, a spiral notebook in his pocket and his entire bullet proof vest before coming to rest superficially in his outer chest wall.

The suspect left the scene but the wounded officer was able to radio for assistance. The suspect was shot and killed by other officers shortly thereafter at a nearby location. The great news is that Officer Wilkinson was treated and released from a Tampa hospital later that same day. Officer Wilkinson's life was spared because he prudently prepared for a life-threatening confrontation on the day he will remember for the rest of his life. This officer did exactly what the "objectively reasonable" police officer should do, that is, prevent the preventable.

Vital Equipment on Your Body or Within Your Reach

Officers must, to the extent possible, carry all of the equipment necessary to win a deadly confrontation on their person. Side arms, rifles, and flashlights locked in the trunk of a patrol car will be of no value to an officer suddenly confronted with an armed and dangerous adversary. There will be no time to run to the trunk, open it, and reach for your firearm. Rifles and shotguns should be maintained inside the passenger compartment of police cruisers, secure but immediately accessible, loaded and ready for battle.

Likewise, officers should carry several (at least two) extra fully loaded handgun magazines on their person in the event they become involved in a protracted firefight. The Los Angeles Police Department (LAPD) became involved in a 44-minute shootout with two heavily armed bank robbers in 1997. The bank robbers wore homemade body armor with metal plates and carried fully automatic assault rifles with 100 round magazines. They entered the bank carrying 3,300 rounds and fired 100 rounds inside the bank.

The "Objectively Reasonable" Officer Defined

During the shootout that followed, the bank robbers fired 1,100 rounds at the LAPD officers who responded to the robbery in progress. LAPD officers fired 650 rounds at the bank robbers. When it was over, ten officers, and seven civilians were wounded. The two bank robbers were killed. A word to the wise should be sufficient. Imagine the feeling of horror that would follow the realization that your adversary is continuing to shoot at you and you are out of ammunition.

Every police vehicle should be equipped with extra ammunition for rifles and pistols in the event of a protracted firefight. This extra ammunition should likewise be secured but immediately accessible. This will provide a proximate source of ammunition in the event that an officer uses up all of the ammunition on his/her person during a shootout.

Chapter 6

FIREARMS AND DEADLY FORCE TRAINING

The "objectively reasonable" law enforcement officer knows that regular recurrent firearms' training is necessary to function safely on the often deadly streets of America today. Likewise, the "objectively reasonable" officer is well aware that he/she is not fighting under military style rules of engagement but instead is required to adhere to the constitutional and departmental policy standards that govern the use of deadly force.

Mandatory Firearms Skill and Marksmanship Training

Proficiency in shooting and marksmanship skills regarding both handguns and shoulder weapons (i.e., rifles and shotguns) derives directly from repetitive practice using the methods taught by expert firearms trainers. Skills of this nature are initially taught to law enforcement recruits in their training academies. Recruits unable to master them after sufficient remedial training should be denied graduation from the basic training academy. This skill is an essential element of the job.

The skill of shooting a firearm, especially handguns, will diminish over time. Preventing diminishing marksmanship skills requires recurrent repetitive In-Service firearms training.[1] Diminished marksmanship skills for police officers are a recipe for disaster. It is predictive of negative safety consequences for the officers themselves, fellow officers, and the general public.

During my service as an FBI Special Agent, agents were required to shoot and qualify at an outdoor firearms range four times a year. In addition, during the cold winter months, we were offered the option to shoot indoors for an additional four times.

During the four mandatory outdoor qualification sessions, FBI agents had to meet or exceed qualification standards during each of the four shoots. There were no exceptions. Performance records were maintained by the FBI firearms instructors and remedial

---

[1] In-Service firearms training is designed for active duty law enforcement officers who have already graduated from the basic police academy. This training is sometimes referred to as Professional Development training and is ordinarily administered once or more times annually.

Chapter 6

training was given to those failing to qualify. Agents who were unable to attend a given mandatory training session were marked absent and were required to attend a make-up session at a later time. Agents were not excused from training and those unable to qualify were not given a pass. They received remedial training until they qualified.

There is no minimum national standard and no legal mandate regarding how many times annually active duty officers must shoot and qualify with respect to firearms.[2] I understand that many state and local departments across America are unable to meet the FBI standard due to budget and manpower constraints. Nonetheless, the FBI requirement of four mandatory qualification shoots per year serves as worthy goal. At a minimum, In-Service firearms training must adhere to all State, and if more stringent, departmental standards for all state and local officers.

In February 2007, Ken Forbus, an NRA Certified Firearms Instructor, posted a blog that reviewed an FBI Study entitled "Violent Encounters: A Study of Felonious Assaults on Our Nation's Law Enforcement Officers." The FBI Study was published in 2006 and according to Forbus's review, the Study focused on 40 violent encounters between 43 violent offenders and 50 law enforcement officers.

One disturbing finding of the Study was that 80% of the offenders practiced regularly with handguns. In fact, these offenders averaged 23 practice sessions per year. In contrast, the victim officers in these violent encounters averaged 14 hours of handgun training annually and 2.5 qualifications annually. This indicates that many of the victim officers officially practiced training with their weapons substantially less than their on-the-street adversaries. This Study alone sends a clear message—More firearms training for law enforcement officers is necessary.

Law enforcement trainers should be selected carefully by police administrators. These men and women must not only excel at shooting but also must exhibit strong leadership skills and be capable of sharing their wisdom effectively. Law enforcement trainers and administrators must take all necessary steps to insure that all recruit and In-Service training is taken completely

---

[2] See, Urey Patrick and John Hall, "In Defense of Self and Others," 2005, p. 84.

Firearms and Deadly Force Training

seriously by trainers and participants. No officer should ever be excused from training. Make-up sessions must be held for those unable to attend. Participants who attend each session must qualify by the end of each session. Officers unable to qualify must receive remedial training until they qualify. Anything less is unacceptable and must not be tolerated.

Trainers must keep proficiency records on all officers. Trainers should be aware that these records may be subject to subpoena, judicial review and disciplinary hearing scrutiny in the event of an officer involved shooting. In the event of a shooting incident, training officers and police administrators are likely to be required to testify **under oath** in a civil lawsuit, grand jury or a disciplinary hearing about the firearms training received by involved officers. Great care should be taken to insure that those records are accurate, correct, and truthful in every respect.

Falsification of training records could result in criminal charges, including perjury, against the offending officials. There can be no doubt that once false records are entered, the likelihood of perjury is greatly enhanced during legal proceedings that may follow. The best way to avoid a cover-up is to avoid false record keeping from the outset. Integrity in firearms training and honest record keeping will always occur when strong-willed, dedicated, and professional firearms instructors manage a department's training program.

Police administrators must insure that all reasonable training actions and decisions by their firearms trainers are fully supported and never undermined. The cardinal sin of a firearms trainer and police administrator would be to allow an unqualified officer to take a loaded firearm onto the street while on duty.

Decisions of this nature are manifestly unfair to the unqualified officers, their fellow law enforcement officers, and the general public. Such a decision places all these categories of persons in jeopardy of death or great bodily harm. Being called to answer for allowing this to happen after a tragedy occurs would be my worst nightmare. Trainers and administrators must take all necessary steps to avoid a local news headline like the following: "Local Officer Shoots Innocent Bystander; Firearms Training Records Falsified."

Chapter 6

One final point to be made regarding firearms marksmanship skills is obvious for law enforcement officers. If your Department does not offer regular repetitive firearms training, officers should seize the initiative and join a local rifle and pistol club to enhance these skills on their own. It is similar to obtaining preventive maintenance on your automobile. You pay for it yourself but such maintenance is a prophylactic to disaster. Likewise, enhancing firearms skills privately will likely be a significant factor in saving one's life down the road.

Even when your Department schedules regular firearms training, shooting on your own will contribute substantially to saving your life someday. I am a member of a local gun club and have been for many years. I pay $100 annually for the privilege and shoot often. It has been money well spent.

Firearms Training—Beyond Marksmanship

As described previously, regular marksmanship training is necessary and essential for the "objectively reasonable" law enforcement officer but it is not sufficient. The degree of danger in deadly force confrontations is so great that firearms training must go beyond good or even excellent marksmanship. Firearms training must also be made as realistic to actual street shooting confrontations as possible. Realistic firearms training at a minimum must include realistic targets with actual pictures of armed perpetrators. It should also include interactive video simulator training with realistic laser-style weapons involving shoot and don't shoot scenarios.

Likewise, force on force training scenarios should be created in which "real bad guys" (i.e., law enforcement officers acting as bad guys) and law enforcement officers confront each other with realistic looking paint bullet (marking cartridges) or airsoft weapons and ammunition. Training should also include requiring officers to shoot on the move because many gunfights involve substantial movement by perpetrators and officers alike. Finally, officers should be constantly trained and reminded to seek available protective cover during regular training sessions to lower the chances of being shot and killed or wounded.

All of this training should be regularly repeated so that officers will not have to pause and think about what they need to do. The training must be so ingrained in their psyche that it becomes second nature as though they are acting on autopilot. This is the kind of training that will allow officers to not only survive a firefight but definitively win it.

Training on Realistic Targets

Lt. Colonel Dave Grossman, a well-known and renowned instructor and author in law enforcement (and military) use of deadly force, in his book *On Combat*, speaks extensively on the kind of targets that law enforcement officers should be shooting at during regular firearms training.[3] Grossman has summarily dismissed bulls-eye (i.e., circle targets) and silhouette targets (i.e., targets with the image of a human torso and head) as grossly inadequate. Instead, he recommends that targets be "photo realistic" and contain a picture of a real looking human holding a firearm or some other dangerous weapon.

Grossman believes that officers who train consistently with photo realistic targets will become mentally prompted to act immediately to defend themselves from being shot and killed or wounded by a menacing adversary. In other words, because of repetitive training involving realistic targets, officers will react without hesitation to the danger confronting them. Hesitation in such dire circumstances significantly raises the likelihood of death or serious bodily harm for the officer and others. (Remember the Deputy Dinkheller shooting, supra.) Repetitively shooting at targets containing armed and dangerous human images will cause the officer to react instantly without conscious thought or delay during an actual shooting event.

Colonel Grossman reinforces his point by contrasting the training of the US Military in World War II and the Vietnam War.[4] Grossman points to a study conducted during World War II, which revealed that unless ordered to fire by a superior, only 15 to 20% of US soldiers would fire at an exposed enemy soldier. He concludes that, "when soldiers were left to their own devices, the vast majority of them ... could not kill."[5] Grossman correctly

---

[3] Lt. Col. Dave Grossman with Loren W. Christensen, *On Combat*, 2004, p. 71.

[4] Id., p. 74.

[5] Id.

Chapter 6

points out that this was a problem with training that could not be allowed to continue. In war and officer involved shootings, failure to quickly shoot at your adversary exponentially raises the probability of your own demise.

Colonel Grossman reports that our Soldiers in WWII were trained to shoot at bulls-eye targets. He observed that bulls-eye targets present no threat, don't shoot back and don't condition the soldier/law enforcement officer to immediately shoot in self-defense. US Military trainers recognized this gross deficiency in training after WWII and corrected it before the Vietnam War.

Colonel Grossman reports that soldiers who have served in our military since Vietnam have been universally trained to shoot at man-shaped targets that pop up in their field of view, "thus ingraining in them a conditioned response. The stimulus appeared and they had a split-second to respond."[6] This kind of training was repeated time and again and resulted in a sea change in mindset. In fact, during Vietnam, the shooting response rate of our soldiers increased from 15 – 20% to 95%.[7] Certainly this extraordinary increase is shooting rates is directly related to better training and kept many of our soldiers from death and serious injury.

Law enforcement officers in America today deserve to receive the same lifesaving training that has proven to be the best for our military. Anything less is grossly inadequate and unconscionable. Paper targets must contain photos of life-like armed adversaries. Firing ranges should be equipped to the extent possible with targets of armed subjects that appear suddenly in the path of trainees. Constant repetitive shooting at targets of this nature should be the norm rather than the exception.

Video Simulators and Force on Force Training

By now it should be abundantly clear to readers that firearms training that is limited to shooting at paper targets for qualification purposes is grossly inadequate. Such limited training amounts to a monumental failure to protect the safety of those

---

[6] Id. at p. 76.

[7] Id. at p. 74.

Firearms and Deadly Force Training

who protect us from evil perpetrators. Our brave law enforcement officers deserve much more.

It is the duty and obligation of law enforcement administrators, public officials, and police firearms trainers to provide the best training that is financially feasible for their officers. This training should attempt to condition officers and expose them to what it is like in actual officer involved shooting situations. Officers exposed to realistic training scenarios requiring deadly force are much more likely to survive and win real life deadly force confrontations.

Accordingly, training should include regular exposure to computer-controlled video simulators that involve life-like video scenarios that permit officers to interact with the video taking place before them. Realistic-looking firearms are used to connect the officer mechanically to what is occurring on the video screen before him/her. Places of cover and concealment should be set up adjacent to the officers to allow them to choose available cover to protect themselves as though the simulation is real. Interaction with the video will teach officers when to shoot or not shoot. It will drive home how quickly "routine" interactions turn into life-threatening confrontations. It will demonstrate to officers the split-second decision making that makes the difference in life-and-death situations.

The most realistic method of recreating real life deadly force incidents involves force on force training. Force on force training involves actors (police officers or otherwise) involved in assuming the role of armed and dangerous perpetrators. These actors are provided a script and will directly confront law enforcement officers involved in the training session. All participants will be dressed in protective gear and both trainees and "bad guys" will be armed with training firearms that are designed to fire paint bullets, aka marking cartridges, or air-soft projectiles.

In his book, Colonel Grossman comments about force on force training and observes: "There is a powerful obligation to participate in this type of realistic training. There are many officers who do not want to participate in paint bullet training for fear of having to lay their training skills on the line in front of their peers, fear of feeling the sting of a round impact their skin, and a general fear of having to function outside their comfort zone.

Chapter 6

Yes, these factors do exist in this valuable, realistic training—but they also exist in a real gun battle."[8]

As mentioned previously, the point of force on force training is to condition officers to the extent possible on what it is like to be involved in a real firefight before they are actually in one. Imagine the impact on an officer in a force on force training session that is shot once or multiple times with paint bullets. This is especially effective when one realizes that the velocity of handgun paint bullets is approximately half the speed of real handgun rounds. Being shot in a paint bullet training exercise will have a lasting positive impact upon involved officers.

Officers involved in force on force training will learn to rely on their safety training in a more positive way. They will approach potentially dangerous subjects more cautiously. They will learn to take cover and not to expose large portions of their bodies to their adversaries. They will draw their firearms to the ready position in dangerous situations to react more quickly to dangerous actions by suspects. They will learn to move laterally in the face of danger and shoot before being shot. They will realize in an unforgettable way, the lifesaving value of wearing protective body armor. They will also experience the positive and negative aspects that the release of adrenaline will have on their minds and bodies during life-threatening situations.

In the Line of Enemy Fire—Move and Shoot

The concept of "Action v. Reaction," which will be examined at great length later in this book, reveals that when a shooter has made up his mind to shoot and has his finger on the trigger of a pointed handgun, he will be able to fire nearly 4 bullets in one second. A law enforcement officer who finds himself/herself on the wrong end of that firearm is threatened with a life-ending situation. The officer will never be able to draw a holstered weapon and respond to the threat in time to stop it. Even if the officer has already drawn his/her own weapon, the end result will be the same. Before the officer can fire his/her weapon at the offender, the offender will fire three or four bullets at the officer. Of course, this is an unacceptable result and outcome.

---

[8] Id. at p. 102.

Firearms and Deadly Force Training

When I was still in the FBI in the late 1990s, the FBI trained its agents to take several steps to the right when facing this situation and fire multiple rounds at the offender while moving.[9] Dave Spaulding, a well-known law enforcement firearms trainer, wrote an article on this subject for Policeone.com in July 2006 entitled, "Firearms: Don't be a Sitting Duck." In the article, Spaulding speaks about the necessity of officer movement in the above described situation. He says, "We all know hitting a moving target is harder than hitting a stationary one. Sitting ducks in a gunfight get hurt or killed. So, don't just stand there—move."

In my view, Spaulding is spot on in his thinking. By moving in the above circumstance, the officer is immediately altering the Action v. Reaction dynamic. The suspect who initially had the advantage is now required to react to the officer's movement. The officer is no longer standing where the suspect thought he was. There will follow the inevitable suspect need for split-second adjustment both mentally and physically to the officer's position change. Meanwhile, if the officer has drawn his weapon, he can begin to fire at the suspect before the suspect has adjusted to the change of position. The concept of Action v. Reaction has been turned in favor of the officer and rounds are now traveling directly at the offender. Moreover, the officer is also creating distance between himself and the offender. Distance increases the odds of not being shot by the offender.

Spaulding's excellent analysis can be found in its entirety on the Policeone.com website but for now I would like to focus on one of his suggestions. Spaulding states, "The most common and best utilized movement in a gunfight is the lateral movement. In fact,

---

[9] Moving either way is acceptable. However, a study conducted in 2007 (Force Science News-Transmission #66-2/23/07) by Dr. William Lewinski, Force Science Research Center Ltd. (FSRC), Minnesota State University, Mankato, MN and one of its technical advisors, Ron Avery, involving 103 non-law enforcement shooters, some who had never fired a gun before, determined that the many of the initial rounds fired by study participants, "tended to go **to the right of the target (from the shooter's perspective)**. This contradicts conventional wisdom, [Avery] said, which holds that shots fired from a right-handed shooter often end up going to the left. If this apparent discrepancy is sustained in further testing, officers who are taught to move to their left in hopes of avoiding early rounds may, in fact, be stepping into the field of fire." (Emphasis added.)

It should be noted that moving aggressively behind close available protective cover is another available and even preferred option to facing a dangerous shooter head on. Standing still is not a wise choice.

you should incorporate the lateral movement just about every time you practice the draw. Consider this: You confront an armed suspect [and both draw your weapons]. He ... attempts to deliver his gun in your direction, but you aren't there. You've sidestepped (i.e., moved laterally), which gives you just enough time to get into his reaction/response loop, creating lag time for him and allowing you to deliver the first accurate shot. ... This move has saved cops ... time and again."

In a later article titled "Shooting While Moving" written for LawOfficer.Com. in June, 2010, Spaulding once again speaks about the concept of lateral movement and states, "The truth is getting off the line [the direct line of fire between the bad guy and the officer] does work, but the single lateral step taught on many square ranges doesn't accomplish this. Lateral movement, to be effective, must be explosive and is more likely to work, if your opponent is [at] twelve o'clock and you're [at] six o'clock ... drawing and shooting as you ..." move laterally in an aggressive manner away from your opponent.

Officers need not wait for their next Department-sponsored training session to practice this technique. It can be practiced over and over again with a safe and empty duty firearm. Place a target of an armed subject holding a firearm on your basement/garage wall. Stand between 5 and 10 feet away and repetitively practice moving laterally away from the target while dry firing multiple rounds at the target. It may someday save your life.

Repetitive Regular Firearms Training—A Necessity

Lt. Colonel Grossman in his book *On Combat* is a major proponent of regular recurrent and repetitive firearms training for both law enforcement officers and the US Military. He reports that in 2003 while training US Marines before their deployment to Iraq, he was approached by a marine who told Grossman what a veteran marine once told him about training and combat. The marine said, "Colonel, my old Gunny taught me that **in combat you do not rise to the occasion, you sink to the level of your training.**"[10]

---

[10] Lt. Col. Dave Grossman with Loren W. Christensen, *On Combat*, 2004, p. 71.

Firearms and Deadly Force Training

Colonel Grossman believes that "Whatever is drilled in during training comes out the other end in combat."[11] Grossman believes that when officers practice life-saving techniques over and over again in training drills and on their own, the techniques become part of their very nature. The techniques become so ingrained in the officers psyche that when confronted by a deadly adversary, they react without conscious thought, if you will, on autopilot.

Firearms Training in Close Quarters

As mentioned earlier in this book, FBI LEOKA statistics for the ten-year period between 2002 and 2011 reveal that 500 law enforcement officers were murdered by firearms and 399 (approximately 80%) of those officers were standing between 0 and 20 feet from their killers when shot. This statistical data is highly instructive and cries out for change in the manner that firearms' training is delivered to officers throughout the United States. When the well-known **"Kill Zone"** is twenty feet or less, why do we spend scarce training time shooting from distances of 25 yards or beyond? Shouldn't the training focus be on training officers to not only survive but win deadly confrontations in the "kill zone"?

Kevin Johnson, a journalist for *USA Today,* reported on January 7, 2013, that the FBI has radically changed its firearms training to reflect the need to focus on what historically has taken place in the "kill zone." Johnson reports that the FBI reviewed nearly 200 shootings involving FBI agents over a 17-year period and found that 75% of them involved suspects who were within 3 yards of agents when firing took place.

Johnson reports that flowing from that review was a dramatic shift in FBI firearms training that for several decades focused on longer range marksmanship training. Prior to the change, FBI agents qualified with their pistols by firing 50 shots, more than half fired from the 15 yard line and the 25 yard line. The new qualification course involves firing 60 rounds, and 40 of them are fired from seven yards and up to three yards from the target.

The article reports that in addition to the change in live-fire training, there is a renewed emphasis in FBI training on the use of virtual simulation technology that permits shooting skills

---

[11] Id. p. 72.

developed during live fire exercises to be tested in life like situations. Agents are able to confront realistic-looking "bad guys" who appear as virtual killer adversaries during computer simulated video scenarios. The performance of the agents is simultaneously videotaped for instructor evaluation and critique later on.

Regular Training on Constitutional and Departmental Deadly Force Standards

I have been training law enforcement officers on the constitutional requirements for the use of deadly force for over thirty years. I trained FBI agents on the FBI policy regarding use of deadly force from 1980 until I retired in 1999. I believe that law enforcement training (constitutional and policy standards) regarding use of deadly force is an absolute necessity. Training of this nature or the failure to train will be closely scrutinized in any lawsuit arising out of an officer involved shooting. All officers carrying firearms for a department must receive this training at least annually or more if state or department standards so dictate. All officers must attend this training or receive training at a make-up session. There must be no exceptions. Records of this important training must be maintained in the event of future court or grand jury proceedings.

Marksmanship with a firearm and combat shooting are only part of the full required training picture. The rest of the picture involves a complete understanding of constitutional and departmental policy standards regarding use of deadly force. Sending officers out on the street with shooting skills but no understanding of when they can be used would be like sending football players into a game without knowing football field rules. Failure and chaos are sure to follow.

Inadequate Firearms Training and Municipal Liability

In October 1990, while serving as FBI Chief Counsel for the Boston FBI Division, I wrote an article for the FBI Law Enforcement Bulletin entitled "Deliberate Indifference, The Standard for Municipal and Supervisory Liability." In that article, I reviewed the history of municipal liability and the newly articulated US Supreme Court standard of liability for failure to properly train police officers.

The article examined the history of municipal liability beginning with a discussion of the U.S. Supreme Court's opinion in, *Monell v. New York City Department of Social Services*.[12] In that case, the Court ruled that a municipal corporation may be liable pursuant to 42 U.S.C. §1983 (hereinafter §1983) for adopting and executing a **formal policy through its official policy makers** that results in a constitutional deprivation. Moreover, the Court ruled that liability can also have its genesis in constitutional violations caused by municipal **"customs" or informal policies**, even though they have not been officially approved by municipal policy makers.

The Court made clear that municipal liability is based solely on the unconstitutional conduct and decisions of municipal policy makers. The Court specifically rejected the idea that municipal liability could be based upon the legal theory known as "Respondeat Superior," which imposes liability on supervisory officials because of the illegal acts of their subordinates even though the supervisors have not acted improperly in the matter. In other words, under this theory, supervisors or employers are liable simply because of their position, regardless of an absence of personal fault.

There is no such thing as "Respondeat Superior" liability or "vicarious liability" for a municipality and its policy makers for constitutional violations committed by subordinate personnel. Municipal liability and personal liability for municipal policy makers will only occur when policy makers act unconstitutionally themselves by adopting and implementing an unconstitutional policy or custom which causes a deprivation of constitutional rights.

Two years after *Monell*, the Supreme Court decided another §1983 case entitled *Owen v. City of Independence, Missouri*.[13] In *Owen*, the Court rejected the City's assertion of the qualified immunity defense in a §1983 action. The Court ruled that rejection of this defense was necessary because permitting its use

---

[12] 436 U.S. 658 (1978).

[13] 445 U.S. 622 (1980).

by municipalities would defeat the twofold purpose of §1983. The statute was created to (1) provide a remedy for persons wronged by abusive government conduct, and (2) to deter future violations of similar abusive conduct.

The Court observed that individual government defendants in §1983 lawsuits may assert the qualified immunity defense, which is often successful in defeating liability. The Court concluded that allowing the municipality to benefit from asserting this defense would leave aggrieved victims without a remedy. This was unacceptable to the Court.

Following *Monell,* federal courts handled a myriad of lawsuits directed against municipal corporations across America based on claims of inadequate police training. There was considerable disagreement among the various federal appellate courts (i.e., federal circuits) concerning the correct standard of liability for municipal failure to properly train law enforcement officers.[14]

City of Canton, *Ohio v. Harris*

The Supreme Court resolved the above mentioned disagreement between the federal circuits when it decided *City of Canton v. Harris,*[15] in 1989. In Canton, the Court ruled that inadequate police training can serve as the basis for municipal liability **only where the failure to train amounts to *deliberate indifference* by municipal policy makers to the constitutional rights of persons interacting with police officers.** The Court explained that inadequate training meets the deliberate indifference standard **only when the need for more or different training is obvious and the failure to implement such training is likely to result in constitutional violations.**

The Court offered two examples of deliberate indifference to an obvious need for training. Not surprisingly, the first of the Court's examples involved failure to train police officers regarding the use of deadly force. This example involved the situation wherein municipal policymakers (e.g., local police chiefs) know that officers are required to apprehend fleeing felons. Moreover,

---

[14] See, Michael Callahan, "Municipal Liability for Inadequate Training and Supervision," FBI Law Enforcement Bulletin, March 1989, pp. 24 – 30.

[15] 489 U.S. 378.

Firearms and Deadly Force Training

they know that officers are equipped with firearms to assist them in accomplishing that goal. The Court observed that in this situation, the need to provide training on the constitutional limitations regarding the use of deadly force is so obvious that the failure to do so would amount to deliberate indifference.

The second example provided by the Court involved a pattern of officer misconduct that placed municipal policy makers on notice that a certain type of training is required. For example, hypothetically, suppose that policy makers are on notice that officers have in the recent past physically abused suspects while attempting to arrest them. This kind of pattern of past abuse puts them on notice and mandates that they take steps to train officers that such abuse is unconstitutional. Failure to do so when the need for training is so obvious amounts to deliberate indifference.[16]

---

[16] It should be noted here that failure to supervise subordinate officers on the part of superior officers can also lead to **personal** constitutional liability on the part of these officers. Deliberate indifference on the part of superior police officials may result in liability for the failure to properly supervise lower level officers. **Personal liability** is likely when high level police officials knew or should have known of a subordinate officer's past unconstitutional actions and took no steps or inadequate steps to provide appropriate discipline. Under these circumstances, the supervisory officials may be found deliberately indifferent to the constitutional rights of the next victim of the rogue subordinate officer. See, for example, *Gutierrez-Rodriguez v. Cartagena*, 882 F.2d 553 (1st Cir. 1989); *Dobos v. Driscoll*, 537 N.E. 2d 558 (1989) and *Bordanaro v. McLeod*, 871 F.2d 1151 (1st Cir. 1989). See also, *Campbell v. City of Springboro, Ohio*, 700 F.3d 779 (6th Cir. 2012).

The United States Supreme Court in its *Ashcroft v. Iqbal*, 129 S. Ct. 1937 (2009) decision has raised a serious question concerning the continued efficacy of the constitutional doctrine of liability for law enforcement supervisors arising out of the unconstitutional conduct of subordinate employees. In fact, in a 5-4 decision, the Court stated, "In a §1983 suit or a Bivens action—where masters do not answer for the torts of their servants—the term 'supervisory liability' is a misnomer. Absent vicarious liability, each Government official, his or her title notwithstanding, is liable for his or her own misconduct."

Since *Ashcroft*, the Seventh and Tenth Circuits have eliminated the possibility of supervisor liability based upon a pre-*Ashcroft* standard of deliberate indifference. See, *T.E. v. Grindle*, 599 F.3d 583 (7th Cir. 2010) and *Dodds v. Richardson* , 614 F.3d 1185 (10th Cir. 2010). Conversely, at least two other Circuits have concluded that supervisory liability pursuant to a §1983 claim, based upon a deliberate indifference standard, can still exist after the Ashcroft decision. See for example, *Lluveras v. Merced* (No. 11-2339, 13-1169) (1st Cir. 2014) and *Starr v. Baca*, 652 F.3d 1202 (9th Cir. 2011). Because of this split among Circuits another Supreme Court decision on this issue is likely.

Chapter 6

Connick v. Thompson

In 2011, the U.S. Supreme Court provided further guidance in the failure to train field when it decided *Connick v. Thompson*.[17] Connick was the Orleans, Louisiana Parish District Attorney and his Office prosecuted Thompson for attempted armed robbery in 1985. Prior to Thompson's arrest, a crime scene technician removed a swatch of the unknown perpetrator's blood from the victim's pants. The blood was tested and determined to be type B. A lab report of this finding was prepared and provided to the District Attorney's Office. An Assistant District Attorney was aware of the potential exculpatory evidence but never disclosed it to defense counsel or the court. Thompson was convicted.

Following his conviction, Thompson was tried in a separate criminal matter for murder. Because of his earlier conviction, Thompson chose not to take the stand in his own defense at trial. Thompson was convicted and received the death penalty.

In late 1999, Thompson's private investigator discovered the lab report from the armed robbery investigation in the Crime Laboratory files. Thompson's blood was subsequently tested and found to be type O. Thompson moved to have his murder conviction reversed. He argued that his armed robbery conviction which was tainted by the withholding of critical evidence by the prosecution prevented him from testifying during the murder trial. Thompson's murder conviction was reversed. After a new trial, Thompson was found not guilty of murder.

Thompson subsequently sued Connick and the District Attorney's Office, pursuant to §1983, for creating an unconstitutional policy of failure to train prosecutors in their constitutional obligation to turn exculpatory evidence over to defense counsel in criminal cases. The case reached the United States Supreme Court and the Court ruled 5-4 in favor of Connick and his Office.

The Supreme Court observed that Thompson had the burden of proving that Connick was deliberately indifferent to the need to train his prosecutors about their obligation to turn over exculpatory evidence and that this lack of training caused the constitutional violation against him.

---

[17] 131 S. Ct. 1350 (2011).

The Court observed that deliberate indifference is a stringent standard of fault, requiring proof that municipal policy makers disregarded the known or obvious consequences of their actions (or failure to act). The Court further noted that when municipal policy makers have actual or constructive knowledge that an omission in a training program has caused subordinate employees to violate constitutional rights, the municipality and the policy makers are deemed to be deliberately indifferent to the constitutional violations that follow.

The Court ruled that "**[a] pattern of similar constitutional violations by untrained employees is 'ordinarily necessary' to demonstrate deliberate indifference for purposes of failure to train.** Policymakers' continued adherence to an approach that they know or should know has failed to prevent [unconstitutional] conduct by employees [in the past] may establish ... the deliberate indifference necessary to trigger municipal liability."[18]

Thompson argued that Connick's need to train his subordinate Assistant District Attorneys' regarding their legal obligation to turn over exculpatory evidence to defense counsel in criminal cases was so obvious that the failure to do so amounted to deliberate indifference . He claimed that because the need for this training was so obvious, he had no obligation to demonstrate a pattern of prior similar unconstitutional failures. In other words, Thompson claimed that when the need for training is so obvious, deliberate indifference can be established on the basis of a "**single [unconstitutional] incident.**"[19]

The Court reviewed its decision in Canton and observed that in a **narrow range of circumstances** a pattern of prior similar misconduct might not be required to establish deliberate indifference in the failure to train context. The Court reviewed the example that it set forth in Canton to demonstrate when this was possible.

The Court's example in *Canton* involved knowledge by municipal policy makers that police officers will be required to arrest fleeing felons and that officers are provided with firearms. **In this**

---

[18] Id. at 1360.

[19] Id. at 1361.

Chapter 6

situation, the Court observed that failure to train officers regarding the constitutional limitations on use of deadly force has "highly predictable consequence[s],"[20] namely, violations of constitutional rights. The Court concluded that while deliberate indifference is possible based upon a single incident as described in the above example, such situations are rare indeed.

The Court distinguished Connick's failure to train situation from its deadly force example in *Canton*. The Court observed that "the obvious need for specific legal training that was present in the *Canton* scenario is absent here. **Armed police must sometimes make split-second decisions with life-or-death consequences. ... Under those circumstances there is an obvious need for... training.**"[21]

The Court ruled that police officers cannot be expected to know the law in the absence of specific legal training but this is not the case with Assistant District Attorneys who are already well trained in legal matters. The Court concluded that Thompson could not establish deliberate indifference on the basis of proof of a single unconstitutional incident alone. He needed proof of a pattern of similar unconstitutional incidents to prevail. However, he was unable to establish the required pattern.

The significance of the Supreme Court's decision in *Connick* cannot be understated. Twenty-two years after the Court's landmark failure to train decision in *Canton*, the Court once again **used a failure to train on deadly force legal issues as its only example of automatic municipal liability based on a single constitutional violation.** A word to the wise should be sufficient. Failure to train on deadly force related issues may result in dead bang liability after only one bad shooting. Municipal policymakers must insure that appropriate basic and in-service deadly force legal training is provided to police officers under their jurisdiction to protect themselves and their municipalities from liability for failure to train in this critical area of the law.

---

[20] Id.

[21] Id.

Firearms and Deadly Force Training

Failure to Train and its Consequences— The Zuchel Case

Failure to train law enforcement officers in the deadly force arena will have significant negative monetary consequences for police administrators and their jurisdictions. A clear example of this is found in *Zuchel v. City of Denver*.[22] On the evening of 8/6/85, Zuchel created a disturbance at a restaurant in Denver, Colorado. Police were called but Zuchel left the restaurant before they arrived. Denver officers tried to locate him in the vicinity of the restaurant. Meanwhile, Zuchel became involved in a heated argument with four teenagers on bicycles nearby.

As officers approached Zuchel from behind, one of the teenagers shouted that Zuchel had a knife. Zuchel turned and faced two officers, one male and one female. The male officer told Zuchel that he needed to shut up. The female officer testified that they were about 15 feet away from Zuchel and that her fellow officer drew his gun when Zuchel turned to face them. She heard her fellow officer say "Drop it, drop it."

She said that she saw nothing in Zuchel's right hand but did not get a clear view of his left hand. She stated that Zuchel kept moving forward at a slow pace and that she was standing right next to Zuchel when the other officer shot him. At that point, Zuchel was about four to five feet away from the male officer's extended firearm. She testified that she was surprised when she heard the first of four shots and had not expected the other officer to shoot Zuchel. Zuchel died and a pair of fingernail clippers was found near his body.

Zuchel's family sued the officer who killed Zuchel and the City of Denver in federal court. They alleged that Zuchel's shooting was unconstitutional and the City of Denver, through its police department, failed to adequately train its police officers regarding the use of deadly force. The family subsequently settled its claim against the defendant officer and the case proceeded to trial

---

[22] 997 F.2d 730 (10th Cir. 1993). See also, *Allen v. Muskogee, Oklahoma*, 119 F.3d 837 (10th Cir. 1997). In this case, the Tenth Circuit ruled that the City's alleged failure to train its police officers in how to respond to encounters involving emotionally disturbed persons (EDP) can be the basis of municipal liability. Liability for the municipality may flow from the situation wherein untrained officers use unreasonable force against an EDP that results in his death and municipal policy makers were deliberately indifferent to the obvious need for EDP encounter training.

Chapter 6

against the City. At the conclusion of the trial, the jury returned a verdict against the City for $330,000. The City filed an appeal with the Tenth Circuit Court of Appeals.

The Tenth Circuit affirmed the jury verdict against the City. The court first ruled that the jury's decision that the shooting of Zurchel was unconstitutional was correct. The court moved on to examine the verdict against the City for failure to train.

The court observed that in February 1983, the local District Attorney sent a letter to the Denver Police Chief concerning six police shootings that occurred in a six-week period from the beginning of January 1983. The court reviewed the content of the letter and testimony from the Zuchel's expert witness (a former police officer and a then current criminal justice professor). The court concluded that the jury correctly found that the Zuchel shooting was the product of a usual and recurring circumstance [a pattern] that confronted Denver police officers, that is, the use of deadly force against citizens.

In the letter, the District Attorney recommended that the Denver Police Department institute or expand firearms training to include **strategic skills development involving situational analysis, and options development that would lead to minimizing violent citizen-police encounters. He also recommended that the Department establish, "[p]eriodic target course 'shoot-don't shoot' live training under street conditions, particularly for officers on the front line."**[23]

The court observed that the Denver Police Department did not institute periodic live range training as recommended by the District Attorney. The court noted that the female officer present at the Zuchel shooting testified that her training included only a lecture on decisional shooting and that she never received live shoot-don't shoot training at a firearms range.

Reinforcing the absolute necessity for expert testimony in cases of this nature, the Tenth Circuit credited the testimony of Zuchel's expert in reaching its decision. The court stated, "we note that Mr. Fyfe (plaintiff's expert) ... stated his belief that failure to institute periodic live range training left Denver far below

---

[23] Id. at p.738 (emphasis added).

Firearms and Deadly Force Training

generally accepted police custom and practice and constituted deliberate indifference to the rights of Denver citizens."[24]

The Tenth Circuit concluded that Denver's failure to implement the District attorney's recommendation on periodic live range training constituted deliberate indifference to the constitutional rights of Denver citizens.

Spending cuts by federal, state, and local governments and law enforcement agencies on critical firearms and deadly force training programs are penny wise and pound foolish. The relatively small amount of money saved will be swallowed up in the failure to train lawsuits that follow. More important, our frontline officers who risk their lives daily to protect and serve will be placed at a distinct personal safety disadvantage by these short-sighted money saving measures. These officers deserve the best available deadly force training to save their own lives and the lives of innocent civilians they represent.

---

[24] Id. at 740.

Chapter 7

ACTION VERSUS REACTION—THE DEADLY REACTIONARY GAP

In times of war between nations, it is generally accepted that soldiers representing either side may take preemptive action to shoot at and attempt to kill or wound an enemy soldier. This is not the case for law enforcement officers in America. Law enforcement officers in the United States do not have the authority to preemptively strike at their adversaries by shooting them. Our officers are not permitted to initiate a deadly action against an adversary because they think he might possibly be a danger to them or others. Instead, "objectively reasonable" officers in America, absent extraordinary circumstances, must wait and respond to a perceived life-threatening move or action directed against them by an adversary. In the law enforcement field, this concept is known as **action v. reaction.**

The action v. reaction concept begins with an actual or reasonably perceived dangerous hostile action taken by a suspect against an officer or other innocent person. Obviously the safest way to handle a dangerous situation of this nature is to take precautionary moves to prevent the suspect from making a dangerous move against the officer in the first place. However, this is not always possible. Once the suspect makes a dangerous move against an officer, it is now incumbent upon the officer to react as quickly and effectively as possible to counter the suspect's hostile action against him/her. The time that it takes (i.e., the time lag) for the officer to react to the suspect's hostile action is sometimes referred to in law enforcement jargon as the **"reactionary gap."**

The reactionary gap is the suspect's best friend and the officer's worst enemy. This short interval of time provides the suspect with the opportunity to not only shoot first at the officer but also deliver multiple deadly rounds before the officer can respond. This deadly reactionary gap provides the best explanation for why only 17 of the 50 officers killed with handguns in 2011 returned fire at their killers.

Chapter 7

Most law enforcement deadly force encounters begin and end within three seconds.[1] Moreover, 327 of the 500 officers murdered by firearms in the ten-year period ending in 2011 were positioned within 10 feet or less from their killers when shot. These statistics confirm that most law enforcement gun battles occur suddenly without warning in close quarters. The suspects have a clear advantage. They have the element of surprise. The officer is usually close by and the suspect doesn't have to be an accomplished marksman. All the suspect has to do is point and fire. In these encounters, it is the suspect who will almost always shoot first.

Reaction time is a real substantive factor in every law enforcement shooting incident. Simply put, the "objectively reasonable" law enforcement officer knows that **action (from a suspect) will always beat reaction (from a law enforcement officer)**.[2] In an officer-involved shooting, the officer is almost always behind the curve. The suspect is already shooting at the officer before he/she can respond.

Reaction Time Components

Reaction time has three main components. The first component is **decision time.** Decision time involves the time it takes for an officer to perceive a threatening action by a suspect, identify it and make a decision as to how to respond to it.[3] The second component of reaction time is **response time.** Response time includes the time it takes for the officer's brain to deliver the message through his/her nervous system to the arms, hands and fingers to draw and fire or fire an already drawn handgun.[4] This would include gripping the weapon, aiming it and placing a finger upon the trigger. The third component of reaction time is referred to as **mechanical time.**[5] Mechanical time involves the officer pulling the trigger of his/her weapon, causing the hammer to fall on the primer of the bullet and the bullet traveling through the barrel of the weapon and exiting at the muzzle. These three

---

[1] John C. Hall and Urey W. Patrick, "In Defense of Self and Others," 2005, p. 101.

[2] Id. p. 103.

[3] Id. p. 302.

[4] Id.

[5] Id.

Action versus Reaction—The Deadly Reactionary Gap

components together comprise an officer's reaction time. Combined, they comprise the elements of the so-called reactionary gap. Although short in duration, the reactionary gap is very deadly for the "objectively reasonable" law enforcement officer.

Reaction Time Studies—"The Tempe Study"

During recent years there have been various time and motion studies conducted in an attempt to scientifically capture what can realistically happen to law enforcement officers during the reactionary gap time frame. One of the best studies was conducted by Dr. Bill Lewinski and Dr. Bill Hudson from Minnesota State University.[6] Dr. Lewinski's study was entitled, "Time to Start Shooting? Time to Stop Shooting? The Tempe Study" (hereinafter, The Tempe Study). This study was reported in the September/October 2003 edition of *The Police Marksman* magazine.

The Tempe Study involved participation by 102 officers from the Tempe, Arizona Police Department. The study was conducted in a very controlled laboratory situation. The equipment for the study included a light bearing stimulus board. On the board were 9 clusters of lights in a 3 by 3 pattern. Each cluster contained three separate lights (red-yellow-green). The stimulus board was operated by a computer that created certain light patterns.

The second piece of equipment for the study was a training handgun developed by Glock. The handgun was primarily based on the Glock standard 9mm. semi-auto pistol. The handgun had a trigger pull of just under ten pounds and a trigger reset based upon a mechanical spring rather than a bullet explosion. The trigger of the handgun was connected to a computer that was able to time each trigger pull.

The third piece of equipment was a master computer that was able to combine information from the light stimulus board and the Glock to determine how long it took each officer to pull the trigger in response to the appropriate light stimulus. The participating officers were instructed to focus on the light clusters in

---

[6] Dr. Lewinski was a professor of Law Enforcement at Minnesota State University at Mankato, MN until 2010 when he retired to become Executive Director, Force Science Research Center (a non-profit organization also based at the University). Dr. Hudson is the Chairperson of the Computer Engineering Department at the same University. See, www.forcescience.org.

Chapter 7

the upper left quadrant of the stimulus board. They were told to pull the trigger once when a specific green light appeared in this area of the board.

The test results demonstrated that the average trigger pull reaction time to the green light stimulus was 31/100ths of a second. The study broke this time into two additional time components. The first involved the time from the appearance of the green light on the stimulus board to the time the trigger finger received the message from the brain to pull the trigger. The average time for this to happen was 25/100ths of a second. The second measured the time it took for each officer to actually pull the trigger on the handgun. The average time for each trigger pull was 6/100ths of a second. This was the average time it took for the participants to move the trigger from its normal position to the rear of the trigger guard.

The Tempe Study demonstrates how quickly a handgun can be fired once the decision to shoot has been made. It does not include the **decision time component** of reaction time, that is, the time it takes for the officer to decide whether shooting is appropriate. For example, the participating officers were instructed to shoot when a particular green light appeared on the stimulus board. They basically had no decision to make. As soon as the green light appeared, they were told to fire, that is, see the green light—pull the trigger. The Tempe Study basically eliminated **decision time** from the reaction equation.

The Tempe Study measured the **response time component** and the **mechanical time component** of reaction time. The study is extremely valuable because it definitively establishes how quickly a handgun can be fired once the shooter has made the decision to fire. The study scientifically demonstrates that when a shooter has his finger on the trigger of a handgun and has made the decision to shoot, the first bullet will be fired in 31/100ths of a second. According to Doctor Lewinski, in a research paper he authored in 2009, the average time for an officer to cycle through trigger pulls (after the first trigger pull) on a Glock semi-auto pistol while firing multiple rounds is approximately a quarter second (.25) per trigger pull.[7]

---

[7] See, William J. Lewinski and Christina Redmann, "New Developments In Understanding The Psychological Factors In the Stop Shooting Response" 2009, p. 38.

Action versus Reaction—The Deadly Reactionary Gap

What is true for the average officer will also be true for the average violent offender. Thus, a suspect who has made up his mind to shoot an officer with a pointed firearm and finger on the trigger can fire approximately 4 bullets at the officer in approximately 1.06 seconds.[8]

Some might counter that the Tempe Study involved trained police officers and that is the reason they could fire so quickly. However, the Alexander Jason study, reported in the *Investigative Sciences Journal* in 2010, included a 26 year old individual who was not a police officer and who never fired a handgun before. This individual was able to fire 7 consecutive shots from a 9mm. Glock semi-auto handgun in 1.81 seconds. Her first shot was fired in .32 of a second, the second shot in .30 of a second, and her third shot in .29 of a second. She was able with no prior experience to fire 3.31 rounds in one second.

When one takes into account that the FBI publication entitled "Violent Encounters" involving interviews with 43 violent offenders who engaged 50 police officers in 40 separate gun battles, the ability of these offenders to shoot handguns becomes clearer still and decidedly more ominous.[9] In "Violent Encounters" the FBI reported that 80% of these violent offenders claimed that they practiced regularly with firearms and averaged 23 practice sessions annually. Moreover, 60% of the offenders purported to be point shooters rather than sight shooters. Simply put, the majority of these offenders do not take the slight extra time it would take them to use the weapon's sights before firing a shot.[10] This means that their ability to fire even more quickly is

---

[8] A separate study conducted by Alexander Jason, Certified Senior Crime Scene Analyst, for the *Investigative Sciences Journal* in January 2010, involved 32 police officers. In this study the average time between shots (not including the first shot that was fired after a holster draw) was 23/100ths of a second or one round every .23 of a second.

[9] Anthony J. Pinizzotto, Ph.D., Edward F. Davis, Charles E. Miller (all employees of the FBI), "Violent Encounters," 2006, Executive Summary, p. iii.

[10] In a separate study conducted by Dr. Lewinski and reported in the Nov/Dec 2002 edition of *Police Marksman* magazine involving 68 officers from the Los Angeles Police Department, Dr. Lewinski determined that it took an average of 3/100ths of a second for officers to obtain a sight picture (by using the weapon's sights) on their handguns before discharging a shot. They were instructed to place their finger on the trigger, obtain a sight picture and fire at the sound of a buzzer. Obtaining a sight picture insures better accuracy but takes slightly longer to fire a round.

Chapter 7

enhanced. Use of sights in shooting becomes more critical at distances of ten yards and beyond from a target.

The "Violent Encounters" publication also points out that 70% of the violent offenders shot the officers they engaged while only 40% of the officers were able to shoot them. The reason for this disparity is likely to include the fact that all but three of the 43 offenders fired the first shot in the deadly encounters.

According to former FBI Academy Firearms Trainers' Hall and Patrick in their book *In Defense of Self and Others*, the "generally accepted rule of thumb is that it takes 0.7 to 1.0 second for an individual to first recognize another's [hostile] action, identify the nature of the action, then formulate and initiate a response **[decision time]**. This is an immutable physiological reality. The response itself will then entail additional time, depending on its nature, before an effect can be expected."[11]

In 2002 Dr. Lewinski conducted a separate study involving 68 Los Angeles police officers. This study, entitled "Biomechanics of Lethal Force Encounters Officer Movements," was reported in the *Police Marksman* magazine (Nov/Dec 2002 edition, pp. 19 – 23). The officers were instructed at the sound of a buzzer to draw and fire one sighted round from a snapped level one holster.[12] The average time it took to draw and fire the round was 1.71 seconds. When the officers drew from a snapped level two holster, the average draw-fire time sequence increased to 1.92 seconds. Drawing and firing from a snapped level three holster increased the average time to 2.0 seconds.

Consider the number of shots that a "bad guy" can fire at an officer who takes a second to recognize a threat and decide to shoot, and 1.71 seconds to draw and fire from a level one holster. The total response time is 2.71 seconds. The "bad guy" will be able to fire 4 rounds in 1.06 seconds and continue to fire for

---

[11] p. 108.

[12] A level one holster has only one level of protection to prevent an unauthorized draw by a third party. The level of protection is most likely a snap or a strap to hold the weapon in place. A level two holster has one additional level of protection to prevent an unauthorized draw and a level three holster has a total of three levels of protection for this purpose. Obviously, the level three holster provides the most protection from an unauthorized draw but also takes longer for the officer to draw the weapon from the holster as well. Regularly practicing draws from any holster will reduce the time it takes to draw a firearm from them.

Action versus Reaction—The Deadly Reactionary Gap

another 1.65 seconds (1 round every quarter of a second) before the officer fires his first shot.

Decision Time—Laboratory v. Reality

Decision time for officers involved in shooting incidents is likely to be much more complicated and time consuming than simply responding to a green light or auditory buzzer when activated in a controlled laboratory setting. Obviously, the longer it takes for an officer to clearly observe a sudden hostile action, process the deadly nature of the threat and formulate a response, the risk to the officer's life rises exponentially.

Officers on the streets of America are frequently operating alone in one person squad cars. They are not only alone but no back up may be immediately available. Officers often have little or no background and intelligence data on the person/persons they are approaching. They may be engaging the person for a minor infraction and have little obvious reason to be concerned for their safety. Weather conditions may be less than ideal and darkness/visibility issues may be present. There will often be traffic safety concerns or other distractions that will interrupt the officer's focus and attention.

Under these conditions, the suspect retains the strategic element of surprise. A surprised officer is likely to hesitate in making a quick decision. Failure to make a quick self-defense decision in response to a deadly threat substantially increases the probability of a bad outcome for the officer.

The Reactionary Gap Hypothetical

Let's return to the action v. reaction discussion and consider a likely hypothetical. Suppose that an officer approaches the driver of a vehicle for a moving traffic violation at night, for example, a speeding violation. While standing at the driver's side window, the officer requests the operator's driver's license and vehicle registration. The driver reaches over and opens the glove box ostensibly to comply with the officer's request. The officer's handgun is holstered in a level two protective holster.

Instead of producing a registration, the driver grabs a pistol from his glove box and points it at the officer. The officer is taken by complete surprise and takes approximately one second to mentally process the threat. It will take him an additional 1.92 seconds to draw and fire his handgun from his level two holster. A total of 2.92 seconds will pass before the officer's first bullet leaves the muzzle of his sidearm.

Meanwhile, the driver (wanted for murder in another state) has already decided to shoot the officer. All he needs to do now is fire his weapon. The driver's first shot will leave his weapon in 31/100ths of a second. Each subsequent shot will leave his weapon at quarter second intervals. It will take him 1.06 seconds to fire 4 rounds. By the time 2.06 seconds have elapsed, the driver will have fired 8 rounds at the officer.

Remember, the officer will not fire his first round until 2.92 seconds have elapsed. By then, if the suspect chooses, 11 rounds will have been fired at the officer. Hard to comprehend but true nevertheless. Hard science supports this result. This example clearly illustrates what is meant by the **deadly reactionary gap**. It comes as no surprise that only 17 of the 50 officers killed by handguns in 2011 were able to fire back at their killers. Many of the dead were surely victims of the deadly reactionary gap.

The Blair Reaction Time Study

On May 26, 2011 Dr. William Lewinski, Executive Director, Force Science Research Center, Mankato, Minnesota reported on a new reaction time study conducted by Dr. J. Pete Blair, Associate Professor of Criminal Justice, Texas State University (TSU) (The Blair Reaction Time Study). Dr. Blair was assisted in his study by the Advanced Law Enforcement Rapid Response Training Center at Texas State University and the Criminal Justice Division of the Texas Governor's Office.

The Blair Reaction Time Study included 30 male and female criminal justice students from TSU who were to play the role of "suspects." It also included 24 male police officers who were participating in a regional SWAT training conference at TSU. Each officer averaged nearly 10 years as a police officer and nearly 5 years as a SWAT officer.

Each officer was armed with a Glock training pistol that fired marking cartridges (i.e., paint bullets). They were told that they were responding to a person with a gun call. They had to progress through 10 rooms in an abandoned school. In each room, the

Action versus Reaction—The Deadly Reactionary Gap

officers were confronted with a "suspect" armed with a similar pistol at a distance of 10 feet. In some cases the suspect's gun was at his/her side pointed at the floor. In others, the suspect had the gun pointed at his/her own head in a suicidal pose.

Eighty percent of the suspects were told to shoot the officers at any time after a command was given for them to drop the gun. The rest of the suspects were told to surrender. Each officer was instructed to have their gun up and pointed at the suspect as soon as they entered each room. They were instructed to shoot first as soon as the suspect made a move to shoot them.

The Blair Reaction Time Study Results

Test results disclosed that the suspects who had their guns at their sides were able to raise the guns and fire at the officers in an average time of .36 of a second. The suspects who held the gun at their heads were able to move the gun from their heads and fire at the officers in .40 of a second.

In response, the average time for officers to react to suspects raising guns from their side and shoot at them was .38 of a second. Officers responded to gun threats originating from the suspects' heads in an average time of .40 of a second.

The results of this study are quite sobering indeed. Here we have experienced SWAT officers vs. untrained students. The officers have drawn their weapons and pointed them at the suspects. The officers know they are likely to face a person with a gun before they enter the room (i.e., no surprise). The officers are able to clearly see a weapon in the suspect's hand before the suspect makes a threatening move. All of this notwithstanding, the suspects were able to raise the weapon from their side and fire a shot at the officer before the officer could fire back (i.e., .36 vs. .38). The result of the suspects shooting at the officers by lowering the weapon from their heads was only slightly better for the officers, a virtual draw (i.e., .40 vs. .40). This is hardly a reassuring situation for responding police officers.

The Supreme Court in its *Graham* and *Garner* decisions has determined that an officer may use deadly force when he/she has **probable cause, that is, an "objectively reasonable belief" that a suspect poses a significant threat of death or serious bodily harm to the officer or others.** The Blair Reaction

Time Study demonstrates the significant threat to officers posed by a suspect with a gun in hand even when the gun is not pointed at an officer. Officers may have their guns pointed at the suspect but the extraordinary danger remains unabated. Given the results of the study, a suspect with a gun in hand, even if it is not pointed directly at an officer, still poses a significant risk of death or serious bodily harm to the officer or others.

Once the officer's order to drop the gun is not immediately complied with, the officer has the legal right to fire at the suspect. Waiting for the suspect to make the first move places the officer on the wrong end of the reactionary gap equation. The Blair Reaction Time Study demonstrates the deadly outcome for the officer. The suspect will shoot faster than or at least as fast as the officer. In close quarters where marksmanship is not required, the officer is very likely to be shot. Officers do not have to wait to be shot at before responding to a deadly threat. Those who do are likely to end up as a murder victim statistic in the FBI's annual Law Enforcement Officers Killed and Assaulted (LEOKA) report.

The Blair Study's Potential Impact on Civil Litigation

On July 30, 2013, the United States Court of Appeals for the Ninth Circuit decided *George v. Morris*.[13] At 7:44 am on March 6, 2008, Carol George placed a 911 emergency call to the California Highway Patrol (CHP). The recorded call disclosed that Mrs. George was hysterical, screaming and shrieking. She can be heard yelling loudly that her husband, Donald George (age 64), has a gun and repeatedly saying "No, No, No." After a moment of calm, she can be heard in a blood curdling scream yelling "No, No, No, Stop it." The phone suddenly went dead. The CHP transferred the matter immediately to a Santa Barbara Sheriff's Office (SBSO) Dispatcher because the call originated from Santa Barbara.

The SBSO Dispatcher made a telephone call to the George residence and Mrs. George answered. Mrs. George told the Dispatcher that her husband had left the room and gone outside. She also stated that he had a gun and had cancer. Three SBSO

---

[13] No. 11-55956.

Action versus Reaction—The Deadly Reactionary Gap

deputies were dispatched to the George residence and arrived twelve minutes after the initial 911 call. At the time of arrival, they knew that a case of domestic violence was in progress; that Mr. George was armed with a firearm; that Mrs. George had suddenly hung up the phone while conversing with the Dispatcher; and that Mr. George had a license to possess firearms in his residence.

Shortly after arrival at the George residence, Deputies Schmidt, Rogers, and Morris observed Mr. George standing on the patio at the rear of his home. They saw him holding on to a walker with one hand and holding a handgun in the other hand. Deputy Schmidt ordered George to drop the gun. Another Deputy observed George manipulate the rear portion of the handgun as though attempting to rack a round into the chamber of his weapon. He also heard George answer "No" in response to the order to drop the gun.

Deputy Rogers observed George with the gun in his left hand pointed at the ground. Suddenly he saw George turn toward him, raise the gun and point it directly toward him. At that point, Deputy Rogers fired directly toward George. Simultaneously, the other two Deputies, fearing for the safety of Deputy Rogers, also fired their weapons at George. A total of nine shots were fired at George. George was killed and a semi-automatic handgun loaded with hollow point bullets was found next to his body.

A houseguest of the Georges later stated that before she heard the gunshots, she heard a Deputy order Mr. George to drop his gun twice. Prior to being diagnosed with brain cancer, Mr. George told a friend that if he was ever diagnosed with cancer, he would get a gun, call the sheriff, and have them shoot him.

Four hours after the shooting, Mrs. George informed the SBSO that her husband became an angry man after his brain cancer operation and stated that he did not want to live like this. He became so angry that the family locked up all the guns that were in the house. She told the SBSO that on this particular morning, her husband found a gun in the trunk of the family car. She stated that she tried to yank the gun away from him but was not successful. She stated that she observed her husband insert a loaded magazine into the handgun.

Chapter 7

True to form, Mrs. George, the victim of domestic violence and the 911 caller, sued the deputies who tried to protect her pursuant to 42 U.S.C. §1983 and claimed excessive use of force against her deceased husband. After the lawsuit was filed, Mrs. George claimed that her husband was so impaired by his condition that he was not physically able to raise a handgun and point it at a deputy. However, only four hours after the shooting, as described above, Mrs. George told quite a different story. At that time, she said that her husband was ambulatory, angry, "pretty strong," and able to resist her attempt to yank the handgun from his hand. She also stated that when she called 911, her husband told her that if she didn't put the phone down he would use the gun.

The Federal District Court Judge denied the Deputies' Motion for Summary Judgment and their claim of qualified immunity. The Judge ruled that a genuine issue of material fact existed as to whether the Deputies could reasonably have believed that the life of one of them was in jeopardy at the time they fired at Mr. George. The Judge ordered that the case proceed to trial. The Deputies filed an appeal with the Ninth Circuit Court of Appeals.

The Ninth Circuit in a 2-1 decision affirmed the ruling of the lower court judge and the case was designated for trial. The two judge majority relied on Mrs. George's assertion that her husband was not physically strong enough to raise a pistol and point it at a deputy. In doing so, the court ignored her statement to investigators four hours after the shooting that she tried to yank the gun out of his hand before Deputies arrived without success. Likewise, the majority declined to consider her statement that Mr. George told her that if she didn't put the phone down, he would use the gun. Moreover, the majority refused to consider the statement of George's friend who said that George told him that if he ever got cancer, he would get a gun, call the sheriff, and have them shoot him. Instead of considering these undisputed salient facts in the record, the majority chose to rely on Mrs. George's questionable assertion that her husband could not have raised and pointed a pistol, even though she was not a witness to the actual shooting.

The two-judge majority ruled that in deciding the defense claim of qualified immunity, they were bound to adopt Mrs.

Action versus Reaction—The Deadly Reactionary Gap

George's view of the facts and could not consider the [clear and cogent] testimony of the three deputies involved in the shooting to the contrary. All of the deputies that fired saw George raise his pistol and point it at Deputy Rogers. The majority concluded [by considering only Mrs. George's so-called facts] that if the Deputies shot a man who held a pistol in his hand pointed at the ground, a reasonable jury could find that excessive force was used.

Federal Appellate Judge Trott filed a dissenting opinion. Judge Trott sharply criticized his fellow judges on their misapplication of the qualified immunity doctrine. As previously discussed in this book, prior to the Supreme Court's opinion in *Scott v. Harris*, 550 U. S. 372 (2007), lower federal courts generally adopted the plaintiff's version of disputed material facts in deciding motions for summary judgment and the assertion by law enforcement defendants of the qualified immunity defense.

Judge Trott astutely pointed out that the Supreme Court modified this course of action in *Scott* and ruled that when the lower court record taken as a whole reflects that plaintiff's version of material facts is not credible; the court should reject that version in reaching a decision on qualified immunity for the defendant officers. Of course, in this particular case, the two judge majority failed to follow the Supreme Court's direction in *Scott*.

Judge Trott reviewed the court record as a whole and found the statements of the three defendant Deputies entirely credible on the issue of whether Mr. George raised and pointed his pistol at Deputy Rogers. Judge Trott also carefully reviewed Mrs. George's so-called facts and stated that "plaintiff's evidence is demonstrably not competent either to resolve the ultimate issue of excessive force or the Deputies' credibility." He further proclaimed "What we are inexorably left with is a situation (1) where the deputies had incontrovertible cause to believe Mr. George posed 'a threat of serious physical harm, either to the officer[s] or to others' (2) where he threatened them with a weapon, and (3) where he had been given a warning to drop the gun. *Tennessee v. Garner*, 471 U.S. at 11-12." Judge Trott correctly concluded that "[n]o reasonable fact finder [i.e., jury] could conclude on this record that the disputed use of force was unreasonable or excessive."

Chapter 7

Judge Trott should be congratulated for his thoughtful and well-reasoned opinion. His opinion was based primarily on his correct conclusion that Mr. George raised and pointed a loaded handgun at one of the Deputies. It was undisputed that Mr. George held a loaded semi-auto pistol at his side and refused to drop it when ordered to do so. The entire controversy in the case was based upon a dispute about whether or not George raised and pointed a loaded pistol at a deputy.

What was never raised or discussed by any of the involved judges or parties was whether Mr. George presented an imminent threat of death or serious bodily harm to the Deputies when he held a loaded pistol at his side and refused to drop it when ordered twice to do so. If he presented an imminent threat of death or serious bodily harm to the Deputies in this situation, there was no material factual dispute, the shooting would be justified and the case could have dismissed in favor of the Deputies on qualified immunity grounds. That brings us to the Blair Reaction Time Study previously discussed in depth in this book.

To refresh your memory, the Blair Reaction Time Study involved 30 college students who played the role of "suspects" and 24 police SWAT trained officers. Each officer was armed with a Glock training pistol that fired marking cartridges (i.e., paint bullets). They were told that they were responding to a person with a gun call. They had to progress through 10 rooms in an abandoned school. In each room, the officers were confronted with a "suspect" armed with a similar pistol at a distance of 10 feet. **In some cases the suspect's gun was at his/her side pointed at the floor.**

The suspects were told to shoot the officers at any time after a command was given for them to drop the gun. The officers were instructed to have their gun up and pointed at the suspect as soon as they entered each room. They were instructed to shoot first as soon as the suspect made a move to shoot them.

Test results disclosed that the suspects who had their guns at their sides were able to raise the guns and fire at the officers **in an average time of .36 of a second.** In response, the average time for officers to react to suspects raising guns from their side and shoot at them was **.38 of a second.**

Action versus Reaction—The Deadly Reactionary Gap

The officers had drawn their weapons and pointed them at the suspects. The officers knew they were likely to face a person with a gun before they entered the room (i.e., no surprise). The officers were able to clearly see a weapon in the suspect's hand before the suspect made a threatening move. **All of this notwithstanding, the suspects were able to raise the weapon from their side and fire a shot at the officer before the officer could fire back (i.e., .36 vs. .38).**

The Supreme Court in its *Graham* and *Garner* decisions has determined that an officer may use deadly force when he/she has **probable cause, that is, an "objectively reasonable belief" that a suspect poses a significant threat of death or serious bodily harm to the officer or others.** The Blair Reaction Time Study demonstrates the significant threat to officers posed by a suspect with a gun in hand even when the gun is not pointed at an officer. Officers may have their guns pointed at the suspect but the extraordinary danger remains unabated. Given the results of the Study, a suspect with a gun in hand, even if it is not pointed directly at an officer, still poses a significant risk of death or serious bodily harm to the officer or others.

The Santa Barbara Deputies would clearly and unequivocally have benefitted from expert witness affidavits that included an explanation of the Blair Reaction Time Study. The study scientifically proves beyond a shadow of a doubt that the three Deputies in the George matter were faced with extreme danger as soon as Mr. George refused to drop the pistol at his side in the face of a command to do so. Had the Deputies waited until George made a move to shoot Deputy Rogers, he would have been able to fire at Rogers before any of the Deputies could respond. Once again, the George case highlights the value of expert testimony in defending officers in excessive force litigation.

Action v. Reaction—The Bottom Line

The bottom line in the discussion of action v. reaction and the reactionary gap is that officers must always remain on alert when interacting with potentially dangerous individuals. No human interaction between citizens and police officers is ever truly "routine." Officers who are surprised by a deadly threat directed against them by a suspect will take longer to process the threat,

Chapter 7

decide what to do and initiate an appropriate response. The longer it takes to react, the further behind the reactionary curve the officer will find him/her self. This will only enhance the likelihood for a somber outcome.

Officers must try to avoid surprise and take all reasonable steps to protect themselves from a deadly assault. This would include approaching suspects with caution and where possible with back-up. It would also include a command presence and close observation of a suspect's demeanor and hand visibility. If the officer develops reasonable suspicion to believe the person is armed, a pat down of the suspect's clothing and vehicle should be done. Waiting for appropriate back-up should be done before placing hands on the suspect if possible.

If all preventative measures fail and the officer is suddenly confronted with a suspect pointing a firearm at him/her, as mentioned earlier in this book, the officer cannot stand still. Standing still in this situation, while at the wrong end of the reactionary gap, will result in multiple shots being fired first at the motionless officer. The officer must move laterally in an aggressive fashion away from the suspect.[14] At the same time, if solid cover is not close by and available, the officer should fire multiple rounds at the suspect while moving away.

Lateral aggressive movement by the officer accomplishes several things. First it adds to the distance between the officer and the suspect. More distance decreases the chances of untrained suspects actually hitting the officer with their unsighted shots. Second, it reverses the reactionary gap in favor of the officer. Now the suspect must react to the officer's movement. The officer is no longer where the suspect thought he

---

[14] Moving forward toward the suspect is not a viable option. Moving forward closes the distance between the suspect and the officer and makes the suspect an even better shot. Since the suspect is likely to fire first, the odds of the officer being shot rise rather than fall with forward movement. Likewise, moving backward while continuing to face the suspect is not a good choice. The officer will continue in the direct line of the suspect's fire and cannot see where he/she is going. Furthermore the risk of falling while backpedaling is significantly increased.

If cover is nearby and available, the officer may also consider turning and running aggressively for cover in a diagonal motion. This is certainly preferable to backpedaling. Obviously, having a plan of what to do before approaching the suspect is the best course of action. The officer should always formulate a plan of action in the event the encounter turns deadly before the suspect begins to take hostile action.

was. The deadly time interval now turns in the officer's favor. Meanwhile, the officer is not only moving away but also directing multiple rounds at the suspect which places the officer in a much better position to survive and win the battle for his/her life. Getting off the straight line between the officer and the suspect is critical for the officer's survival. Standing still in such dire circumstances is an invitation to disaster.

How Long Does It Take to Stop Shooting?

Law enforcement shooting incidents often involve one or more officers firing multiple shots at their adversary. In the aftermath of these incidents, officers often face media criticism, internal departmental disciplinary review, grand jury inquiry, and civil litigation concerning the number of shots each officer fired during the incident. There are usually several reasonable explanations to account for the number of rounds fired by officers in these situations.

One reason for "extra" rounds being discharged by an officer in a gun battle is found in time reaction studies. Dr. Lewinski's renowned reaction time study, "The Tempe Study," not only scientifically measured the time it would take for an officer to start shooting but likewise measured the time it would take an officer to stop shooting once it had begun.

In this phase of the Tempe Study, participating officers (102) were instructed to immediately and repeatedly pull the trigger when the light came on. **They were further told to stop immediately when the light went off.** The officers did not know when the light would go off. According to the Tempe Study, "The scientific literature says that a stop reaction time where a person is actively engaged in doing something and then has to react to a new stimulus is approximately one-half of a second or a little less."[15] In the Tempe Study the participants were actively engaged in repeatedly pulling the trigger on the handgun when the light went off. They were supposed to immediately stop pulling the trigger when the light went off. They were physically unable to do so.

---

[15] Dr. William Lewinski and Dr. William Hudson, "Time to Start Shooting? Time to Stop Shooting? The Tempe Study," The *Police Marksman Magazine,* Sept/Oct 2003 edition, p. 28.

Chapter 7

The result of this phase of the study revealed that the **average time** for the participants to stop firing when the light went off was 35/100ths of a second. Some of the officers took as long as 5/10ths to 6/10ths of a second to stop firing. The study reveals a time lag between the time the brain recognizes a stop function signal and the time the brain transmits the message to the hand and finger to stop pulling the trigger. As mentioned above, in an ideal laboratory setting, where the officers were not confronted with a real deadly situation, the average stop time or lag time was 35/100ths of a second.

The Tempe Study disclosed that "in this simple experiment... the time to termination of a trigger pull response, when the officer was engaged in a chain of trigger pulls, **was at least two and sometimes three [additional] trigger pulls or more.**"[16] In other words, during the time lag between the brain recognizing that the trigger pull action should cease and actually stopping the trigger pull action, at least two additional trigger pulls occurred.

If an officer is engaged in a real gun battle on the street, the time it takes to stop shooting once begun, is likely to be substantially increased. This is true because a whole host of additional complicating factors are likely to be in play. For example, fear of death; adrenaline rush; tunnel vision; auditory exclusion, that is, hearing loss; darkness or low light conditions; inability to see whether shots actually hit the suspect; the suspect remaining upright and holding on to a weapon (rather than falling to the ground) are just some of the factors that will make it difficult for an officer to even begin to realize that his/her adversary is no longer in the fight.

The officer will in many cases not stop shooting when the suspect is **actually no longer a threat.** The suspect may have given up the fight or is no longer physically able to continue but this is not yet obvious to the officer. The officer will decide to stop shooting when he/she **reasonably perceives/believes that the suspect is no longer a threat.** This is what is necessary and all that the Supreme Court in *Graham* requires. Through the terrible

---

[16] Id., p. 29. In a sequence of trigger pulls, one-quarter of a second is the average time between pulls. If it takes an average of 35/100ths of a second to stop the pull sequence, an average of two additional trigger pulls will happen in that time frame, i.e., one in .25 of a second and another will be started in the second .25 sequence. It is highly unlikely that this second trigger pull can be stopped once initiated.

Action versus Reaction—The Deadly Reactionary Gap

trauma of a fight for life, an officer is required by the Supreme Court to act with objective reasonableness, not perfection. The suspect may no longer be able to continue his mayhem but the officer is not required to cease self-defense until he/she reasonably perceives this to be the case.

Reaction Time / Knife and Edged Weapons Attacks

FBI LEOKA statistics show that between 2002 and 2011 three law enforcement officers in the United States were murdered by persons using a knife or other cutting instrument. Although being killed by a knife is relatively rare for police officers in this country, being assaulted by a knife-wielding suspect is a far more common problem for officers on the streets of America. In fact, in 2011, FBI LEOKA statistics reveal that there were 997 officers in the United States that were attacked with a knife or other cutting instrument. Almost 16% of those victim officers were stabbed or cut by their assailants. Similarly, LEOKA statistics also disclose that in the ten-year period ending in 2011, over 10,000 officers were attacked with edged weapons and almost 13% of them were cut or stabbed.

Given the dangerous threat presented to officers by knife-wielding suspects, the question arises as to how officers should respond to situations involving edged weapons. Once again, Dr. William Lewinski, Force Science Research Center, Mankato, Minnesota has conducted a productive reaction time study that provides significant insight into the correct law enforcement protocol and response. Dr. Lewinski's study was reported on 4/22/05 in Transmissions #17 and #18 of the Force Science News (www.forcesciencenews.com).[17] In his study, Dr. Lewinski points out that for more than 20 years, the so-called "21-Foot Rule" has been a core component of law enforcement self-defense training concerning protection from knives and other edged weapons.

Dr. Lewinski reports that the "21-Foot Rule" originated from research conducted by law enforcement trainer Dennis Tueller from Salt Lake City, Utah. The 21-Foot Rule states that **"in the time it takes for the average officer to recognize a threat, draw his sidearm and fire 2 rounds at center mass [i.e., the**

---

[17] The Study was named, "Edged Weapon Defense: Is the 21-Foot Rule Still Valid? Was It Ever?"

Chapter 7

torso of a body], an average subject charging at the officer with a knife or other cutting or stabbing weapon can cover a distance of 21 feet [and stab the officer]."[18]

Dr. Lewinski conducted his time reaction study in 2005 to determine the continued validity and efficacy of the rule. The study participants included attackers and officers. The attackers were standing 21 feet away from the officers on a flat surface offering good traction. The officers were standing in a fixed position, with their side arms holstered and snapped in a Level 11 holster (i.e., a snap plus one other protective feature designed to prevent unauthorized draw), on the same plane/line as the attacker. The attackers were instructed to run headlong at the officer from their fixed position.

The study revealed that it took the average officer 1.5 seconds to draw from a snapped level 11 holster and fire one unsighted round at the center mass of the attacker. It took an average additional 1/10th of a second to obtain a sight picture before firing the weapon. It took the officers an additional ¼ of a second to fire a second round.

The average attacker in the study was able to travel 21 feet from his starting position to the location of the officer with an edged weapon raised in an overhand position in 1.5 to 1.7 seconds. According to Dr. Lewinski the best attacker covered the 21 feet in 1.27 seconds. Lewinski opined that a suspect in a real street confrontation, experiencing intense rage, high agitation or the influence of stimulants may even shorten the time to cover the distance. Lewinski concluded, **"Bottom line: Within a 21-foot perimeter, most officers dealing with most edged-weapon suspects are at a decided—perhaps fatal—disadvantage if the suspect launches a sudden charge intent on harming them."**[19]

The "objectively reasonable" law enforcement officer must be aware of the danger he/she faces when confronted by a suspect with a knife or other cutting instrument. Officers must understand that when facing a suspect with an edged weapon, standing within 21 feet of the officer, the suspect will be able to charge and

---

[18] Id.

[19] Id.

Action versus Reaction—The Deadly Reactionary Gap

stab them at approximately the same time they can draw and fire one shot. Obviously, the danger is enhanced as the initial distance between officer and suspect narrows. In the game of baseball, the rule is that a tie goes to the runner. In the real world of law enforcement a tie signals death or serious injury for an officer. This is not an acceptable outcome.

With this in mind, the "objectively reasonable" officer must attempt to maintain sufficient distance between the suspect and him/herself. According to the Lewinski study, some trainers recommend that officers position themselves 30 feet or more from a suspect with an edged weapon. The officer must recognize the need to draw his/her sidearm and raise it in the direction of the suspect to reduce the time it takes to fire if the suspect charges. Further, in the event the suspect charges forward, the officer must aggressively move off the direct line between him/herself and the suspect.

Moving laterally while firing at the attacker is the correct option. Moving aggressively in a lateral direction at a 90 degree angle is appropriate. Dr. Lewinski believes that a better option for the officer is to move obliquely forward at a 45 degree angle to the oncoming attacker with a maneuver called the "Tactical J." Lewinski believes that this maneuver is likely to confuse the attacker and require a more radical change in direction to reach the officer. This, of course, works in the officer's favor because it provides additional time to draw and shoot the attacker.

Edged weapon attacks are deadly threats and must be treated as such. Responding to such an attack with a wrestling move, a baton, billy club, chemical spray, flashlight, or taser is not appropriate and is likely to result in death or serious injury for the victim officer. The "objectively reasonable" officer knows that it is lawful and reasonable to react to these attacks with deadly force.

The "objectively reasonable" officer also knows that firing only one or two shots in this situation is highly unlikely to immediately terminate the life-threatening assault. Unless the first shot enters the suspect's brain or damages his upper spinal column, the suspect will be able to continue the edged weapon assault for several more seconds/minutes until sufficient blood has been lost to stop blood flow to the brain. Thus, firing to end the threat may continue until the suspect is no longer a threat.

Chapter 7

Officers should understand that it is not appropriate to shoot a suspect with a knife simply because he is standing within 21 feet of an officer. The officer in this situation should draw his weapon and point it at the suspect, increase the distance between them, order the suspect to drop the weapon, and if possible wait for help. The time to move and shoot is when the suspect begins to move forward toward the officer or begins to move toward other innocent people.

Chapter 8

WOUND BALLISTICS

Most Gunshot Wounds Are Not Fatal

The "objectively reasonable" law enforcement officer must be cognizant of the fact that most gunshot wounds (with the exception of suicides) are not fatal. The Firearm & Injury Center at the University of Pennsylvania (FICAP) provided statistics in 2011 in a report entitled, "Firearms Injury in the US"[1] that disclosed that in the United States between 2003 and 2007 there were 63,018 persons killed in felonious homicides by bullets fired by other persons.[2] A large number, indeed, but it pales in comparison to the 242,466 persons who, according to the same report, received non-fatal bullet wounds in attempted felonious homicides during the same time frame.[3] In 2007 alone, 12,632 persons were murdered by firearms in America and 48,676 persons were feloniously wounded.[4] Close to 80% of persons shot in America survive.

Far more people are shot and wounded by other people in America annually than are shot and killed by other people. This fact is also true for law enforcement officers. According to FBI LEOKA statistics for the years 2002 – 2011, 500 law enforcement officers were shot and killed in the line of duty. LEOKA statistics reveal that in the same ten year time frame, over 21,000 officers were injured by firearms.

Although these statistics are in general good news for law enforcement, they also send a clear and ominous message as well. The bottom line is that when a perpetrator of a deadly assault against an officer is shot, he is not likely to die or be immediately incapacitated. Even if he does die, he is not likely to die immediately. This has potentially disastrous consequences for law enforcement officers because in these violent encounters they are dealing with violent offenders who are trying to kill them. If the perpetrator's deadly assault on the officer is not immediately

---

[1] p. 27.

[2] Id. The source of this figure was obtained from statistics compiled by the Federal Centers for Disease Control, National Center for Injury Prevention and Control.

[3] Firearms Injury in the US, p. 27.

[4] Id. p. 15.

stopped, the perpetrator, even if shot one or more times, will be able to continue shooting at the officer with potentially deadly consequences.

Deadly Force and Immediate Incapacitation—An Elusive Goal

During a gunfight between police officers and violent offenders, **the goal of the police officer is to bring the encounter to a stop as quickly as possible.** The goal is not to kill the perpetrator but rather to stop him from committing further acts of violence. Death of the offender may result but this is not the goal of the officer. Ideally, the closer the officer gets to immediate incapacitation of the offender, the more likely the officer is to survive. The longer the violent offender is able to continue his attack on the officer, the greater the probability that the officer will be killed or seriously harmed. The faster that the officer can bring the violent encounter to an end, the safer the officer, other officers and members of the public will be.

The "objectively reasonable" officer must understand that violent offenders, who are shot, even with non-survivable gunshot wounds, are not likely to be stopped or die immediately. Retired FBI Firearms expert, Special Agent Urey Patrick, in his excellent book written for the FBI, entitled "Handgun Wounding Factors and Effectiveness," commented on this topic and observed:

> "[p]hysiologically, a determined adversary can be stopped ... immediately only by a shot that disrupts the brain or upper spinal cord [i.e. the central nervous system]. Failing a hit to the central nervous system, massive bleeding from [bullet] holes in the heart or major blood vessels of the torso causing circulatory collapse is the only other way to force incapacitation ... and this takes time. For example, there is sufficient oxygen within the brain to support full, voluntary action [by a violent offender] for 10 – 15 seconds after the heart has been destroyed."[5]

---

[5] "Handgun Wounding Factors And Effectiveness" (1989), p. 8 (emphasis added). Urey Patrick was a firearms trainer at the FBI Academy, Quantico, Va. for many years.

Wound Ballistics

Continuing, Patrick observed, "In fact, physiological factors may actually play a relatively minor role in achieving rapid incapacitation. **Barring central nervous system hits, there is no physiological reason for an individual to be incapacitated by even a fatal wound, until blood loss is sufficient to drop blood pressure and/or the brain is deprived of oxygen.**"[6]

Patrick also noted that **pain caused by bullet wounds** is ordinarily not an immediate contributor to quick physiological incapacitation because the "effects of pain ... are commonly delayed in the aftermath of serious injury such as a gunshot wound."[7] He points out that in times of serious injury, the human body goes into survival mode and temporarily suppresses pain because it is irrelevant to survival.

Gunshot Wounds—Blood Loss—Physical Incapacitation

As previously mentioned, the desired goal for law enforcement officers in a gun battle with a violent perpetrator is to bring that gun battle to a halt as close to instantaneously as possible. The desired goal is often elusive and unable to be achieved. Gun battles often occur suddenly without warning. They are likely to occur in darkness or low light conditions. Unlike shooting at fixed paper targets, real life offenders may be firing from behind cover or moving quickly in one direction and then another. Targets are likely to be brief and fleeting. Under these conditions, especially when the officer is being fired upon by the offender, shot placement for the officer becomes extremely problematical.

As discussed earlier, the only way to bring an immediate end to a violent firearms encounter is to shoot the offender in the head or upper spinal column. Shots of this nature, under the dynamic and life threatening conditions of a firefight **require extraordinary marksmanship or pure luck.**

The "objectively reasonable" law enforcement officer understands that the **only other way to end a gun battle** with a determined offender involves bullet wounds delivered to the

---

[6] Id. (emphasis added).

[7] Id.

Chapter 8

offender that result in massive blood loss. Blood loss from bullet wounds takes time to result in incapacitation.

Lt. Colonel Dave Grossman in his 2004 book, *On Combat*[8] speaks about the effects of blood loss from bullet wounds. While encouraging officers wounded in a gun battle to keep on fighting, he observes, "If you get holes punched in your body, blood will come out ... How much? Well, your body holds approximately one and a half gallons of blood, and you can lose 30 percent, approximately a half a gallon, without losing your hydraulics. To see what that much blood looks like, take a half gallon of strawberry milk and pour it on the ground. Yes, it is a large puddle, but tell yourself that that is the volume of blood you can lose and still fight. ... **Know that if you stop before you lose that much blood, it is your will that failed, not your body.**"[9]

Doctor Maurizio A. Miglietta, Assistant Professor of Surgery, NYU School of Medicine, and Chief, Division of Trauma & Critical Care, Bellevue Hospital declared in an article titled "Trauma and Gunshot Wounds" that "The average adult male has 5 liter(s) of blood in the body. Typically blood pressure begins to drop ... when 20 – 30% [of the blood] is lost. Death can occur when 40% of blood loss occurs and the volume is not replaced." He states further that there are several areas within the body where bleeding is likely to be more profuse and this will cause the body to go into shock. Some of these areas are identified as the chest, abdomen, and pelvis.

Non-Survivable Wounds and the Continuing Threat

Retired FBI agents Hall and Patrick report in their book *In Defense of Self and Others,* 2005,[10] on a study conducted in Dade County, Florida concerning the activity of gunshot and knife

---

[8] P. 148.

[9] Id. (emphasis added). See also, Urey W. Patrick and John C. Hall, "In Defense of Self and Others," 2005, pp. 62 – 63. Patrick states that "[i]n a healthy standing adult, adequate blood pressure can be maintained until at least a 20% loss of blood volume occurs at which point the effects of decreased blood pressure begin to be felt." Obviously, some torso injuries from bullet wounds are likely to cause massive blood loss more quickly than others. For example, Patrick states that if the thoracic aortic artery "is severed (the largest artery), it will take almost five seconds at a minimum for a 20% blood loss to occur in an average size male."

[10] P. 64.

Wound Ballistics

wound victims who died from their wounds. The study, entitled "Survival Time in Gunshot and Stab Wound Victims"[11] indicates that 64% of gunshot victims shot in the chest and abdomen survived for five minutes or more after being shot. Moreover, 36% of the victims shot in the head and neck also survived five minutes or more after being shot. This study suggests that even head shots may not always bring an instantaneous halt to a gunfight.

Violent offenders who are shot and wounded by police officers during a gun battle still present a serious threat of death or serious bodily harm to the officers on the scene. Wounded offenders, even those who have non-survivable wounds are capable of continuing their violent assault until they lose approximately 30% of their blood. As mentioned above, even a direct hit to the heart will not immediately stop a violent perpetrator. He will still have 10 to 15 seconds before collapse. In 10 seconds, that offender would be able to fire 16 rounds from a semi-auto 9mm pistol, reload and fire another full magazine at a police officer.

Gunshot Wounds and the Immediate Fall— A Hollywood Myth

Americans have been exposed to many Hollywood movies where they have witnessed actors purportedly being shot with handguns and rifles and immediately falling to the ground. If the Hollywood portrayal of reality were true, law enforcement officers in America would be much safer on the job. The Hollywood view of reality is that one shot by an officer equals one kill. "Dirty Harry" Callahan confronts the bad guys with his .44 caliber magnum Smith & Wesson revolver and kills several bad guys in a row, one a time, with one shot for each villain. Each bad guy falls directly backward to the ground, through a glass window or down a flight of stairs; immediately killed by one well-placed shot and all is well in the world. In the mythical Hollywood world, one shot equals one drop.

Sadly for law enforcement and the law-abiding public, Hollywood's "reality" and real world reality are worlds apart. Former FBI firearms trainers' Patrick and Hall, both experts on deadly force issues, comment on this issue in their book, *In Defense of*

---

[11] See, *The American Journal of Forensic Medicine and Pathology*, 1988; 9(3).

Self and Others, 2005.[12] They observe, "**A bullet simply cannot knock a man down.** If it had the energy to do so, then equal energy would be applied against the shooter ... and he too might be knocked down or would certainly have trouble retaining control of the weapon. That is simple physics, and has been known for hundreds of years. The amount of energy deposited in the body by a bullet is approximately equivalent to being hit with a major league fastball. Tissue damage is the only physical link to incapacitation, but excluding [bullet hits to the] central nervous system, it is not a causative factor for incapacitation within the desired time frame, i.e., instantaneously."[13]

Patrick and Hall further note that, "the actual destruction [to the human body] caused by any small arms projectile is too small in magnitude relative to the mass and complexity of the target. An effective bullet will destroy about 2 ounces of tissue in its passage through the body. That represents .07 of one percent of the mass of a 180-pound man. Unless the tissue destroyed is located within critical areas of the central nervous system, it is physiologically insufficient to force incapacitation upon the unwilling [i.e., determined violent offender] ... target."[14] In other words, most bullet hits will not result in immediate incapacitation. The offender may eventually reach the point of incapacitation or even succumb to his wounds but in the meantime, he will be able to remain on his feet in a gun battle; a deadly adversary.

In 2003, the Discovery Channel examined the issue of bullet knock down power in its *Myth Busters* television show. The show was entitled "Brown Note" (the title had nothing to do with the bullet examination portion of the show). The issue posed by the show's producer was whether a bullet has enough kinetic energy to knock a person down. The producers used real weapons, that is, handguns, rifles, and shotguns and real ammunition in the experiment.

They needed a target that would approximate the body of a 180-pound human being. They chose a recently killed 150-pound pig for the target and added sand bags to reach the desired

---

[12] P. 69.

[13] Id.

[14] Id. p. 71.

Wound Ballistics

weight. They set up a wooden rig and hung the pig from the rig with chains and hooks that were attached to the hooves of the pig. Before they began to fire at the pig, they gave it a slight push by hand and the pig immediately fell to the ground.

Now they were ready to proceed. The producer enlisted the assistance of Sergeant Alan Normandy of the South San Francisco Police Department to help with the experiment. Sgt. Normandy was the Chief Firearms Instructor for his department, and he supplied numerous firearms with corresponding ammunition for the experiment. Included among the firearms was an MP5-9mm submachine gun that fires 9mm hollow point bullets; a Thompson Submachine gun that fires .45 caliber bullets; a shotgun that fires one ounce rifle slugs at approximately 1800 feet per second (fps); a Colt M-4 rifle that fires .223 rounds (used by the U.S. Military in Iraq and Afghanistan) at approximately 3200 fps; a .308 sniper rifle that fires .30 caliber rounds at approximately 2600 – 2900 fps; and a .44 caliber magnum revolver that fires bullets at approximately 1300 fps.

During the experiment, members of the *Myth Busters* cast fired the various weapons at the hanging pig one at a time from a distance of 22 feet. Neither "Dirty Harry's" handgun of choice, the .44 magnum revolver, nor any of the enumerated rifles were able to move or dislodge the hanging pig. Remember the pig had been dislodged from the rig before the experiment began with a slight hand push. Bullet after bullet was fired into the body of the pig with no discernible movement. In fact, at one point several members of the cast fired the pistol and the rifles simultaneously and repeatedly at the target without dislodging it from the rig.

Finally, the shotgun loaded with the rifle slugs was used by a participant in the experiment. The shotgun was fired one time; the rifle slug dislodged the pig from the rig and it fell straight down to the ground. It should be noted that the pig's body was not propelled backward in any way; it simply fell directly downward and landed on the ground.

The rifle slug weighs approximately 437.5 grains (one ounce) versus, for example, a .40 caliber bullet used in most American police issued handguns that weighs 180 grains. The experiment demonstrated the raw power of the rifle slug fired from a shotgun. This was the round fired by the bank robber in my first FBI

Chapter 8

shooting incident in Richmond, Virginia in 1972. As mentioned at the beginning of this book, the Richmond police officers who were on the receiving end of that shot were richly blessed that a bullet of this power and size missed them.

More important, the *Myth Busters* experiment demonstrates for all to see that bullet wounds from all other types of weapons normally used by police officers will not knock adversaries to the ground.

Real World Reality—The FBI Miami Shootout

On the morning of April 11, 1986, FBI Supervisory Special Agent (SSA) Gordon McNeill and 13 other FBI agents set out on a mission to capture two armed and dangerous bank/armored car robbers. These men had been extremely active in southwest Miami, Florida in the previous six months.[15] During that time frame the unidentified robbers held up two local banks and two armored cars. During the two armored car robberies they shot and wounded two guards. In addition, they shot and killed the owner of a stolen car that they used in one robbery and shot and seriously wounded the driver of a second stolen vehicle used in their last bank robbery on March, 19, 1986. It was later learned, in the aftermath of the shootout with the FBI, that one of the suspects (William Mattix) was the prime suspect in the murder of his former wife and her coworker in Ohio. Needless to say, these guys were aggressive, reckless, and extraordinarily dangerous.

The stolen vehicle used in the March 19 bank robbery was a black Chevrolet Monte Carlo, 2-door sedan, bearing Florida license plate NTJ891. It had not been recovered after the March bank robbery and was believed to possibly be still in the

---

[15] Information for this section of the book was obtained from several different sources. One source for the information was an FBI Training Academy Division Video entitled "Firefight," that was produced by the FBI Academy Firearms Training Unit. The second source of information on the shooting incident involved reviewing an actual FBI Administrative Inquiry Report dated 6/5/86, entitled "Shooting Incident: 4/11/1986—Miami Florida" (BuFile 62-121996). This report was released pursuant to the Freedom of Information Act and is available on the Internet at an FBI website entitled "FBI Records: The Vault—Miami Shooting: 4/11/86." The third source of information is an Internet site entitled "Firearms Tactical Institute" (www.firearmstactical.com). In July, 1998, the latter site had for its primary source of information on the Miami FBI shootout, a publication written by W. French Anderson, M.D., USC School of Medicine, Los Angeles, California. Dr. Anderson's publication is entitled, "Forensic Analysis of the April 11, 1986, FBI Firefight."

Wound Ballistics

possession of the serial robbers. SSA McNeill was in charge of the surveillance operation on April 11. He instructed his cadre of FBI agents to spread out over a 60 block area in southwest Miami and watch for the stolen Monte Carlo. This particular area had several banks located within its perimeter. SSA McNeill was acting on an educated "hunch" that it was about time for these dangerous criminals to strike again in this particular area. His "hunch" turned out to be prophetically but tragically correct.

Shortly after 9:30 am on April 11, Special Agents Benjamin Grogan and Gerald Dove, riding together in an unmarked FBI vehicle, observed a black Chevrolet Monte Carlo, bearing Florida License plate NTJ891 drive past their location. The vehicle contained two white males in the front seat. The occupants matched the general description of the robbers who had covered their faces with masks in the prior robberies. The agents pulled in behind the suspects and began to follow them. Agent Dove radioed to his fellow agents and informed them of their observations and location. The other agents began to immediately respond. However, several of them were not located in the immediate vicinity of the moving vehicle surveillance and did not reach the shooting scene in time to participate in the shootout.

Three FBI vehicles containing four agents were able to respond quickly to the call for assistance. The Monte Carlo pulled off the main highway and traveled through a residential area with many private homes. The agents quickly decided to stop the Monte Carlo and extract the suspects from the vehicle by means of a "felony car-stop" procedure.[16] They made this decision because they believed that the robbers had "made" the surveillance. It was time to act to prevent the suspects from entering a major well-traveled road and the probability of a high speed pursuit. Special Agents Grogan and Dove activated a flashing blue light and siren in an attempt to stop the Monte Carlo. The suspects refused to yield.

An FBI vehicle occupied by Special Agents Hanlon and Mireles attempted to force the Monte Carlo off the road. After some initial physical contact between the Monte Carlo and the FBI vehicle, the Monte Carlo was able to disengage; make a

---

[16] This is a procedure used by law enforcement officers that is designed to safely extract dangerous "high risk" occupants from a vehicle after it is stopped.

Chapter 8

U-turn and proceed in the opposite direction. One FBI vehicle was able to drive parallel with the Monte Carlo, engage it on the driver's side and force it to crash into a tree on the right side of the street. The FBI vehicle came to rest directly beside the Monte Carlo, effectively keeping it from getting back on the street. The Monte Carlo now was wedged between the FBI vehicle and a third party vehicle that was located to its immediate right. The location was 12201 South West 82nd Avenue in southwest, Miami. At this point in time all manner of hell broke loose.

In the next four plus minutes, well over 100 gunshots were exchanged between FBI agents and the two bank robbers, later identified as William Mattix and Michael Platt. These two men, aged 34 and 32 respectively, had met previously while serving as Military Police officers in the US Army. Prior to becoming a Military Police officer, Platt had graduated from the US Army Airborne Ranger—Paratrooper Air Assault Training School. Mattix, prior to his US Army service, had served as a US Marine.

Because of their prior military service training, these men were well schooled in handling firearms. On this particular day, Platt was armed with a Ruger Mini-14, military style assault rifle. This rifle had a 30-round magazine and fired .223 rounds at approximately 3200 feet per second. Platt was also armed with a .357 magnum revolver. Mattix was armed with a 12-gauge shotgun and a .357 magnum revolver.

Mattix was driving the Monte Carlo when it was forced to stop on South West 82nd Avenue and Platt was sitting in the front passenger seat. During the next four minutes Platt fired at least 42 rounds from his Ruger Mini-14. Platt emptied one 30-round magazine during the gun battle, reloaded and fired several more rounds from his second 30 round magazine. Mattix fired at least one round from his 12-gauge shotgun. A total of three rounds each were fired from the two .357 magnum revolvers in the possession of Platt and Mattix during the shootout.

Shortly after the shootout commenced, another FBI vehicle arrived on the scene containing two additional FBI agents Orrantia and Risner. At the outset of the shootout, SSA McNeill took up a kneeling position behind the engine block of the FBI vehicle that initially forced the Monte Carlo to crash into the tree. It was parked to the immediate left of the Monte Carlo. He fired

Wound Ballistics

four shots with his .357 magnum revolver into the front passenger compartment of the Monte Carlo. Platt fired several rounds directly at McNeill with his Mini-14 and hit him in his gun holding hand with a .223 round. McNeill, although bleeding profusely, basically ignored being shot and fired his last two rounds directly at Mattix. One of those rounds hit Mattix just forward of his right ear, below the temple. The bullet, a .38 Plus P round (FBI standard issue at the time for a revolver) shattered Mattix's cheek bone, fractured the base of his skull, entered the right sinus cavity under his eye, bruised his brain but did not penetrate through the skull into his brain.[17]

A medical doctor from the University of Southern California (USC) Medical School conducted a comprehensive and thorough post shooting examination of the shootout and opined that McNeill's bullet probably rendered Mattix instantly unconscious.[18] McNeill's last round hit Mattix in the right side of his neck, penetrated the neck at a downward angle, severed blood vessels behind his collar bone, ricocheted off a rib near his spine and came to rest in his chest cavity.[19] The wound also disrupted the nerves and blood supply to his right arm and probably paralyzed that arm as well. Bleeding from this wound resulted in pooling of almost a liter of blood in his chest cavity within 2 – 3 minutes after receiving the wound. **The doctor later opined that this wound would have ultimately been fatal for Mattix.**[20]

These dire bullet wounds notwithstanding, in the following few minutes, Mattix, on his own power, would exit the Monte Carlo through the passenger side front window, circle around undetected, enter the passenger front seat of an FBI vehicle, and assist Platt in an attempt to start the vehicle to escape the scene.

Meanwhile, after Platt shot SSA McNeil in the hand, he decided to quickly remove himself from the Monte Carlo. Because

---

[17] See, the July 1998 "Firearms Tactical Institute" website report on the FBI Miami Shooting and in particular its report of USC Medical School Doctor. W. French Anderson's analysis of the shootout in his publication "Forensic Analysis of the April 11, 1986, FBI Firefight."

[18] Id.

[19] Id.

[20] Id.

Chapter 8

the passenger side door of the two-door sedan was jammed shut, he exited through the passenger side window of the Monte Carlo.[21] While Platt was climbing through the window, Special Agent (SA) Dove fired several shots with his 9mm semi-auto pistol at Platt from behind an FBI vehicle parked behind the Monte Carlo. Platt was hit with a 9mm round in his upper right arm.[22] The bullet passed through Platt's arm, severing the brachial artery, exited near his armpit, penetrated his chest, and passed almost entirely through his right lung before stopping in the lung. The bullet stopped an inch short of penetrating Platt's heart wall.[23]

At autopsy, Platt's right lung was completely collapsed and contained 1300 milliliters of blood. **The USC medical doctor believes that the wounds Platt received from this bullet (Platt's first in the gun battle) were non-survivable and the primary cause of Platt's death.**[24] After being hit initially, Platt was quickly shot twice more, probably by SA Dove, in the right rear thigh and the left foot.[25] Platt rose to his feet after rolling off the hood of the third party vehicle parked to the immediate right of the Monte Carlo. At this time, Platt was hit by a grazing wound to his back that may have been fired by SA Orrantia from across the street. Platt fired back at SA Orrantia and his partner SA Risner across the street and then turned to face SA Dove, SA Grogan, and SA Hanlon at their location behind the Monte Carlo.[26]

At that point, Platt was shot a fifth time by either Orrantia or Risner. The shot entered Platt's right forearm, fractured the radius bone in his forearm, and passed through the arm.[27] He was immediately shot a sixth time with a bullet fired by SA Risner. The bullet entered his upper right arm, exited below the armpit,

---

[21] Id.
[22] Id.
[23] Id.
[24] Id.
[25] Id.
[26] Id.
[27] Id.

Wound Ballistics

entered the right side of his chest, and came to rest in the soft tissues of the right side of his back.[28] It was a non-fatal wound.

After being shot multiple times, with one non-survivable wound, Platt was on his feet and firing the deadly Mini-14. He fired two shots at SSA McNeill, who, although shot in the hand with a .223 round, had partially reloaded his revolver and stood up to see where Platt was. Platt shot McNeill in the neck with another .223 round. The bullet stunned his spinal cord, causing McNeill to collapse and become temporarily paralyzed.

Platt suddenly left his fixed location and with military style aggression moved forward with a slight flanking maneuver. He rapidly closed the distance between himself and the three FBI agents located behind the FBI vehicle that was parked behind the Monte Carlo. Platt arrived at the passenger side rear of the FBI vehicle, leaned over it and left large arterial blood spurt patterns on the rear of the vehicle.[29]

Platt's audacious move apparently caught the agents by surprise. SA Hanlon, already wounded in the hand by a shot from Platt, saw Platt's feet on the passenger side of the FBI vehicle while lying on his back on the ground, but it was too late. Platt shot and killed SA Grogan with a .223 round to the chest. He shot and wounded SA Hanlon in the groin area after Hanlon attempted to wedge himself beneath the vehicle to protect his head and torso from Platt. Platt immediately shot SA Dove twice in the head, killing him instantly. None of these three agents were wearing bullet-resistant vests.[30]

---

[28] Id.

[29] Id.

[30] Ordinary bullet resistant vests would not have protected any of the FBI agents involved in the shootout from Platt's Ruger Mini-14 rifle. The velocity of the .223 round that it fires will cause the round to penetrate right through the ordinary Kevlar protective vest. For law enforcement officers to protect themselves from bullets fired from military style assault rifles such as the AR-15; Mini-14; M-4 etc., officers must wear body armor that contains large protective plates made of steel, ceramics, or polyethylene.

Nevertheless, because gun battles occur suddenly and are often over in less than 3 seconds, law enforcement officers must have their handgun-stopping Kevlar body armor on at all times to protect them in the event of a surprise gun battle. The Federal Office of Justice Programs, National Institute of Justice website, www.ojp.usdoj.gov/nij reports that since the 1970s over 3100 law enforcement officers lives have been saved in the United States because the victim officers were wearing body armor when they were violently assaulted.

Chapter 8

Most shocking is the fact that all of this mayhem was caused by Platt, a man bleeding profusely from a non-survivable bullet wound. A bullet wound that severed the brachial artery in his upper right arm and almost completely passed through his right lung. He had become the FBI agents' worst nightmare.

At that point in the battle, neither Platt nor Mattix were done. Platt, intent upon escape, began to enter an FBI vehicle through the driver's side door. Simultaneously, SA Mireles attempted to shoot Platt with a 12-gauge shotgun that he could only operate with one hand. Earlier in the gunfight, Mireles had received a devastating bone-breaking (clear through) wound to his left forearm from a .223 round fired by Platt. The wound was so severe that the bones were literally sticking out from his forearm. His left arm was basically useless.

Mireles miraculously managed to operate the pump-action shotgun with one hand from a sitting position behind the rear of another FBI vehicle. Mireles fired five consecutive rounds at Platt as he was entering and after he entered the FBI vehicle. Each round fired had to be racked into the shotgun chamber with one hand. Mireles fired 00 Buckshot at Platt (each round contains 9 .32 caliber bullets). The first round hit Platt in both of his feet. The other four rounds missed.[31] Platt sustained broken bones in his feet from the shotgun blast but was able to continue his escape attempt. He closed the driver's side door and apparently ducked down to avoid the remaining shotgun blasts from Mireles.[32]

Meanwhile, Mattix had regained consciousness and joined Platt in the front seat of the FBI vehicle. Platt and Mattix were both attempting to start the FBI vehicle when SA Mireles approached the driver's side window with his .357 magnum revolver in his right hand. Mireles fired all six shots (.38 caliber plus P rounds) into the front seat of the FBI vehicle. The first shot missed. A fragment from the second shot hit Platt just above the right eyebrow but the bullet had apparently hit a part of the

---

[31] See, the July 1998 "Firearms Tactical Institute" website report on the FBI Miami Shooting and in particular its report of USC Medical School Doctor. W. French Anderson's analysis of the shootout in his publication "Forensic Analysis of the April 11, 1986, FBI Firefight."

[32] Id.

Wound Ballistics

vehicle before hitting Platt and most of the bullet went in another direction.[33] Instead of penetrating Platt's brain, the remainder of the round traveled along the exterior surface of the forehead and stopped above the right temple.[34]

Mireles' third shot hit Mattix in the face just below his left cheekbone. The bullet fragmented and did not cause significant damage. Mireles' fourth round hit Mattix just below the right eye, traveled downward through his lower jaw, into his neck and severed his spine.[35] Mireles fired his fifth shot directly into Mattix's chin. This round penetrated his jaw bone; went through his neck and came to rest next to his spine.[36] Mattix was done.

By this time, SA Mireles was standing right next to the driver's side open window of the FBI vehicle. He had one round left and pointed his revolver through the open window of the vehicle. He aimed directly at Platt and fired. The bullet hit Platt in the chest, just below the left collar bone, traveled through his shoulder and neck and bruised his spinal cord.[37] Platt was finished. The battle was over but the outcome was devastating.

The entire event, from the moment the FBI agents first observed the Monte Carlo until the last shot was fired, took only nine and a half minutes. The gun battle itself took slightly more than 4 minutes from beginning to end. During the gun battle well over 100 rounds were fired by the combatants. At the end of the fray, two FBI agents were killed, five FBI agents were wounded, and the two violent offenders were dead. April 11, 1986, tragically became the most violent day for FBI agents since the inception of the Bureau in 1924.

During the gun battle Mattix was shot six times and Platt was shot twelve times. Both had received non-survivable wounds early on in the gunfight. Although both were seriously wounded, both were not only still alive at the end but actively trying to escape when SA Mireles shot them sitting in the front seat of the FBI

---

[33] Id.

[34] Id.

[35] Id.

[36] Id.

[37] Id.

Chapter 8

vehicle. The Miami shootout was truly an eye-opening experience for all of law enforcement across America.

The Miami Shootout—Aftermath and Lessons Learned

The FBI shootout in Miami sent shockwaves across the Bureau and all law enforcement agencies in the United States. After all, the FBI outnumbered the violent offenders 8 to 2 at the scene of the shootout and 6 more agents were desperately trying to reach the scene of the confrontation as it unfolded. Local police were alerted and on the way to help. No reinforcements were coming to assist the robbers. Nonetheless, seven agents were shot before the deadly encounter was over and two were killed. This shootout was not your average 3 second or less gunfight. It took over four minutes to end; four minutes of unadulterated terror.

It was simply unthinkable that two violent offenders could cause so much damage to so many FBI agents. Even more incomprehensible, was the realization, that in reality only one of the offenders, Michael Platt, was responsible for virtually all of the carnage inflicted upon those brave agents. The reason is simple to comprehend. Platt was well trained; extremely aggressive; never going to surrender, and armed with superior firepower. He was a package of human dynamite ready to explode.

Platt demonstrated to the FBI and to law enforcement everywhere what one aggressive, well-trained, and well-armed man on a mission could do. He proceeded forward with no regard for human life including his own. The tragically shocking outcome was on display in the middle of a Miami residential street for all to witness. The FBI had inexplicably been outgunned and outmaneuvered by Michael Platt. The incident changed everything for the FBI and for all law enforcement in the United States. These changes were designed to meet the challenges provided to law enforcement by modern-day violent offenders.

Changes After Miami

Included among the changes for the FBI after the Miami shootout were the types of handguns and ammunition issued, access to and availability of shoulder weapons, firearms training, policy, and tactics. After the shootout, the FBI discontinued its traditional and long-standing policy of issuing revolvers to its field agents. In 1992, I transitioned from carrying a Smith & Wesson .357 magnum revolver containing six .38 caliber bullets for the first 20 plus years of my career, to carrying a Sig Sauer 9mm semi-auto pistol containing sixteen 9mm bullets. I went from carrying six extra rounds in a small leather pouch on my belt to carrying two full magazines on my belt with fifteen 9mm rounds in each magazine.

Shoulder weapons including MP5-submachine guns and M-4 rifles were now readily available to agents who investigated violent crime. The weapons were kept in the FBI vehicles during investigative activities and not in the FBI gun vaults where they were virtually useless to the agents who needed them. Dangerous and high risk arrests were now being regularly handled by highly trained FBI SWAT teams instead of regular investigative agents. Agents were now required to wear soft body armor when making any arrest.

The FBI Handgun and Ammunition Transition

During the Miami firefight in 1986, SA Dove was armed with a Smith & Wesson, Model 459 semi-auto pistol.[38] According to retired FBI firearms experts' John Hall and Urey Patrick in their book *In Defense of Self and Others*,[39] SA Dove's handgun was loaded with a "lightweight, high velocity round widely popular throughout law enforcement at the time. It was designed to expand rapidly and limit penetration, 'dumping' its energy totally within the target and thereby eliminating any danger of 'over penetration.' The round [in the Miami shootout] did exactly as it was designed to do."[40]

Patrick and Hall report that during the initial stages of the Miami shootout, a round from SA Dove's weapon penetrated armored car robber/murderer Michael Platt's right upper arm and

---

[38] See, Charles E. Petty, "The Gun Zone," www.thegunzone.com/Miami-ammo.html. Apparently in 1986 some FBI field agents were permitted to carry semi-auto pistols. I know that FBI SWAT team members and Hostage Rescue Team members were armed with 9mm semi-auto pistols well before regular field agents began receiving the new 10mm semi-auto pistols in 1989.

[39] P. 73.

[40] Id. (emphasis added).

Chapter 8

came to rest deep into his right lung. Patrick and Hall state that "[t]he path of the bullet would have penetrated the upper heart/aorta if the bullet had continued to penetrate."[41] Of course, the bullet stopped short of Platt's heart/aorta and **only penetrated into his body 6 or 7 inches.**[42] Patrick and Hall correctly observed that this bullet performed exactly as it was designed to do but they also correctly characterized the bullet as a "failure."[43] The wound to Platt's upper arm (which included severing the brachial artery) and lung was non-survivable, but the bullet that struck him failed to take him quickly out of the fight. If the bullet had entered his heart and severed his aorta, the killing of two FBI agents and the severe wounding of two more would likely have never happened.

In 1989 the FBI issued a report entitled "Handgun Wounding Factors and Effectiveness" authored by FBI Firearms expert SA Urey Patrick. In the report Patrick observed that handgun rounds cause two major negative impacts on the human body. The first involves **permanent tissue destruction (i.e., permanent cavitation) along the path of the bullet** caused by the size, that is, diameter of the bullet and the expansion of the bullet (if it is a hollow point round). The second involves the **degree or length of penetration into the body.** Patrick concluded that a bullet must be able to **penetrate at least 12 inches into the body from any angle to reach and damage major organs including the heart.**

Patrick states that a "handgun bullet must penetrate 12 inches of soft body tissue at a minimum regardless of whether it expands or not. If the bullet does not reliably penetrate to these depths, it is not an effective bullet for law enforcement use."[44] Patrick teaches that greater bullet diameter and expansion is valuable because expansion will damage more blood vessels, cause more bleeding and permanent tissue destruction. However, between the two, penetration of at least 12 inches is by far the most important.

---

[41] Id. p. 74.

[42] Id.

[43] Id.

[44] P. 11.

Wound Ballistics

By 1989 the FBI had decided to replace its standard issue revolvers with semi-automatic pistols. There were several reasons for this decision.[45] First, the semi-auto pistol had the capability of firing several more rounds than the revolver without reloading. Second, when reloading was required, it could be done much quicker with a semi-auto pistol. Third, according to FBI firearms expert John Hall, semi-auto pistols are "generally easier to shoot quickly and accurately due to the self-cocking operation of the slide ... and the more efficient transmission of recoil."[46]

Following the Miami shootout, the FBI convened a Wound Ballistics Seminar at the FBI Academy in 1987 for the purpose of determining which semi-auto bullet would be most effective to incapacitate a deadly adversary.[47] Noteworthy individuals from the scientific and medical communities with knowledge of wound ballistics were invited to attend.

Although the seminar did not conclusively resolve the issue of which bullet would be most effective, participants unanimously agreed that physiological incapacitation (i.e., bringing about the cessation of hostile actions as quickly as possible) can be accomplished in two ways.[48] First, incapacitation is most effectively accomplished through direct bullet hits to the brain or upper spinal column of a deadly adversary (hits of this nature are likely to result in immediate incapacitation). Second and less immediately effective are bullet wounds to major body organs that generate massive bleeding.[49] Seminar participants concluded that with respect to the latter, **bullet penetration** sufficient to pass through major arteries and blood-bearing organs was necessary to produce the amount of bleeding required to result in incapacitation. Finally, seminar participants decided that the **size of a bullet and bullet expansion** would play an important

---

[45] See, Supervisory Special Agent/Unit Chief, FBI Firearms Training Unit, John C. Hall, "The FBI's 10MM Pistol," The FBI Law Enforcement Bulletin, November 1989.
[46] Id.
[47] Id.
[48] Id.
[49] Id.

Chapter 8

role in the incapacitation process through tissue damage and the rate of hemorrhage.[50]

After the seminar, the FBI Firearms Training Unit at Quantico, Virginia set out to determine through bullet testing which bullet would perform the best in terms of body penetration and expansion.[51] The FBI tested .45 caliber, 9mm, and 10mm (180 grain hollow point) bullets. The majority of the bullets were fired from a distance of 10 feet into 10% ballistic gelatin, which simulated soft human muscle tissue. During several of the tests, the FBI added a t-shirt, flannel shirt, and an outer down denim jacket material to the gelatin to reflect real life conditions.[52]

Before the tests, the FBI had already concluded that when considering the concept of human incapacitation, penetration of a bullet into the body is more important and critical to incapacitation than bullet expansion.[53] Accordingly, the FBI set up a minimum standard of 12" of penetration to judge the effectiveness of each round fired. Furthermore, as a point of reference, the FBI also tested the standard revolver bullet that FBI agents had been carrying in their issued revolvers for several years, that is, the .38 caliber 158 grain hollow point bullet. Forty rounds of each caliber were fired by FBI personnel during the testing process.[54]

The test results disclosed that the FBI standard issue .38 caliber 158 grain hollow point revolver round was able to meet or exceed the 12" minimum standard for penetration only 67.5% of the time. Likewise the 9mm rounds fired during the test met or exceeded the 12" minimum standard 67.5% of the time. The .45 caliber rounds fired during the test performed much better and met or exceeded the 12" minimum standard 92.5% of the time. Finally, the 10mm (i.e., .40 caliber) rounds fired during the test performed even better than the .45 caliber rounds. In fact, 39 out of the 40 ten millimeter rounds fired met or exceeded the

---

[50] Id.

[51] Id.

[52] Id. For a more complete explanation of each test, see the article written by SSA/Unit Chief John C. Hall, "The FBI's 10MM Pistol" in the FBI Law Enforcement Bulletin, Nov. 1989.

[53] Id.

[54] Id.

Wound Ballistics

minimum 12" standard for body penetration. Thus 97.5% of the 10mm rounds fired penetrated 12" or more during the test.[55]

The test results also revealed that the 10mm and .45 caliber rounds also outperformed the 9mm and .38 caliber rounds in the category of tissue displacement, that is, permanent cavitation. The 10mm and .45 caliber rounds displaced 4.11 and 4.22 cubic inches of tissue respectively within the desired length of penetration (12" or more), whereas the 9mm and .38 caliber rounds displaced only 2.82 and 2.16 cubic inches of tissue respectively.[56] The 10mm rounds fired during testing were also "by far the most accurate round tested."[57] At the conclusion of the testing, the FBI decided that the 10mm round was the best and most effective and accurate round for FBI agents to carry.

Smith & Wesson won a bidding process and contracted with the FBI to produce a new 10mm pistol for FBI agents to carry going forward. The first distribution of the S&W 1076 10mm pistol to FBI field agents occurred in late 1989. As time went on all FBI field agents were carrying semi-auto pistols.

Eventually the FBI transitioned to the Glock 23, .40 caliber semi-auto handgun that is the standard issue of today. The Glock 23, .40 caliber pistol fires the .40 S&W bullet (a slightly shorter version of the 10mm round). Currently, most law enforcement agencies in America issue as their primary handgun .40 caliber semi-auto handguns made by such noted manufacturers as Smith & Wesson; Glock; Beretta; and Sig-Sauer.

On December 12, 2012, ATK, Inc. was awarded a contract to supply the FBI with .40 caliber handgun ammunition. ATK's affiliate Speer LE is now supplying the FBI with .40 caliber Gold Dot 180 grain jacketed hollow point bullets for its Glock 23 duty semi-auto pistols. According to a Speer LE Senior Technician, the .40 caliber round supplied to the FBI by Speer LE has performed to the following standards in ballistic testing: **Penetration into Bare Gelatin—12.19 inches; Expansion—.640** (original diameter .40); **Bullet Weight Retention—179.9 grains.**

---

[55] Id.

[56] Id.

[57] Id.

Chapter 8

Speer LE ballistic tests on its FBI .40 caliber round also disclose that when fired into gelatin covered by heavy clothing, that is, t-shirt, flannel shirt, and denim-covered down jacket, the round performed as follows: **Penetration—13.25 inches; Expansion .709; Bullet Weight Retention—180.3 grains.** We can see from the performance of the Speer LE .40 caliber round that the work accomplished by FBI firearms experts Patrick and Hall after the Miami shootout was extremely important and infinitely valuable to not only FBI agents but also to all American law enforcement agents. The .40 caliber bullet now available to all US law enforcement agencies is far superior to the rounds used by American law enforcement agencies at the time of the Miami shootout. US Law enforcement agencies across the board owe a great debt of gratitude to now retired FBI Supervisory Special Agents Patrick and Hall for their pioneering work in the field of wound ballistics.

Officers of today, who would have been killed or seriously wounded by bad guys, after shooting the bad guys with non-survivable wounds, are now less likely to be shot by those bad guys. This is because the rounds used by the law enforcement officers of today will penetrate much deeper into the bodies of the bad guys, hitting major organs and causing more profuse bleeding.

The .40 caliber round of today will also greatly expand while retaining its original weight. This expansion will lead to more permanent body cavitation that will also cause greater internal bleeding. Remember the cardinal rule, absent a round entering the brain or upper spinal column, the only way to neutralize an adversary trying to kill you with a firearm is through massive blood loss. The quicker the bad guy loses blood, that is, the more massive the blood loss, the quicker his life-threatening actions will end. This inevitably results in more officers going home safely at the end of their tour of duty.

Other Lessons Learned from the Miami Shootout

There are many other lessons to be learned by the "objectively reasonable" law enforcement officer from the FBI shootout in Miami on April 11, 1986. These important and life-saving lessons are outlined as follows:

Wound Ballistics

- Officers who are designated for involvement in potential life-threatening operations must take proper precautions before the operation is initiated. **This must include wearing appropriate soft or hard body armor.** Placing the right kind of body armor for the assignment in the back seat or trunk of a vehicle is simply unacceptable.
- If a high-risk extremely dangerous operation is anticipated, **Special Weapons and Tactics (SWAT) teams should be deployed to directly confront the violent offenders.**
- When there is a potential for a confrontation with violent offenders, **shoulder weapons, including M-4 carbines; M-16 or AR-15 riles; MP5 sub-machine guns; and shotguns should be immediately available to participating officers.** Once again, weapons locked in gun cases in the trunks or back seats of a police vehicle (or even worse, in a vault at the police station) will sit there when a firefight suddenly begins. These weapons must be ready for immediate use if a gun battle erupts.
- Officers on "routine" assignments, that is, normal patrol duties, must also **wear their soft body armor. They must carry sufficient extra magazines to sustain them in a firefight. They should also have shoulder weapons (as mentioned previously) in their patrol cars and immediately available if needed.** Weapons of this nature located in a locked vault at police headquarters will be of no value to street officers facing a gangbanger armed with an AK-47 assault rifle; a bank robber armed with an AR-15 or an active shooter with an M-1 carbine in the local high school.
- During a vehicle pursuit, **officers should keep their handguns holstered or in their hands until they intend to fire them.** During the FBI pursuit of Platt and Mattix, two agents placed their handguns on the seat of their vehicles. During the crashes that occurred during or at the end of the pursuit, the handguns fell to the floor and were not available to the agents during the gun battle. Entering a gun battle without a gun is not a desired outcome.

Chapter 8

- All law enforcement officers should **receive appropriate EMT training to include handling bleeding from bullet and knife wounds** received by fellow officers or themselves in the event of violent confrontation. An appropriately stocked medical survival kit should be located in every vehicle as well.
- Officers should expect that some violent offenders will become extremely aggressive and even reckless during a confrontation. **They should be ready for some violent offenders to move aggressively forward and/or try to flank them** during the confrontation and attempt to kill the officers at close range.
- Officers must understand that **even if they are able to shoot their adversaries once or several times during a gun battle, this is not likely to stop them from continuing to be a deadly threat.**
- Officers must understand that **unless they shoot their adversary in the brain or upper spinal column, a deadly confrontation is likely to continue for several seconds or minutes until their opponent has lost at least 30% of their blood.**
- Officers must understand that **shooting an opponent one or more times will not knock him to the ground and that even shooting him directly in the heart will give him 10 – 15 more seconds to continue his life-threatening assault.** Michael Platt was shot twelve times before he died in the Miami shootout, including a non-survivable bullet wound to his upper arm (severing the brachial artery) and lung. Nonetheless, true to his military training, Platt went on the offensive; he shot and seriously wounded two agents and shot and killed two more. All the while, he was bleeding profusely but undeterred from his mission of mayhem.
- Officers must understand that **they are likely to be shot in an armed encounter with a violent offender and that if they are shot, they must continue to fight.** Lying down after being shot is an open invitation for the offender to walk up and execute the fallen officer. FBI Special Agent Mireles' heroic action on April 11, 1986,

Wound Ballistics

stands as a proud example of this principle. He was shot during the gunfight and severely wounded. His left arm was rendered totally useless and yet he continued to fight. It was Mireles in the end who prevented the killers from escaping the scene in an FBI vehicle and possibly running over a wounded FBI agent lying behind the car.

- **Officers must understand that they also can lose up to 30% of their own blood and remain in the battle.** As Lt. Colonel Dave Grossman has remarked, "know that if you stop before you lose ... [30% of your blood during a violent encounter] it is your will that failed, not your body."
- The "objectively reasonable" law enforcement officer must understand that **it is legally permissible to continue firing at a violent offender in a gun battle until that offender no longer represents a threat to the officer, other officers, and the public.**
- **Law enforcement officers must be clear in their mind that they will use deadly force in defense of themselves or others before being actually confronted with the necessity of using such force.** Waiting to make such an important decision until that horrific moment will result in hesitation. **Hesitation will result in death or great bodily harm to the officer and fellow officers.**

Shooting to Wound—"A Fool's Errand"

Wikipedia describes the term "A Fool's Errand" as attempting an **impossible task.** Likewise, The Free Dictionary defines it as an attempt to do something with **no chance of success.** For law enforcement officers who find themselves in a life-threatening deadly force encounter, shooting to wound is without question "A Fool's Errand." Nonetheless, there are many uninformed people in society who believe that law enforcement officers are so well trained and so skilled that this is not only possible in a deadly force encounter but required.

For example, PoliceOne.Com News reported in 2006 that David Paterson, a New York State Senator, introduced legislation that would require police officers in the State of New York to try to shoot violent offenders in the arms or legs to stop them during

Chapter 8

a deadly force encounter. Paterson proposed the legislation after four New York City police officers were acquitted of criminal charges in connection with the shooting death of Amadou Diallo. The officers fired 41 shots at Diallo and hit him 19 times after they believed that he was trying to draw a firearm in response to their attempt to question him in a rape investigation. It turned out that Diallo was unarmed and was not involved in the rape investigation.[58]

Senator Paterson believed that shooting to wound a suspect in the arm or leg would be sufficient to neutralize the suspect's deadly threats, thereby obviating the necessity of shooting him in areas of the body that are more likely to result in death, that is, the head or chest. Although Senator Paterson later withdrew the bill, he is certainly not the only one to adopt this fallacious manner of thought. This kind of erroneous thinking is often offered by news media commentators/reporters, public advocacy and civil liberty groups, politicians, and attorneys after officer involved shooting incidents.

As we have already discussed and examined at length in this section of the book, a law enforcement officer's sole objective in a gun battle is to bring the confrontation to an end as quickly as possible. The longer the confrontation goes on, the more likely the officer, other officers, and the public will be killed or seriously wounded.

I have demonstrated previously that until a deadly adversary is shot in the head or upper spinal column or until his brain is deprived of oxygen from massive blood loss, he will be fully able to continue to try to kill officers attempting to capture him. **Shooting to wound such an adversary will not bring a violent encounter to an immediate halt. To the contrary, minor wounds will do little or nothing to bring a violent offender under control.**

---

[58] Diallo matched the description of a serial rapist that had been active in the area. When approached by the officers during the nighttime hours, he disobeyed orders to stop and ran up the stairs into the vestibule of an apartment building. He was ordered to show his hands and instead reached into a pocket and withdrew a dark object that the officers thought was a gun. The object was later determined to be a wallet. The officers were found by an NYPD shooting review Board to be acting properly. They were subsequently indicted by a grand jury and acquitted after a jury trial.

Wound Ballistics

As we have seen in the FBI Miami shootout and elsewhere, even a deadly non-survivable wound did not bring an immediate end to that deadly confrontation. In fact, a violent offender killed two FBI agents and seriously wounded several more after receiving a non-survivable wound. **Let me say it emphatically once more, shooting to wound a deadly adversary will fall far short of the desired goal, which is to bring the violent encounter to an immediate halt.**

Furthermore, shooting to inflict minor wounds is exceedingly difficult, if not impossible. Common sense tells us that shooting at the arm on the torso of a human displayed on a stationary paper target would be much harder to hit than the actual torso displayed on the target. Now add multiple additional hurdles that are found in real gun battles, for example, a violent offender with a firearm shooting at you; the offender moving rapidly back and forth; the offender ducking and crouching or charging aggressively in your direction; poor lighting conditions; bad weather. Now try to shoot the offender in the arm. It becomes infinitely more difficult. Hitting a rapidly moving target in the arm would amount to pure luck.

Meanwhile the offender is taking dead aim at your torso. Why? Because it presents the largest target. Even if you hit the offender in the arm by total luck, he is not affected adversely. He is still on his feet, still moving quickly toward you, still armed and shooting at you and trying his best to take your life.

Dr. William Lewinski, Executive Director of the Force Science Research Center, Minnesota State University—Mankato, has observed, "In reality, most deadly force encounters, unfold very rapidly and very dramatically. Shooting to wound is rarely an option. Given the training most officers have, they are lucky to put bullets into center mass [the torso of the offender—a much larger target] without trying to hit limbs that can be moved faster and more radically than larger parts of the body."[59]

Lewinski points out that "[h]ands and arms can be the fastest-moving body parts. For example, an average suspect can move his hand and forearm across his body to a 90-degree angle in 12/100

---

[59] See, "Special Force Science series: Why shooting to wound doesn't make sense, scientifically, legally or tactically," PoliceOne.com News. 4/5/06.

Chapter 8

of a second.[60] He can move his hand from his hip to shoulder height in 18/100 of a second." Lewinski explains that "[t]he average officer pulling the trigger as fast as he can on a Glock, one of the fastest cycling semi-autos, requires one quarter of one second to discharge each round."[61]

The suspect's arm/hand is capable of moving so much faster than the officer's trigger pull, making a direct hit highly unlikely and to what end? Even a direct hit to the suspect's arm is not going to stop him from continuing deadly mayhem. During the Miami shootout, SA Mireles was hit with a .223 rifle round in his left forearm which completely shattered the bones in his forearm. He continued in the fight and in the end was the agent who killed both of the armored car robbers who were trying to escape in an FBI vehicle.

Trying to shoot a deadly offender in the leg is also nothing but folly. Again the target is likely to be on the move, making it much more difficult to hit. A person's leg is a much smaller target than the torso. Even if a shot to the leg is successful, it will not put the suspect on the ground and the suspect will still be able to use his hands to fire a pistol or rifle at the officer.

Police officers are trained to fire at the center mass of a deadly threat offender because this is the largest target. The goal is to stop the deadly threat as rapidly as possible. Shooting to wound is not only exceedingly difficult but is contrary to the sole objective: that is, to stop the offender from shooting the officers or other innocent persons.

Senator Paterson's legislative proposal reaches far beyond what the constitution and the Fourth Amendment requires. **This book demonstrates clearly and unequivocally that an officer's conduct will be lawful if it is "objectively reasonable."** It is totally beyond reason to expect an officer to act at skill levels that are virtually impossible to reach. Moreover, it is entirely unreasonable to require officers to expose themselves to greater degrees of danger than they already face in trying to keep us safe from dangerous predators. Shooting to wound is a bad idea. It is an idea born in ignorance and it must be vigorously opposed and defeated when raised. It is truly a "Fool's Errand."

---

[60] Id.

[61] Id.

Chapter 9

TENNESSEE V. GARNER—DEADLY FORCE AND THE FLEEING FELON

In 1985, the United States Supreme Court decided *Tennessee v. Garner*.[1] The case combined the issues of the fleeing felon and law enforcement use of deadly force and brought them squarely before the Court for the first time. At the time this case happened several states still had statutes that authorized law enforcement officers to shoot fleeing felons regardless of whether they were considered armed or dangerous. Tennessee was one of those states.

During the night time hours of October 3, 1974, two City of Memphis, Tennessee police officers responded to a residential burglary in progress call. After speaking to a neighbor who heard glass breaking next door, one officer went to the front of the house and the other to the rear.

The officer at the rear heard a door slam and observed a suspect run from the house across the backyard. The suspect, a 15-year-old male, headed directly for a six-foot high chain link fence at the rear of the yard. The officer used a flashlight and was able to see that the suspect had no weapon in his hands. The officer ordered the suspect to halt and identified himself as a police officer. The suspect refused to comply and began to climb over the fence. The officer drew his revolver and fired one shot at the suspect from behind. The bullet struck the suspect in the back of the head and he died shortly thereafter in a nearby hospital.

The father of the suspect brought suit in the local Federal District Court pursuant to 42 U.S.C. §1983 (the federal civil rights statute). He sued the officer who fired the shot and other defendants not relevant to this discussion. After a trial before a Federal District Judge, a verdict was issued in favor of the defendants. The Judge ruled in favor of the officer who shot the suspect because he acted pursuant to the Tennessee "fleeing felon" statute. The statute authorized the shooting of a fleeing felon as long as the police had probable cause to believe that he

---

[1] 471 U.S. 1 (1985).

had committed a felony and was likely to escape, even if he was not considered armed or dangerous.

The plaintiff filed an appeal with the US Court of Appeals for the Sixth Circuit. The Sixth Circuit reversed the District Court and ruled that the Tennessee fleeing felon statute was unconstitutional insofar as it authorized the shooting of an unarmed and non-dangerous fleeing felon. The Sixth Circuit dismissed the officer from the lawsuit on qualified immunity grounds. The State of Tennessee intervened in the lawsuit to defend its fleeing felon statute and petitioned the Supreme Court for review.

The Supreme Court accepted the case for review; affirmed the decision of the Sixth Circuit; **and ruled that the Tennessee "fleeing felon" statute violated the Fourth Amendment in so far as it authorized the shooting of an unarmed and non-dangerous fleeing felon.**

Prior to declaring the Tennessee statute unconstitutional, the Supreme Court ruled that an apprehension of a person by law enforcement officers by means of deadly force is a **"seizure,"** which implicates the Fourth Amendment. The Court explained that once there is a **governmental seizure** of a person, the Fourth Amendment mandates that the seizure must be **reasonable** to be constitutional.[2]

The Court next declared, as mentioned above, that the Tennessee "fleeing felon" statute was unconstitutional (i.e., unreasonable) to the extent that it authorized law enforcement officers to use deadly force against unarmed and non-dangerous fleeing felons. Following *Garner,* it was no longer permissible for law enforcement officers to shoot unarmed or non-dangerous fleeing felons to prevent them from escaping arrest.

It must be noted, however, that the Court did not prohibit the shooting of all fleeing felons but limited its ruling to those who were unarmed and non-dangerous. The Court made clear that use of deadly force by law enforcement officers against fleeing felons was constitutionally permissible as long as three conditions were met.

---

[2] The Fourth Amendment to the United States constitution prohibits **unreasonable** searches and **seizures.** In order for a search or seizure to be reasonable under the Fourth Amendment, law enforcement officers must, in most cases, possess probable cause to justify the search and/or seizure.

Tennessee v. Garner—Deadly Force and the Fleeing Felon

First, the law enforcement officer intending to use deadly force against a fleeing felon must possess **probable cause to believe that the suspect poses a significant threat of death or serious physical harm to the officer or others.**[3] **Second,** the officer must have a reasonable belief that the use of deadly force is **necessary to prevent the suspect from escaping arrest.** In other words, the officer must reasonably believe that there is no other safe alternative to the use of deadly force to prevent escape.[4] **Third,** the officer must **warn the suspect** of an intention to use deadly force, **if it is feasible** to do so.[5] The Court's warning requirement is accompanied by the words, "where feasible."[6] These carefully chosen words signal the Court's clear recognition that there will be times when officers will not be able to warn a suspect that they are about to use deadly force because a warning is likely to increase the danger to officers or other innocent third parties.[7]

---

[3] Probable cause is a legal term of art that requires law enforcement officers to have a **reasonable belief** based upon **articulable facts and circumstances** that a certain fact exists. For example, the officer must possess knowledge based upon facts and circumstances that the suspect is in possession of a firearm or other dangerous weapon.

[4] For example, the officer may reasonably believe that because he is younger and in better shape than the suspect, he is likely to catch the suspect running away with a gun in his hand, but this is not a safe alternative to the use of deadly force. It is unreasonable to require the officer to choose an alternative that is inherently unsafe and, if used, would place the officer in significantly greater danger than he was in before choosing it. Catching up to a suspect with a firearm is likely to result in dire consequences for the pursuing officer.

[5] John Michael Callahan Jr., "Deadly Force, Constitutional Standards, Federal Guidelines and Officer Survival," 2001, pp. 1 – 2. There are times when a warning is simply not feasible, i.e. to provide a warning is likely to increase the danger to officers or innocent third parties. For example, there have been several incidents that the author is familiar with over the years in which bank robbers and murderers have taken innocent bystanders as hostages at gunpoint. FBI agents have shot and killed them without warning. Warning them would simply provide them with the chance to kill the hostages and discover the precise location of FBI snipers. Warnings under such conditions are simply not feasible.

[6] 471 U.S. 1, at p. 12.

[7] See for example, *Napier v. Town of Windham, et al.*, 187 F.2d 177 (1st. Cir. 1999). Napier fired a rifle several times in his yard but no one was injured. When officers arrived at his home, he pointed a firearm at one officer. Both officers fired at him but did not hit him. Napier turned toward the second officer with his gun still raised. The second officer fired several more shots at Napier and he was wounded. Napier claimed that the officers never warned him to drop his firearm. Both officers disputed this claim. He further alleged that he never pointed his firearm at either officer. The First

Chapter 9

The Court's first requirement that the suspect pose a significant threat of death or serious bodily harm can be characterized as the Court's **dangerousness component**.[8] Referring to this component, the Court explained that deadly force may be used against a fleeing felon "if the suspect threatens the officer with a weapon or there is probable cause to believe that **he has committed a crime involving the infliction or threatened infliction of serious physical harm....**"[9]

The court's use of the disjunctive "or" signals its belief that there are two categories of suspects that can independently meet its dangerousness component.[10] First, this includes those suspects who threaten an officer or others with a weapon. This would include suspects running from officers with a weapon in their hands.

Second, it includes those who have committed a crime involving the infliction or threatened infliction of serious bodily harm. The latter category of suspect meets the dangerousness component of *Garner* because of the violent or potentially violent nature of the crime committed regardless of whether they are believed to be actually armed at the time of their attempted capture.[11]

Circuit Court of Appeals ruled in favor of the officers and found the shooting of Napier to be reasonable. The court dismissed Napier's claim that a warning was necessary in these circumstances and further ruled that Napier need not have pointed his gun directly at the second officer before the officer could believe that he was in mortal danger.

See also, *Colston v. Barnhart,* 130 F.3d 96 (5th Cir. 1997). Texas State Trooper Barnhart stopped a vehicle that Colston was riding in for a traffic violation. Barnhart instructed Colston, a passenger, to step out of the vehicle and asked him for identification. A second officer arrived on the scene and both officers became involved in a violent physical altercation with Colston. Colston, young, large and strong, was able to render the other officer unconscious and knocked Barnhart to the ground as well. Barnhart observed Colston begin to move toward his patrol car, which contained a loaded shotgun. Without warning Colston, Barnhart drew his firearm and fired three shots at him from his position on the ground. Two of the shots hit Colston and he was seriously wounded. The Fifth Circuit ruled that in this situation, Barnhart's failure to warn Colston was not unreasonable.

[8] John Michael Callahan Jr., "Deadly Force, Constitutional Standards, Federal Guidelines and Officer Survival," 2001, at p. 2.

[9] 471 U.S. 1, at p.11 (emphasis added).

[10] John Michael Callahan Jr., "Deadly Force, Constitutional Standards, Federal Guidelines and Officer Survival," 2001, p. 2; 471 U.S. 1.

[11] John Michael Callahan Jr., "Deadly Force, Constitutional Standards, Federal Guidelines and Officer Survival," at pp. 2 – 3.

Dangerous Fleeing Felons—*Forrett v. Richardson*[12]

Forrett committed a violent home invasion in which he tied up three victims, shot one in the neck with a handgun and fired at another. He fled the scene in one victim's truck with several stolen firearms and 250 rounds of ammunition. Within an hour, police officers found the stolen truck abandoned and the weapons missing. Minutes later, Forrett was spotted in the neighborhood of the abandoned truck and a foot pursuit ensued. Forrett was able to temporarily escape capture and police set up a perimeter around the area where he was last seen.[13]

Police used a helicopter in an attempt to locate Forrett. He was able to avoid capture for a time by running across backyards and climbing fences. Finally, officers confronted him in a yard bounded by a six foot high wooden fence. Forrett turned and looked at the officers who were 20 to 30 feet away from him. The officers shouted at him to stop and surrender. Forrett hesitated and the officers fired seven or eight shots at him which missed. Forrett ran to the fence and began to climb over it. Three officers fired several more times at him but all of the shots missed.[14]

Forrett scaled the fence and fell to the ground on the other side. The officers fired through the fence and hit him twice as he was getting up, once in the back and once in the hip. The officers fired 24 rounds at Forrett before he was captured. No firearms were found on Forrett's person or in the vicinity of his arrest.[15]

Forrett recovered from the gunshot wounds; pled guilty to the home invasion and violent assaults inside the home; and sued the officers who shot him, the Chief of Police, and the City of Riverside, California for use of excessive force and related allegations.

After a jury trial in federal court, the jury ruled in favor of Forrett against the officers who shot him and the Chief of Police. The trial judge reversed the jury's finding of liability and ruled as a matter of law that the officers had used objectively reasonable

---

[12] 112 F.3d 416 (9th Cir. 1997).

[13] John Michael Callahan Jr., "Deadly Force, Constitutional Standards, Federal Guidelines and Officer Survival," p. 18.

[14] Id.

[15] Id.

Chapter 9

force on Forrett. Moreover, the Chief of Police was not liable because the subordinate officers acted within constitutional boundaries when they shot Forrett. Forrett appealed to the Ninth Circuit Court of Appeals.[16]

The Ninth Circuit also ruled in favor of the police officers who shot Forrett and the Chief of Police. In so doing, the court examined the circumstances in which a fleeing suspect can be said to pose a threat of serious harm to police officers or others that would justify use of deadly force by police. The court observed that a fleeing suspect, under certain circumstances, **"need not be armed or pose an immediate threat to the officers or others at the time of the shooting."**[17]

The court examined the Supreme Court's opinion in *Garner* and observed that a fleeing felon is dangerous when he threatens the police with a weapon **or has committed a crime involving the infliction or threatened infliction of serious physical harm.** The court noted that in this case Forrett had committed a crime involving the actual infliction of serious bodily harm, that is, he shot the home invasion victim in the neck. Forrett therefore posed a threat of serious bodily harm to the officers and residents in the neighborhood, regardless of whether or not he was armed. The court also ruled that shooting Forrett was necessary to prevent escape and concluded that the police had adequately warned him before the shooting.[18]

The bottom line is that police officers shot a suspect twice from behind as he was trying to escape capture. No weapons were

---

[16] Id. at p. 19.

[17] *Forrett v. Richardson*, 112 F.3d 416, 420. In this particular case, I would also argue based on the existing evidence that there was probable cause for the officers to believe that Forrett was armed at the time he was shot and represented a real threat of death or serious bodily harm to the officers who confronted him in the back yard. After all, the officers knew that Forrett had shot and seriously wounded a victim of the home invasion and also shot at and attempted to kill a second victim. Forrett brought that weapon to the home invasion and there was no evidence that he left that weapon in the home when he departed. Moreover, he stole several additional firearms during the home invasion and 250 rounds of ammunition. None of these items were found in the stolen vehicle that Forrett abandoned just before he was shot. These facts provide ample basis for the belief that Forrett was armed with one or more firearms at the time he was shot.

[18] John Michael Callahan Jr., "Deadly Force, Constitutional Standards, Federal Guidelines and Officer Survival," at p. 20.

found on his person or in the vicinity of his arrest. Nonetheless, the Ninth Circuit, relying on the Supreme Court's opinion in *Garner,* found him to be a dangerous threat to the officers' safety based upon his prior commission of a deadly assault during the home invasion. **This is a significant part of the *Garner* decision and not generally well known or understood within law enforcement circles.**

The Necessity of Shooting Forrett—A Safe Alternative?

Forrett argued during his appeal to the Ninth Circuit that it was not necessary for officers to shoot him to prevent his escape because they had a safe and available alternative. Forrett contended that a less drastic alternative to shooting him in the back existed which involved officers allowing him to escape from them at the time he was shot and capturing him later. He claimed that his capture was simply inevitable because the police had cordoned off the area, set up a perimeter with numerous officers and were using a helicopter to spot his movements from the air.

The Ninth Circuit rejected Forrett's lack of necessity argument. The court observed that the evidence did not show that the police had actually established an escape proof perimeter at the time Forrett was shot. Moreover, the Court stated, "[e]ven if Forrett's capture was inevitable, it does not follow on those facts that the use of deadly force was unnecessary. The Fourth Amendment does not require law enforcement officers to exhaust every alternative before using justifiable deadly force. The alternative must be reasonably likely to lead to apprehension **before the suspect can cause further harm.**"[19]

The court observed that the officers knew that Forrett was fleeing through a residential area where many school children were located. The court concluded that the officers correctly reasoned that it was highly possible that if they allowed Forrett to continue to elude them, he would seize the opportunity to take an innocent child hostage. In these dangerous circumstances, Forrett's shooting was not a violation of the Fourth Amendment.

---

[19] *Forrett v. Richardson,* 112 F.3d 416, at p. 420 (emphasis added).

Chapter 9

Fleeing Felons—The Fourth Amendment and Deadly Force Policy

The Supreme Court made it abundantly clear in *Garner* that deadly force may be used against a fleeing felon when there is probable cause to believe that the felon has committed a crime involving the infliction or attempted infliction of serious bodily harm upon another person. Deadly force may be used in that situation even in the absence of a reasonable belief that the fleeing felon is currently armed with a weapon. However, the ruling of the Supreme Court notwithstanding, law enforcement officers are often constrained against the use of deadly force in such a situation by their own departmental deadly force policy.

For example, the Supreme Court decided the *Garner* case in 1985. It instantly became the law of the land. However, in 1995 the Attorney General of the United States approved a deadly force policy created by the FBI for all United States Department of Justice agencies.

The policy states with respect to "Fleeing Felons" that, "Deadly force may be used to prevent the escape of a fleeing subject if there is probable cause to believe: (1) the subject has committed a felony involving the infliction or threatened infliction of serious physical injury or death, **and** (2) the escape of the subject would pose an **imminent danger of death or serious physical injury to the officer or another person.**"[20]

The Department of Justice (DOJ) deadly force policy permits the use of deadly force upon a fleeing subject only in circumstances wherein the subject presents an **imminent danger** to the officer/agent or another person. By adding the imminent danger requirement, the DOJ made its policy more restrictive than the constitutional standard articulated by the Supreme Court in *Garner*.

As previously discussed, *Garner* would permit the use of deadly force upon a fleeing felon when there is probable cause to believe that he/she has committed a felony involving the infliction/threatened infliction of serious bodily harm, whether or not there is probable cause to believe the suspect is currently armed. The DOJ policy prohibits the use of deadly force in that circum-

---

[20] See, Memorandum of the Attorney General, October 17, 1995 on Resolution 14, "Policy Statement Use Of Deadly Force" (emphasis added).

Tennessee v. Garner—Deadly Force and the Fleeing Felon

stance and requires something more, that is, that the suspect present an **imminent danger** to the officer or others if allowed to escape.[21] The DOJ policy, in my opinion, would require that the suspect be armed, for example, with a firearm or other dangerous weapon, while fleeing.

For example, James "Whitey" Bulger was an FBI "Top Ten" fugitive for 16 years. He was wanted in connection with a federal racketeering indictment charging him with 19 murders. He was captured in the basement garage of an apartment building by FBI agents in Santa Monica, California in 2011 after being lured into the garage by means of a ruse. He surrendered without a fight and was taken into custody.

Suppose for the sake of argument that Bulger was dressed only in a bathing suit when he entered the garage and was carrying nothing in his hands. Suppose further that when confronted by the FBI, he ran up the ramp leading to the street and started to run down the sidewalk toward a waiting vehicle trying to escape. The agents have not observed a firearm and have no probable cause to believe he is currently armed. The *Garner* decision would permit the FBI, consistent with the Fourth Amendment, to shoot Bulger from behind to keep him from escaping.

The shooting would be constitutionally permissible because there is probable cause to believe that Bulger has committed 19 murders. However, the DOJ policy would not permit use of deadly force in this situation because Bulger would not meet the **imminent danger requirement** of the policy.

The bottom line here is that although the Fourth Amendment to the Constitution may authorize the use of deadly force in certain circumstances, officers must also be thoroughly familiar with their own departmental deadly force policy requirements. Those policy requirements cannot be less restrictive than the constitutional requirements regarding the use of deadly force **but can, and often are, more restrictive than constitutional requirements.** Officers who fail to adhere to their own internal policy dictates regarding the use of deadly force are likely to face disciplinary sanctions up to and including dismissal from the department. A word to the wise should be sufficient.

---

[21] John Michael Callahan Jr., "Deadly Force: Constitutional Standards, Federal Guidelines and Officer Survival" (2001), p. 26.

Chapter 9

It must be noted here, however, that when law enforcement officers are sued for alleged use of excessive force in violation of the Fourth Amendment to the United States Constitution, it is the Fourth Amendment and its "objective reasonableness" standard that will govern the outcome of the case. The deadly force rules, regulations, and policies of individual law enforcement agencies will not determine the outcome of these federal constitutional litigation matters.

For example, in *Thompson v. City of Chicago*,[22] a case involving allegations of excessive force that resulted in the death of a citizen, the Seventh Circuit Court of Appeals ruled that 42 U.S.C. §1983 (the federal civil rights statute) protects persons from constitutional violations and not from violations of state laws, departmental regulations and police policies. In fact, the court stated that violation of police regulations or even state laws is completely immaterial to the question of whether a violation of the federal constitution has been established.[23]

Dangerous Fleeing Felons—The Reactionary Gap / Hide & Ambush

The "objectively reasonable" law enforcement officer knows that foot pursuits of armed and dangerous fleeing felons are inherently unsafe and extremely dangerous. Two examples taken from the most recent publicly available FBI Law Enforcement Officers Killed and Assaulted (LEOKA) report for 2011 highlight the sad and tragic reality of this statement. The first incident involved a Vallejo, California police officer and the second involved a Livonia, Michigan officer. Both officers engaged in foot pursuits of dangerous suspects and both were shot and killed by the subjects of those pursuits.

The California incident began with a bank robbery. Shortly after 1:30 p.m. on November 17, 2011, a masked man entered a Vallejo, California bank. He approached a teller, told her that he had a gun and left the bank with over $3500 in cash. A silent

---

[22] 472 F.3d 444 (7th Cir. 2006).

[23] For other cases holding that violations of police policy and departmental regulations do not control the outcome of excessive force cases, see *Marquez v. City of Albuquerque*, 399 F.3d 1216 (10th Cir. 2005); *Cole v. Bone*, 993 F.2d 1328 (8th Cir. 1993); and *Smith v. Freland*, 954 F.2d 343 (6th Cir. 1992).

Tennessee v. Garner—Deadly Force and the Fleeing Felon

alarm was activated and a witness observed the robber enter a particular vehicle and leave the vicinity of the bank. The witness followed the suspect vehicle in his own vehicle for a time until a Vallejo Officer arrived in a marked police cruiser. The Officer attempted to stop the suspect vehicle and a vehicle pursuit ensued. The chase ended with the Officer using the Pursuit Intervention Technique (PIT) to force the suspect vehicle to stop.

After the suspect vehicle came to a stop, the suspect took off on foot with the Officer in pursuit. The suspect entered the backyard of a nearby residence that was surrounded by a six-foot high fence and waited for the Officer to ambush him. **When the Officer entered the backyard, the suspect fired at him three times with a .40 caliber semi-auto pistol.** One of the bullets entered the Officer's back, below his body armor. This bullet went through the Officer's heart and exited his chest. It was a non-survivable wound. This brave Officer became one of the 72 officers feloniously killed in 2011.

On January 17, 2011, an Officer from the Livonia, Michigan Police Department was participating in a surveillance of two residential home burglary suspects. Officers observed them break into a home and attempted to arrest them. One of the suspects took off on foot and was pursued by the victim Officer. The Officer chased the suspect into a residential backyard that was surrounded by a privacy fence.

The suspect turned and fired five rounds from a .45 caliber semi-auto pistol at close range. The Officer was shot several times but did not give up. Instead, he was able to return fire and discharge two rounds. One of these rounds fatally wounded the suspect. However, before the suspect died, he fired another round at the Officer. This round caused the death of the Officer.

These heroic officers exhibited significant bravery in their effort to protect the citizens of their jurisdictions. Nonetheless, both situations had a horrific outcome and follow in a long line of tragic endings for law enforcement foot pursuits of armed and dangerous suspects. These foot pursuits of armed fleeing felons are inherently dangerous for pursuing law enforcement officers and officers who try to cut them off and block the escape as well. The reason they are inherently dangerous is twofold.

Chapter 9

First, as demonstrated in the Livonia, Michigan officer murder, the **concept of the "reactionary gap"** frequently enters the picture in foot pursuits of armed felons. As we have seen in the "action v. reaction" section of this book, once a person has made up his mind to fire a handgun that is already in his hand, it takes little or no time to fire the first shot and multiple additional shots at the pursuing officer.

Picture a fleeing suspect, firearm in hand, running from the pursuing officer. Picture the officer, firearm in hand, running in an attempt to catch the suspect. Suddenly, the suspect, having already made up his mind to kill the officer, turns and fires multiple rounds at the officer.

After the suspect's surprise and instantaneous turn, he raises his weapon to eye level and fires his first shot in .31 of a second. Successive shots directed at the officer will follow at .25 second intervals. In 1.06 seconds, four shots have left the suspect's firearm.

Meanwhile, even if the officer has a weapon in his/her hand, he/she must first process what is happening, stop pursuit, steady his/her body, raise the weapon to eye level and return fire.[24] The time it takes to process the threat will be approximately .07 to 1.0 seconds. The time it will take to stop, steady the body, raise a firearm and fire the first round will probably take an additional 1.0 second. At best, the officer will be able to return fire in approximately 1.7 seconds. In that time frame, the suspect will be able to fire six or seven rounds at the officer. In the murder of the Livonia, Michigan officer in 2011, the suspect turned and fired five shots at the pursuing officer. The officer was killed. The outcome is both tragic and unacceptable.

The second reason that pursuing armed fleeing felons is so dangerous is the likelihood that the armed fleeing felon will adopt

---

[24] Raising the weapon to eye level and firing a sight picture shot is a disputed method among law enforcement firearms trainers. Some trainers, especially in close quarter combat situations, eschew taking the extra time to fire a sight picture shot and instead adhere to the point and shoot method of firing the handgun, that is, point and fire without using the handgun's sights at all. When I was in the FBI, I was taught to pick up the front sight on my handgun and commence firing in close quarter battles. Use of the point and shoot method will obviously result in a faster response time but it also reduces the likelihood of direct center mass hits on the adversary. One thing is certain; whatever the officer does repetitively in training is what the officer will do in a real life shooting encounter. You will play like you practice.

Tennessee v. Garner—Deadly Force and the Fleeing Felon

a **hide and ambush strategy** against the pursuing officer. Foot pursuits of armed suspects provide numerous opportunities for the suspect to hide and lie in wait for the pursuing officer. In urban areas, apartment buildings, private homes, garages, parked cars, and other objects offer suspects the chance to obtain the tactical advantage of cover and concealment. They can wait until the officer passes them by and shoot them from behind.

Likewise in rural areas, foot pursuits of armed suspects are similarly inherently dangerous. Suspects will be able to hide behind trees, bushes, and dense foliage and shoot pursuing officers as they run by them. Over the years there have been several instances where armed suspects have been able to use the hide and ambush tactic to shoot and kill pursuing officers. For example, most recently in the 2011 Vallejo, California incident described previously, it appears that the bank robbery suspect ambushed the pursuing Vallejo Officer and killed him before he had a chance to defend himself.

My first realization of the inherent danger of this kind of foot pursuit occurred in 1973 while I was serving in the FBI. I learned the details of a foot pursuit that resulted in the shooting death of FBI Special Agent Gregory Spinelli in Charlotte, North Carolina. SA Spinelli was involved in a stakeout of a suspected bank robber by the name of Arthur Mankins on March 15, 1973. Mankins was being sought for his role in a recent bank robbery in which he had exhibited a firearm.

During the surveillance, SA Spinelli observed Mankins take off running and began to pursue him with another agent. After a chase through the woods, during which Mankins shot and killed a dog, Mankins reached a building under construction and disappeared from view. SA Spinelli attempted to intercept Mankins on the other side of the building but was ambushed by Mankins in the process. Mankins shot SA Spinelli twice, once in the head, and he died from his wounds. Mankins engaged the second agent in a shootout and neither was hit. Mankins was finally arrested by the second agent after hand to hand combat with the help of some innocent bystanders.

Another incident is both relevant and instructive. On February 1, 1994, three residential burglary suspects hijacked a town-owned van in Holden, Massachusetts at gunpoint. Soon there-

Chapter 9

after, the van became stuck in the snow and was abandoned by the suspects. The suspects ran into the nearby woods.

Officer Robert Mortell, the Chief of Police from the nearby town of Paxton, Massachusetts responded and arrived at this location as the suspects were running into the woods. He immediately followed them into the woods on foot. During the pursuit that followed, one suspect hid behind a bush and waited for Chief Mortell to run past him. As the Chief ran by, the suspect fired eleven shots at the Chief. One of those rounds passed through Chief Mortell's heart and lungs and he was killed. The Chief never fired a shot and never had a chance.

A third reason why pursuit of armed fleeing felons is inherently dangerous involves the deadly threat it presents to other officers who attempt to cut the fleeing suspect off from another direction and are unaware that he is holding a firearm. Suppose, for example, that officers pursuing the suspect from behind see him holding a firearm but are unable to communicate the observation to officers on the perimeter in front of the suspect. Those officers in front of the suspect may be suddenly confronted by a suspect ready to shoot them before they can adequately defend themselves.

A situation similar to this occurred in one Massachusetts community in 2010. According to a news release issued by the Middlesex County District Attorney's Office on March 31, 2011, an armed robbery of a department store occurred in Woburn, Massachusetts on December 26, 2010, at approximately 8:30 p.m. The news release reported that Woburn Police Officers responded to an armed robbery in progress call. The first officer to arrive saw a possible lookout standing just outside the store and began walking toward him. Suddenly, a second suspect exited the store and pointed a firearm at the officer. The second suspect took off running with the officer in pursuit.

During the pursuit, the fleeing suspect pointed his handgun at a snowplow driver who attempted to block his progress. The suspect was heading for the main street from the store parking lot when a second officer by the name of Jack Maguire arrived in his patrol car. Officer Maguire exited his cruiser as the suspect ran by with his gun in hand. The suspect fired at Officer Maguire and hit him several times. Officer Maguire was able to return fire

Tennessee v. Garner—Deadly Force and the Fleeing Felon

and kill the suspect. Sadly, Officer Maguire died from his wounds. Officer Maguire bravely confronted this extremely dangerous fleeing felon. His death should remind us all of the inherent danger that flows from foot pursuits of armed fleeing felons. The Officer Maguire murder demonstrates that not only are officers pursuing fleeing armed suspects in mortal danger but likewise officers who try to cut them off as well.

Case Law on Deadly Force and Armed Fleeing Felons

The Federal Court of Appeals for the Eleventh Circuit decided a case entitled *Montoute v. Carr*,[25] which deals directly with the issue of the legality of law enforcement use of deadly force against an armed fleeing felon. During the early morning hours of 4/11/93, Sebring, Florida police officers responded to several 911 calls reporting that a fight involving multiple parties and gunfire was occurring at a local bar. Upon his arrival at the bar, Sergeant Carr heard the sound of a shotgun being fired. He looked around and spotted Montoute moving quickly toward him. Montoute was carrying a sawed-off 12-gauge pump-action shotgun in his right hand. The muzzle of the gun was pointed down toward the ground.

Sgt. Carr and a fellow officer repeatedly ordered Montoute to drop the shotgun. Montoute did not drop it and instead told the officers that he was on their side and had taken the gun from someone else. Montoute moved quickly past the officers without dropping the weapon. He began to run and headed down a nearby alley with the gun still in his hand. Sgt. Carr began to follow Montoute, stopped and fired two shots at Montoute from behind. One of those shots hit Montoute in his left buttock. Montoute was taken into custody without further incident.

Montoute later sued Sgt. Carr in the local Federal District Court and alleged that he was the victim of police use of excessive force. The Federal District Judge denied Carr's dismissal motion and ruled that the case should proceed to trial. The Judge explained that if Montoute was shot in the back it was questionable as to whether Sgt. Carr could reasonably believe that Montoute posed a serious threat to him or others. Sgt. Carr filed an appeal of this adverse ruling.

---

[25] 114 F.3d 181 (11th Cir. 1997).

Chapter 9

The Eleventh Circuit Court of Appeals reversed and ordered that the case against Sgt. Carr should be dismissed. At the outset, the court observed that even Montoute agreed that it would have been legally permissible for Sgt. Carr to shoot him as he was approaching Sgt. Carr after he refused orders to drop the shotgun. However, Montoute claimed that once he passed Carr with the weapon still in his hand, he no longer presented a danger of serious bodily harm to the officer. The Eleventh Circuit rejected this claim and ruled that the danger to Sgt. Carr and the other officer continued after Montoute passed them by.

The court observed that once Montoute passed the officers and started to run, there was nothing to prevent Montoute **from turning and pointing his firearm at the officers in a split second.** The court explained that when an officer has ordered a suspect to drop his weapon and his order is ignored; **the officer is not required to wait until an armed and dangerous felon has drawn a bead upon him or others before using deadly force.** (The court appears to grasp the concept of the reactionary gap and the danger that is inherent in it.)

The court further stated that Sgt. Carr could reasonably have believed that Montoute might wheel around and fire the shotgun at him **or might take cover behind a parked car or hide on the side of a building and shoot the officers as they run by.** (The court here appears to fully comprehend the concept of hide and ambush.) The court observed that if any of these things were to happen, Montoute would have presented a greater danger to the officers than when they first saw him approaching with the shotgun at his side. The court ruled that shooting of Montoute, although in the back and from behind, was lawful and in full compliance with the Supreme Court's decision in *Tennessee v. Garner*. The Eleventh Circuit astutely grasped the extreme danger that officers face when they choose to pursue a suspect with a gun in hand.

Another case decided by the Eighth Circuit Court of Appeals is also instructive. In *Krueger v. Fuhr*,[26] Springfield, Missouri police officer Fuhr responded to a call of an armed assault with a knife during the early morning hours. He was provided with a description of the suspect and was informed that the suspect may be a prison

---

[26] 933 F.2d 1358 (8th Cir. 1993).

Tennessee v. Garner—Deadly Force and the Fleeing Felon

escapee. The suspect was believed to be high on drugs and armed with a knife. Officer Fuhr entered the area where the suspect was believed to be and observed him lying down between two cars.

Officer Fuhr stopped his patrol car, drew his firearm and approached the suspect. He identified himself as a police officer and ordered the suspect to freeze. The suspect, Leroy Krueger, did not have a knife in his hands at that point. Krueger disregarded the officer's order and took off running. The officer pursued him for over 200 hundred feet. Several times during the chase, Fuhr ordered Krueger to yield without success. During the chase, Officer Fuhr testified that Krueger drew a knife from his waistband and gripped it in his hand.

Fuhr testified at deposition that he was fearful that Krueger was going to turn and attack him with the knife. He had closed to within three or four yards behind Krueger and was afraid that he would not be able to stop in time to defend himself from a knife attack. Fuhr slowed down, leveled his firearm and fired four shots at Krueger from behind. Two rounds struck him in the back and a third round hit him in the back of the head. Krueger was killed and a knife with an exposed blade was found 43 feet from his body.

Krueger's family sued Fuhr in the local Federal District Court. The Federal District Court Judge refused to dismiss the suit and ordered that it proceed to trial. Fuhr appealed and the Eighth Circuit Court of Appeals reversed and ruled in favor of Officer Fuhr. The court ruled that Officer Fuhr's use of deadly force was objectively reasonable pursuant to existing Supreme Court rulings in *Garner* and *Graham*.

The court observed that Fuhr had probable cause to believe that Krueger was armed with a knife and reason to believe that he faced a serious and immediate danger of physical harm when Krueger pulled that knife from his waistband. Moreover, the court ruled that it was not necessary for the officer to conclude that Krueger was too dangerous to capture and allow him to proceed in the hope that other officers in the area would be able to confront him later on.[27]

---

[27] In my opinion, it would be unreasonable for Officer Fuhr to allow Krueger to escape from him and become an extreme danger to other officers in the vicinity. At least Fuhr knew that Krueger had taken a knife out and represented an immediate danger to anyone who tried to stop him. Other officers in the vicinity may not have had the benefit of this knowledge if they confronted Krueger further down the road.

Chapter 9

Finally, the court observed that Fuhr had ordered Krueger to freeze at the inception of the chase and had continued that order numerous times during the pursuit. The court ruled that although there was no evidence that Fuhr attempted to warn Krueger that he was about to shoot him, given the urgency of the situation and the danger faced by the officer, the failure to warn was not constitutionally unreasonable.

When Krueger pulled the knife from his waistband and gripped it in his hand, he became a deadly threat to Officer Fuhr. At this point there was no way that Fuhr could safely arrest Krueger if he was able to catch up to him. As soon as Fuhr got within striking distance, he would become extremely vulnerable to being stabbed or cut. Furthermore because he was running at full speed, he would have been even more vulnerable to a sudden turn and knife assault from Krueger. He gave Krueger numerous opportunities to stop, drop the knife, and surrender. He was not constitutionally required to give Krueger the opportunity to stab or cut him. Krueger had already displayed his intent to do harm by removing the knife from his waistband.

Another Eighth Circuit case that is important in the discussion of law enforcement use of deadly force in the police foot chase context is *Thompson v. Hubbard,* 257 F.3d 896 (8th Cir. 2001). In *Thompson,* Pine Lawn, Missouri police officers responded to a report of shots fired and two suspects fleeing from the scene of an armed robbery. Officer Hubbard observed Thompson getting into a vehicle. Thompson fit the description of one of the armed robbers and was located in the area of the robbery. Thompson initially appeared to surrender but then turned to flee. A foot chase followed. Thompson climbed over a fence, rose from the ground, looked over his shoulder at Hubbard, and moved his arms as though he was reaching for a weapon in his waistband. Thompson's back was facing toward Hubbard and his hands were not visible to the officer. Hubbard yelled "stop" but Thompson's arms continued to move. Hubbard fired one shot that hit Thompson in the back.

Thompson died from his wound. No weapon was found on his body. Hubbard's family sued Hubbard, his supervising officer, and the City of Pine Lawn in the Federal District Court pursuant to 42 U.S.C. §1983, alleging excessive use of force in violation of

Tennessee v. Garner—Deadly Force and the Fleeing Felon

Thompson's Fourth Amendment rights. The District Court Judge dismissed the lawsuit and the Eighth Circuit affirmed.

The court observed that it had previously held that "deadly force is justified where the totality of circumstances give the officer probable cause to believe that a fleeing suspect poses a threat of serious physical harm to the officer or to others." The court rejected the Thompson family's contention that Officer Hubbard should have recognized that Thompson's sweatpants were not strong enough to hold a firearm in the waistband area. The court responded by stating, "An officer is not constitutionally required to wait until he sets eyes upon a weapon before employing deadly force to protect himself against a fleeing suspect who turns and moves as though to draw a gun."

The Eighth Circuit, in ruling for Officer Hubbard, also reviewed an earlier Tenth Circuit opinion in *Ryder v. City of Topeka,* 814 F.2d 1412, 1419 (1987), in which the Tenth Circuit ruled against requiring that a suspect actually be armed with a weapon in order to justify a police shooting. The court noted that the Tenth Circuit stated that a requirement that a suspect be actually armed with a weapon would place officers in "a dangerous and unreasonable situation."

This case is important because it stands for the proposition that an officer is justified in using lethal force against a suspect as long as he/she has probable cause that the suspect presents a threat of serious bodily harm to the officer or others, even when it is later determined that the suspect was unarmed. As long as the officer had probable cause to believe the suspect was armed and presented a deadly threat, the use of deadly force will be found to be within constitutional bounds.

Law Enforcement Departmental deadly force policies that require officers to chase offenders armed with exposed firearms are unnecessary, not required by existing law, and extremely dangerous for officers to follow.

Chapter 10

DANGEROUS VEHICLE PURSUITS—*SCOTT V. HARRIS*

On 4/30/07, the United States Supreme Court decided *Scott v. Harris*.[1] A Georgia Deputy Sheriff attempted to stop Harris for traveling at 73 mph in a 55 mph zone. Harris refused to yield and began traveling down a two-lane road at speeds in excess of 85 mph. Deputy Scott joined the pursuit along with other officers. During the pursuit, Harris attempted to evade officers by pulling into a shopping center parking lot. The officers attempted to box him in but Harris collided with Deputy Scott's vehicle and escaped.

Back on the road, Harris continued his excessive speed in an effort to get away. Deputy Scott implemented the so-called "Precision Intervention Technique" (PIT) in an attempt to bring the chase to a halt. The PIT maneuver is designed to tap a fleeing vehicle on the corner of its rear bumper to cause the vehicle to come to a spinning stop. During implementation of the PIT maneuver, Harris's vehicle ran down an embankment, overturned, and crashed. Harris was badly injured and became a quadriplegic.

Harris sued Scott and other officials pursuant to 42 U.S.C. §1983 and alleged that Scott's use of the PIT maneuver amounted to excessive force in violation of the Fourth Amendment. Both the Federal District Court and the Eleventh Circuit Court of Appeals rejected Scott's motion to dismiss on the basis of qualified immunity and ruled that the case must proceed to trial. Scott petitioned the Supreme Court, which accepted the case for review and reversed.

The Supreme Court ruled 8-1 in favor of Deputy Scott. The Court observed that normal procedure in deciding cases involving the pre-trial assertion of the qualified immunity defense, where there is a dispute involving material facts, requires the lower courts to accept the plaintiff's [Harris's] version of the facts as true.[2] However, the Supreme Court rejected normal procedure in

---

[1] 550 U.S. 372; 127 S.Ct. 1769 (2007).

[2] As explained earlier in this book, when a defendant police officer asserts the qualified immunity defense before trial, the officer's goal is to obtain an early dismissal of the suit by the trial judge before protracted discovery and trial. In order for the trial judge to rule on the efficacy of the defense, he/she must decide based on the known facts, whether the officer violated clearly established constitutional law. When the material

Chapter 10

this case, because of the existence of clear and unequivocal video tape evidence that displayed for all to see what actually occurred during the pursuit. The video tape was available from the dashboard cameras that were installed in the police cruisers.

The Court observed that the video tape clearly contradicts Harris's version of the facts involved in the pursuit. Harris's version gave the impression that he was driving so carefully that one might conclude that he was attempting to pass a driver's test to obtain his license. The Court noted by way of contrast, that the video tape told a far different story.

The Court observed, "We see Harris's vehicle racing down narrow, two lane roads in the dead of night at speeds that are shockingly fast. We see it swerve around more than a dozen other cars, cross the double yellow line, and force cars traveling in both directions to their respective shoulders to avoid being hit."[3] The Court also noted, "Far from being the cautious and controlled driver the lower court depicts, what we see on the video more closely resembles a Hollywood-style car chase of the most frightening sort, placing police officers and innocent bystanders alike at great risk of serious injury."[4] The Court made clear that in future cases the lower courts must make use of reliable video evidence when resolving qualified immunity claims by police officers.

At the outset of the case, the Court ruled that the Fourth Amendment was implicated and that Deputy Scott's tapping of Harris's bumper was a "seizure" pursuant to that Amendment. The only remaining question was whether that "seizure" was accomplished with "objective reasonableness" pursuant to the Court's earlier decision in *Graham v. Connor*.

Harris argued that *Graham* was not the controlling precedent for this case and that it should be decided pursuant to *Tennessee*

---

facts are in dispute, the trial judge is normally required to adopt the plaintiff's version of the disputed facts in deciding whether the officer violated clearly established constitutional rights. If the trial judge rejects the qualified immunity defense before trial, the case will proceed to a jury trial unless the trial judge's decision is reversed on appeal. In the case at hand, the Eleventh Circuit affirmed the trial judge's rejection of the qualified immunity defense but the Supreme Court reversed and ruled in favor of Deputy Scott. This terminated the lawsuit immediately.

[3] 127 S.Ct. 1769, at 1775.

[4] Id. 1775, 1776.

v. Garner. He argued that *Garner*'s three-pronged analysis should control the outcome of the case, that is, (1) Did Harris's conduct amount to a significant threat of serious bodily harm to the officer or others?; (2) Was it necessary for the officers to use deadly force to stop Harris?; (3) Was it feasible for the officers to warn Harris that deadly force was going to be used against him?

The Court rejected Harris's argument and observed, "Garner did not establish a magical on/off switch that triggers rigid preconditions whenever an officer's actions constitute deadly force. *Garner* was simply an application of the Fourth Amendment's reasonableness test to the use of a particular type of force in a particular situation."[5] The Court explained that *Garner* was a case involving the foot pursuit of an unarmed and nondangerous fleeing felon. The Court observed that the "threat posed by flight on foot of an unarmed suspect [is not] even remotely comparable to the extreme danger to human life posed by [Harris] in this case."[6] The Court concluded that its prior decision in *Graham v. Connor* was the controlling precedent here and the only thing that mattered was whether Deputy Scott's actions were "objectively reasonable."

The Court stated that in determining the reasonableness of Scott's actions, it must balance the nature of the governmental intrusion upon Harris's Fourth Amendment interests against the governmental interests that would justify the intrusion. The Court explained that in "judging whether Scott's actions were reasonable, we must consider the risk of bodily harm that Scott's actions posed to [Harris] in light of the threat to the public that Scott was trying to eliminate."[7] In the latter respect, the Court observed that Harris posed an actual and imminent threat to the lives of any pedestrians, other motorists and the officers involved in the pursuit.[8]

---

[5] Id. 1777.

[6] Id.

[7] Id. at 1778.

[8] Parenthetically, the identical conclusion would be compelled when discussing a fleeing felon on foot with a firearm in his hand. Not only are pursuing officers in imminent danger but also any other persons in the area including innocent civilians and additional officers trying to cut the suspect off from escaping.

Chapter 10

The Court observed that Scott's implementation of the PIT maneuver posed a high likelihood of death or serious injury to Harris but that fact alone did not control the outcome of the case. The Court applied its balancing test and observed that, "it [is] appropriate ... to take into account not only the number of lives at risk [i.e. pedestrians, other drivers, and police officers] but also their relative culpability. It was [Harris], after all who intentionally placed himself and the public in danger by unlawfully engaging in the reckless, high-speed flight that ultimately produced the choice between the two evils that Scott confronted."[9] The Court declared that Harris could have ended the ten-mile pursuit at any time by simply applying the brakes on his vehicle. The Court had no trouble in concluding that Scott acted reasonably under the Fourth Amendment.

Finally, the Court debunked Harris's claim that the police should have terminated the chase instead of using the PIT maneuver upon his vehicle. The Court observed that "Scott's action, ramming [Harris] off the road, was certain to eliminate the risk [Harris] posed to the public, ceasing pursuit was not."[10] The Court explained that there was no way to predict that Harris would realize that the pursuit had been terminated and stop his reckless driving. Moreover, the Court declared, **"[W]e are loath to lay down a rule requiring the police to allow fleeing suspects to get away whenever they drive so recklessly that they put other people's lives in danger."**[11]

The Court concluded by stating, "[i]nstead, we lay down a more sensible rule: A police officer's attempt to terminate a dangerous high-speed car chase that threatens the lives of innocent bystanders does not violate the Fourth Amendment, **even when it places the fleeing motorist at risk of serious injury or death."**[12]

---

[9] 127 S.Ct. 1769, 1778.

[10] Id. at 1779.

[11] Id. (emphasis added).

[12] Id. (emphasis added).

Dangerous Vehicle Pursuits—*Plumhoff v. Rickard*

On May 27, 2014, the Supreme Court of the United States decided the matter of *Plumhoff v. Rickard* (#12-1117).[13] This case is extremely important because it involves a vehicle pursuit, similar to the one in *Scott v. Harris* and the subsequent death of the driver and his passenger. Unlike *Scott,* Rickard, the male driver of the pursued vehicle, and Allen, his female passenger, were shot and killed by pursuing officers rather than run off the road by means of a PIT maneuver.

The Court, in an opinion authored by Justice Alito, ruled 8-1 that officers did not violate the Fourth Amendment when they attempted to terminate a high speed pursuit by shooting the driver of the suspect vehicle. Moreover, the Court ruled, 7-2 that officers did not violate the Fourth Amendment when they fired a total of 15 shots at the driver in an attempt to end the dangerous pursuit. Finally, the Court ruled alternatively 9-0 that the involved officers did not violate clearly established Fourth Amendment law at the time they shot and killed the male driver and therefore were entitled to dismissal of the case upon qualified immunity grounds.

In *Plumhoff,* the driver of a vehicle (Rickard) and his passenger Kelly Allen were stopped by a West Memphis, Arkansas police officer around midnight on 7/18/2004 for driving with only one headlight. Rickard was asked by the officer to step out of the vehicle. Instead, he suddenly drove off and a multi-car police pursuit followed. The chase continued from Arkansas into Memphis, Tennessee. The entire chase and parts of it was captured on several police vehicle video cameras. During the chase, which lasted more than 5 minutes, Rickard drove at speeds exceeding 100 miles per hour. He passed more than two dozen other vehicles during the pursuit.

During the chase, Rickard made a quick right turn that caused contact between a police vehicle and the suspect vehicle. This in turn caused Rickard's vehicle to spinout and collide with another cruiser. At this point, other police vehicles surrounded the suspect vehicle, leaving only one way for Rickard to attempt escape. Rickard's front bumper quickly made contact with

---

[13] 134 S. Ct. 2012. Decision below unpublished opinion, *Allen v. City of West Memphis, et al.*, 509 Fed. Appx. 388 (6th Cir. 2012).

Chapter 10

another police vehicle that blocked Rickard from moving forward. At this point, the wheels on Rickard's car were spinning and his car was rocking back and forth. He was using his accelerator in an effort to break free even though his front bumper was flush against the front of a police cruiser.

Some of the officers exited their vehicles and approached the suspect vehicle on foot. (This of course exposed them to the danger of being hit or run over by Rickard's vehicle). Officer Evans approached on the passenger side and attempted to open the door and gain entry without success. At that time, Officer Plumhoff fired three shots into the Rickard vehicle from the passenger side. Apparently unfazed, Rickard placed the car in reverse and drove in reverse in a 180 degree arc. He maneuvered the vehicle onto another street and almost struck an officer in the process. Rickard placed the car in drive and began to move the vehicle forward. At that point, Officer Gardner fired 10 shots at Rickard's moving vehicle, first from the passenger side and then from the rear as it proceeded forward. At this time a third officer fired two shots at the Rickard vehicle. A total of 15 shots were fired at the Rickard vehicle during the encounter.

Rickard drove down the road but subsequently crashed into a nearby building, not far from the shooting scene. Both Rickard and Allen were killed. Twelve rounds hit Rickard and two hit Allen. They died from bullet wounds and injuries sustained in the final crash.

A survivor of Rickard sued the participating officers pursuant to 42 U.S.C. §1983. The Federal District Court Judge refused to dismiss the lawsuit before trial and rejected the officers' assertion of qualified immunity. The officers filed an immediate appeal with the Federal Court of Appeals for the Sixth Circuit. The Sixth Circuit upheld the District court's rejection of the officers' qualified immunity defense and ordered that the case proceed to trial.

In its decision, the Sixth Circuit noted the similarity between the facts of this case and the facts of the Supreme Court's earlier decision in *Scott v. Harris* (2007). The court observed that normally when material facts are disputed, the appellate court will accept for purposes of deciding the qualified immunity issue, the facts asserted by the party opposing qualified immunity.

However, the court noted that after the Supreme Court's ruling in *Scott,* federal appellate courts are now required to take into account evidence (e.g., videotape) that shows that a plaintiff's version of disputed facts is demonstrably not credible.

In this case, the Sixth Circuit reviewed the available videotape evidence but remained unpersuaded that it required reversal of the District Court's rejection of the qualified immunity defense. The court attempted to minimize the danger to officers and the general public by claiming that unlike the still moving pursuit in *Scott,* the pursuit in this matter was essentially over, and the suspect vehicle was surrounded by pursuing officers. The court further took into account the number of shots fired into Rickard's vehicle and the fact that Allen was also in the passenger compartment of the car.

As mentioned above, the Supreme Court unanimously reversed the Sixth Circuit on the issue of qualified immunity and in a nearly unanimous decision held that the conduct of the involved officers did not violate the Fourth Amendment.

In deciding whether the conduct of the officers violated the Fourth Amendment, the Court analyzed two distinct issues. First, the Court examined whether it was reasonable for officers in the circumstances of this case to use deadly force to terminate the chase. Second, if deadly force was initially permissible, the Court examined whether the firing of 15 shots into Rickard's vehicle amounted to an excessive use of force.

At the outset, the Court quoted language highly favorable to law enforcement from its earlier opinions in *Graham v. Connor* and *Scott v. Harris.* In *Scott,* the Court ruled that a law enforcement officer's successful attempt to end a dangerous high-speed pursuit that threatened the lives of innocent bystanders by using a tactical vehicle maneuver (the PIT maneuver) did not violate the Fourth Amendment. The Court took the position in Scott that such police conduct was reasonable, "even when it places the fleeing motorist at risk of serious injury or death."[14]

The Court saw no distinction between the facts of *Scott* and the facts in *Plumhoff.* The Court observed that Rickard proceeded at speeds in excess of 100 mph in an effort to outrun the pursuit

---

[14] See, *Scott v. Harris,* 550 U.S. 372, 386 (2007).

Chapter 10

and in the process placed the lives of numerous motorists in serious jeopardy. The Court characterized Rickard's driving as "outrageously reckless." The Court noted that when Rickard collided with a police vehicle and temporarily came to a stop, he refused to yield. In less than three seconds, with his front bumper flush against a police cruiser, he pressed down on his accelerator, causing his wheels to spin. He next placed his car in reverse and attempted to get away by backing up in a circular fashion, never yielding to officers who were now on foot in close proximity to his vehicle.

The Court rejected a claim by Rickard's survivor, that police bullets were fired after the chase was over. The Court responded to this claim by stating, "Under these circumstances, *at the moment* when the shots were fired, all that a reasonable officer could have concluded was that Rickard was intent on resuming his flight and that, if he was allowed to do so, he would once again pose a deadly threat for others on the road." The Court observed further, that even after the shots were fired, Rickard continued to drive away and crashed his vehicle into a building down the road away from the shooting scene.

The Court also was critical of reasoning used by the District Court in ruling against the defendant officers. The District Court ruled that the danger presented in a high-speed pursuit cannot justify use of deadly force because it is caused by the officers' decision to continue the chase. In other words, the police have an obligation in such circumstances to discontinue pursuit. The Court responded by stating, "In Scott, however, we declined to 'lay down a rule requiring the police to allow fleeing suspects to get away whenever they drive so recklessly that they put other people's lives in danger.'" The Court ruled that in circumstances like those found here, attempting to terminate a dangerous high-speed pursuit by means of police firearms did not violate the Fourth Amendment.

The Court next addressed Rickard's survivor's contention that even if deadly force was permissible, the officers nonetheless used excessive force by firing 15 shots into the Rickard vehicle. The Court rejected this contention and stated, "It stands to reason that, if police officers are justified in firing at a suspect in order to end a severe threat to public safety, the officers need not stop shooting until the threat is ended."

The Court observed that all of the bullets were fired in a 10-second span and, that during that time frame, Rickard continued his attempt to escape. Even after the firing stopped, Rickard was able to drive his vehicle away from the officers and subsequently crashed down the road away from the shooting scene. The Court stated that its view would be different if Rickard had *clearly surrendered,* or became *clearly incapacitated* as a result of the gunshots. Gunshots fired after that point would cross the line and be viewed as excessive use of force.

The Court also rejected an argument that Allen's presence in the front seat of Rickard's vehicle made the use of force in this instance excessive. The Court observed that the issue before it was whether Rickard's Fourth Amendment rights had been violated, not Allen's. The Court added, "Allen's presence in the car cannot enhance Rickard's Fourth Amendment rights. After all, it was Rickard who put Allen in danger by fleeing and refusing to end the chase, and it would be perverse if his disregard for Allen's safety worked to his benefit."[15]

Finally, the Court unanimously ruled that the shooting in this case did not violate clearly established Fourth Amendment law at the time it occurred. Consequently, the involved officers were alternatively entitled to a judgment in their favor based on qualified immunity. The Court observed that the controlling legal precedent at the time of the Rickard shooting was the Supreme Court's decision in *Brosseau v. Haugen,* 543 U.S. 194 (2004). The Court noted that in *Brosseau,* it ruled that a police officer did not violate clearly established law when she fired at a suspect attempting to flee in a vehicle, to prevent harm to officers on the scene and other citizens who might be in the area. The Court concluded that, "Brosseau makes plain that ... it was not clearly established that it was unconstitutional to shoot a fleeing driver to protect those whom his flight might endanger."

---

[15] In a footnote discussing whether Allen would be able to recover damages on Fourth Amendment grounds, the Court observed that there appears to be some disagreement among the federal circuit courts on this point. At least two federal circuit courts have answered this question in the negative. See, *Landol-Rivera v. Cruz Cosme,* 906 F.2d 791 (1st Cir. 1990) and *Milstead v. Cooper,* 243 F.3d 312 (4th Cir. 2001).

Chapter 10

The decision of the Sixth Circuit in *Plumhoff* provides yet another example of a lower federal appellate court's rejection of the clear direction of the Supreme Court that it should make every attempt to decide cases involving qualified immunity before trial and without protracted discovery. The Supreme Court's decision in *Scott* was a clear and recent example of the Court's intent in this regard. Nonetheless, the Sixth Circuit explicitly rejected the Supreme Court's instruction. In doing so, the Sixth Circuit displayed its total disregard for the significant danger faced by officers and the public in situations like they faced in the *Plumhoff*.

Rickard was not unarmed and clearly not under control. He was the driver of a deadly weapon, a 3000-pound motor vehicle. Under both *Graham* and *Garner*, Rickard was and continued to be a serious deadly threat to officers, pedestrians, and other drivers until he was stopped. The officers acted with "objective reasonableness" in stopping him in the way that they did.

Like the officers in *Scott*, the officers in *Plumhoff* had to act to defend themselves and the public by using the only means available, that is, their firearms. In *Scott*, officers used a police vehicle to end the danger. Here they used their firearms. Once again, the Supreme Court displayed wisdom and understanding regarding the inherent danger faced by law enforcement officers on the roads and streets of the United States.

Plumhoff's Progeny

The impact of the Supreme Court's decision in *Plumhoff* on the lower federal appellate courts is likely to be profound. The predictable derivative benefit to law enforcement officers sued for alleged civil rights violations is also likely to be significant. For example, two months after the Court issued its *Plumhoff* decision, the First Circuit Court of Appeals decided *McGrath v. Taveras* (No. 12-2277) (August 1, 2014).[16] In this case, two Plymouth, Massachusetts police officers responded in separate vehicles to an

---

[16] See also, *Thompson v. Mercer* (No. 13-10773) (5th Cir. 8/7/14) in which the Fifth Circuit found no Fourth Amendment violation after a local Sheriff shot and killed the driver of a stolen car with an AR-15 rifle. Thompson stole a vehicle with the owner inside. He was armed with a firearm and led pursuing police on a reckless and dangerous high speed chase for two hours before being shot and killed by Sheriff Mercer.

Dangerous Vehicle Pursuits—*Scott v. Harris*

activated burglar alarm at a local liquor store during the early morning hours of January 10, 2006. As Officer Almeida approached the immediate vicinity of the liquor store, he observed a Toyota Camry make an illegal left turn. Almeida believing that the Toyota might be connected to the burglary alarm, decided to pull the Toyota over and turned on his lights and siren. The driver of the Toyota refused to yield and a vehicle pursuit began.

Officer Taveras heard about the pursuit over his police radio and joined the chase. The officers pursued the speeding and zigzagging Camry until it reached a T intersection. The speeding Camry driver was unable to make the turn and crashed into a stone wall. The pursuing officers pulled up behind the Camry, one on the driver's side rear and the other on the passenger's side rear. Officer Almeida exited his police vehicle, drew his pistol and ordered the driver of the Camry to come out with his hands up. The driver, later determined to be a 16-year-old male by the name of Anthony McGrath, refused to surrender. Instead, he revved the engine, placed the Camry in reverse and attempted to back up between the two police vehicles. In the process, McGrath hit one of the police cars and crashed into a nearby telephone pole.

Officer Taveras approached the Camry on the front passenger side and ordered McGrath to shut the car off and exit the vehicle. Officer Almeida was positioned to the right of Officer Taveras. Both officers had their handguns drawn and pointed at McGrath. Instead of yielding, McGrath again revved his engine and drove forward in the direction of Officer Taveras. Taveras fired twice at the approaching Camry. One of the bullets penetrated the front windshield and struck McGrath in the upper right arm. The Camry continued forward toward Officer Almeida and Officer Taveras fired two more shots. One of those shots entered the Camry through the front passenger window, struck McGrath in the back and resulted in a fatal wound. Officer Almeida then fired seven shots, none of which struck McGrath. The Camry continued on, hit a curb, became airborne, and came to a complete stop.

Three years after the shooting, McGrath's mother sued the two involved officers, the Chief of Police and the town in federal court pursuant to 42 U.S.C. §1983, alleging, among other things, excessive use of force in violation of the Fourth Amendment.

Chapter 10

Officers Taveras and Almeida moved for summary judgment prior to trial and asserted that there was no violation of the Fourth Amendment and in any event, they were entitled to qualified immunity. The District Court granted summary judgment in favor of Officer Taveras, finding that his conduct was objectively reasonable and did not violate the Fourth Amendment. The Court found no need to address the qualified immunity issue. The District Court likewise ruled in favor of Officer Almeida, finding no Fourth Amendment seizure of McGrath because none of Almeida's bullets hit McGrath. Inasmuch as there was no finding of unconstitutional conduct by the involved officers, the suit against the Chief and the town was also dismissed.

McGrath's mother filed an appeal with the United States Court of Appeals for the First Circuit. The First Circuit affirmed the rulings of the District Court and ruled in favor of the involved officers. First, the court agreed with the District Court that there was no Fourth Amendment "seizure" of McGrath by Officer Almeida, "not solely because none of [his] shots hit [McGrath], but also because Almeida's missed shots did not restrain [McGrath's] freedom of movement."

The court next focused on the conduct of Officer Taveras. Initially, the court set forth the legal standard by which Taveras's conduct must be evaluated. The court observed, **"in the Fourth Amendment context, the use of deadly force is not excessive if an objectively reasonable officer in the same circumstances would have believed that an individual posed a threat of serious physical harm either to the officer or others."**

McGrath's mother claimed that her son never drove directly toward the officers and never represented a direct threat to their safety. In doing so, she relied on crime scene photographs, a forensic map, and a sketch of the scene prepared by Massachusetts State Police Troopers (Accident Reconstructionalists). She provided no expert testimony of her own. The court ruled that in the absence of expert testimony, the plaintiff could not rely on photographs depicting bullet holes in the vehicle alone to establish the location of the officers at the time they fired at McGrath. Moreover, the State Police report prepared by State Police experts concluded that it was not possible to determine the location of the shooters from looking at the bullet holes in the vehicle.

After carefully reviewing the record, the court concluded that when Officer Taveras fired his first two shots at McGrath's vehicle, McGrath was driving toward him. The court observed that Taveras's "choices were to shoot or risk being run over. This is the type of 'split-second judgement' police officers are forced to make, and which we must take into account in assessing an officer's actions. A reasonable officer in this situation could reasonably believe he was facing a threat of serious physical harm, if not death. After all, a car can be used as a deadly weapon."

The court next observed that when Taveras fired his final two shots, the court record revealed (based on the State Police investigation reports and relevant depositions) that "when Officer Taveras fired shots three and four, he believed officer Almeida was to his right and the Camry was headed in that direction." The court ruled that "any reasonable officer in Taveras's position, faced with the same reckless driver who had almost run him over a fraction of a second earlier, could reasonably believe that Officer Almeida was in grave physical harm's way."

In concluding, the First Circuit quoted directly from the Supreme Court's opinion in *Plumhoff* and stated, "[A]t the moment when the shots were fired, all that a reasonable police officer could have concluded was that [McGrath] was intent on resuming his flight and that, if he was allowed to do so, he would once again pose a deadly threat for [the officers, as well as for] **others on the road**." (emphasis added). The mention by the First Circuit of a threat to "others on the road" reflects the Supreme Court's analysis in *Plumhoff*, which focused not only on the danger posed during a high speed pursuit to officers involved **but also to the danger likewise posed to other innocent drivers and pedestrians.** *Plumhoff* **emphasizes the importance of the danger to these innocent bystanders in evaluating the use of deadly force in any high speed pursuit.**

Chapter 11

DEADLY FORCE—THE BODY'S PHYSIOLOGICAL RESPONSE

Lieutenant Colonel Dave Grossman's book, *On Combat*, examines the physiological changes that a law enforcement officer can expect to occur to his/her body while participating in a deadly force encounter with a violent offender.[1] Colonel Grossman instructs that the human body's autonomic nervous system (ANS) consists of the sympathetic nervous system (SNS) and the parasympathetic nervous system (PNS). Grossman teaches that these two systems generally work opposite of one another. For example, the PNS is in control when the body is at rest or asleep. When the PNS is in control, the heart rate is low. It is during times of rest and sleep that the body stores and builds its supply of energy.

Conversely, the SNS "mobilizes and directs the body's [stored] energy resources for action."[2] The SNS is connected to the body's stress response, that is, the "flight or fight" response.[3] When a law enforcement officer is confronted with a potentially deadly threat, the officer's SNS causes the body to release stored energy necessary to face the threat. For example, in a deadly encounter, an officer's body reacts by releasing large amounts of adrenaline into the body. This causes the heart rate to increase (sometimes in dramatic fashion); digestion is inhibited; bronchial tubes and heart vessels become dilated; major muscle groups receive more blood; muscles tense; and blood vessels in the extremities constrict.

These physiological changes are initially very favorable for the officer because they permit him/her to respond in an extraordinary and positive manner to the threat presented. Colonel Grossman reports that ideally, in response to a threat, an officer's heart rate should increase **and remain** at a rate of **between 115 and 145 beats per minute (bpm)**. He describes this as the "optimal survival and combat performance level" and labels it

---

[1] Lt. Col. David A. Grossman with Loren W. Christensen, "On Combat," 2004.
[2] Id. p. 14.
[3] Id.

Chapter 11

Condition Red.[4] He states that in **Condition Red** the officer's *complex motor skills* are at their peak. Complex motor skills involve a combination of **balance and coordination.** For example, twisting or turning the body while aiming and firing a handgun. This requires hand and eye coordination in conjunction with movement of large muscle groups.[5] Likewise, according to Grossman, *visual reaction time* and *cognitive reaction time* are also at their peak.[6] This is the heart rate zone or condition that an officer should be in while engaged in a gun battle.

Grossman points out, however, that once an officer enters **Condition Red** (i.e., the heart rate rises to 115 bpm or higher) *fine motor skills* begin to deteriorate. Fine motor skills involve dexterity with small muscle groups, such as fingers, hands, toes, feet, tongue and lips. The reason for the negative affect on fine motor skills is found in the term "vasoconstriction." Col. Grossman explains that negative symptoms relating to fine motor skills "are the result of early stages of vasoconstriction, a condition that restricts the flow of blood to the extremities."[7] Thus, we see that as the heart rate of an officer rises during a confrontation both good and bad things happen in **Condition Red.**

The "objectively reasonable" law enforcement officer understands and expects these physiological changes to his/her body before he/she enters into a deadly force encounter. Officers must be aware of the fact that upon entering **Condition Red** blood flow to their fingers and hands will begin to dissipate. For example, as the heart rate rises above 115 bpm, it will become increasingly harder to reload a pistol, hold a firearm steadily on a target, clear malfunctions of the firearm and handle misfeeds of ammunition.

Col. Grossman points out that fine motor skill problems can be overcome through repetitive training. He states, "Through intense, high-repetition training [an officer] will turn the skills that he needs to perform into 'muscle memory.' Magazine changes, misfeed drills, weapons handling, and handcuffing are

---

[4] Id. p. 30 (emphasis added).

[5] My example not Col. Grossman's.

[6] Lt. Col. David A. Grossman with Loren W. Christensen, "On Combat," 2004, p. 14.

[7] Id. p. 32.

Deadly Force—The Body's Physiological Response

just a few of the many skills he must rehearse until he can perform these intricate tasks flawlessly."[8] Failure to properly train for a violent encounter will have potentially deadly consequences. The time to first learn that your fine motor skills are not functioning correctly is not when a violent offender's bullets are whizzing by your head.

When an officer is confronted with a deadly threat, the arousal of the SNS is the normal physiological response to the threat. It will automatically result in an adrenaline release and an increase in heart rate. Colonel Grossman explains, "Hormonal induced performance and strength increases can achieve 100% of potential max within 10 seconds, but drop [to] 55% after 30 seconds, [to] 35% after 60 seconds, and [to] 31% after 90 seconds."[9]

He also points out that **exercise induced heart rate increases** do not produce the same results because there is no large release of adrenaline into the body. However, "when you combine ... **the fear induced heart rate increase** with physical exertion or exercise demands, the result seems to be an 'amplifying' effect, which can result in some extraordinarily high heart rates."[10] As we shall soon learn, excessively high heart rates in a gun battle are not welcome and can be disastrous for the law enforcement officer.

Col. Grossman teaches that when "the average police officer experiences a stress-induced (i.e., adrenaline-induced) heart rate increase in the area of 145 bpm [and higher], there is a significant breakdown in performance."[11] The breakdown will begin with a deterioration of complex motor skills.[12] When this happens, complex motor skills involving balance and coordination will become increasingly more difficult.

Grossman teaches, however, that this breakdown of complex motor skills can be forestalled thorough extensive repetitive

---

[8] Id. p. 33.

[9] Id. p. 31.

[10] Id. p. 32.

[11] Id. pp. 34 – 35.

[12] Id. p. 31. We must remember that fine motor skills involving small muscle groups in the hands and the fingers already begin to deteriorate at 115 bpm. This of course adds to the deterioration of the complex motor skills at heart rates of 145 bpm and higher.

practice of the skills required in a gun fight. He explains that, "'you can push the envelope' of Condition Red, enabling extraordinary performance at accelerated heart rate levels [i.e., rates between 145 and 175 bpm]."[13] Grossman labels the heart rate zone [i.e., 145 – 175 bpm] for officers who regularly engage in extensive repetitive training to ready themselves for a gun battle as **Condition Gray.**

Grossman's final designation for stress-induced heart rate increases is **Condition Black.** Condition Black begins for an officer when his/her heart rate during a critical incident reaches and exceeds 175 bpm. Grossman explains, "Cardiologists tell us that at a certain point [i.e. heart rates of 175 bpm and above] an increased heart rate becomes counterproductive because the heart is pumping so fast that it cannot draw in a full load of blood before pumping it back out. As the heart rate increases beyond this point, the effectiveness of the heart, and the level of oxygen ... to the brain, steadily decreases."[14]

Colonel Grossman states that at heart rates above 175 bpm, a catastrophic series of negative changes will occur within an officer's body. Some of these changes involve **tunnel vision** (i.e., loss of peripheral vision and inability to see additional adversaries); **loss of depth perception** (i.e., objects appear closer than they really are); **loss of near vision** (e.g., difficulty in using pistol or rifle sights); **auditory exclusion** (e.g., inability to hear warnings from colleagues or warnings directed at offenders); and perhaps worst of all, **a deterioration of cognitive function** (i.e., inability to think clearly).[15] Moreover, **vasoconstriction (reduction of blood flow to bodily extremities) becomes catastrophic.**

With massive vasoconstriction, blood pools in the body's core and large muscle groups, and blood pressure skyrockets.[16] Although this enhances gross motor skills, for example, running, jumping, charging etc., the ability to think clearly, see, hear, handle a firearm, track a moving target, grab a magazine for

---

[13] Id. p. 35.

[14] Id. p. 43.

[15] Id. p. 31.

[16] Id. p. 45.

reload, insert it into a weapon, and use the sights on a firearm become greatly impaired. Hardly an ideal set of circumstances for an officer involved in a deadly force encounter.

Colonel Grossman reports that Dr. Alexis Artwohl conducted a survey of 141 officers that had been involved in deadly force encounters and found that 85% experienced auditory exclusion; 80% experienced tunnel vision; 65% experienced slow motion time sequencing and 51% suffered memory loss for parts of the event.[17]

Officers facing a deadly threat for the first time must not be surprised by these physiological changes to their bodies. In particular they must prepare for the potential of facing a deadly threat by regular repetitive training that is designed to replicate an actual deadly force encounter. Officers must regularly train in this manner to avoid **Condition Black.** Going into Condition Black simply adds significantly to the deadly threat that is already facing the officer and reduces the odds of a successful outcome with a violent offender. Officers cannot control the timing of when they might have to confront a deadly perpetrator but they do have control over whether their bodies enter Condition Black during that encounter.

Avoiding "Condition Black"— Stress Inoculation

Colonel Grossman tells us in his book *On Combat* that the greatest safeguard against excessively high heart rates and the parade of negative consequences that are bound to follow is what he refers to as "stress inoculation."[18] He teaches that law enforcement officers must be placed in regular training situations that will replicate to the extent possible, real life gun battles. Grossman states that this reality-based training, that is, so-called "force on force training," will result in helping officers to keep their stress reactions in a real gun battle under control. He explains, "[W]arriors can (and must) be inoculated against this stressor [i.e., a gunfight] by experiencing force on force scenarios in which they shoot and are shot at by paint filled gunpowder propelled, plastic bullets [aka, marking cartridges]."[19]

---

[17] Id. p. 55.

[18] Id. p. 205.

[19] Id. p. 38.

Chapter 11

Grossman points out that "[m]any elite military and law enforcement organizations have applied this type of training with remarkable success. Sometimes we see SWAT teams and special ops units whose members think they are good, but they get a rude surprise during their first force-on-force scenario using paint bullets. But then they get better, much better."[20] Grossman states that he "had the privilege of training numerous combat units associated with the US Army, Navy, and Marines as they prepared for the invasion of Iraq in 2003. All of these troops had incorporated extensively the use of paint bullets in their training to inoculate themselves against combat stress. Additionally, the US armed forces ... have integrated state-of-the-art video firearms simulators and laser engagement simulators into unit training."[21]

Grossman points to one quite amazing military success that he attributes to force on force training during the invasion phase of the Iraq war. One Army Captain was leading a Company of eighty soldiers when they were surrounded by 300 enemy soldiers. The Captain was unable to obtain air or artillery support. The Company had never seen live combat before and fought the enemy for eight hours. In the end, 200 enemy soldiers were killed and not one US soldier lost his life.

Avoiding Condition Black — Tactical Breathing

Colonel Grossman examines at length in his book *On Combat*, the technique of "Tactical Breathing" and its efficacy in the control of the human heart rate. He observes that "Tactical Breathing" is very useful in slowing a fear/stress induced rise in the human heart rate. He instructs that it is a "tool to control the sympathetic nervous system."[22] He teaches that the body has a somatic nervous system and an autonomic nervous system.[23] The somatic nervous system is involved with bodily actions that we consciously control, such as raising our hands and moving our legs. The autonomic nervous system refers to physiological opera-

---

[20] Id. p. 101.

[21] Id. p. 207.

[22] Id. p. 320.

[23] Id. p. 321.

tions of our body that we do not have under conscious control, such as our heart rate.[24]

Grossman explains that breathing and blinking are the only two functions of our autonomic nervous system that we can consciously control. He instructs that through "Tactical Breathing," a law enforcement officer can bring a rapidly rising heart rate caused by an adrenaline release under control. Thus, in the middle of a violent deadly force encounter, if there is a momentary pause and an officer is behind protective cover, the officer can bring his/her heart rate down from "Condition Black" to "Condition Red" through the "Tactical Breathing" process.

Grossman explains the process of "Tactical Breathing" by stating that an officer should begin the process "by breathing in through your nose to a slow count of four, which expands your belly like a balloon. Hold for a count of four, and then slowly exhale through your lips for a count of four, as your belly collapses like a balloon with its air released. Hold empty for a count of four and then repeat the process [until the heart rate slows down]."[25] Grossman states that this simple process can be used in a life-threatening situation to control heart rates and the sometimes catastrophic physiological consequences that follow from a large release of adrenaline into the body. The process can be regularly practiced so that in the event of a deadly confrontation, it will quickly come to mind when needed.

Winning the Gunfight—Physical Fitness

Finally, common sense tells us that law enforcement officers who are physically fit are far more likely to survive and win a deadly force encounter. Most, if not all law enforcement agencies and departments across America have developed basic physical fitness standards for new recruits. For example, FBI agent trainees are required to meet fitness standards at the FBI Training Academy, which involve push-ups, sit-ups, pull-ups, timed 1.5 mile runs and a timed 300-meter sprint. However, it appears that in many instances police training academy physical fitness standards are not required for officers once they graduate

---

[24] Id.

[25] Id. pp. 323–324.

Chapter 11

from their law enforcement academies. This failure to require on duty fitness standards or at least offer them on a voluntary basis has obvious long- and short-term negative consequences.

The June 2008 edition of the *Police Chief Magazine* contained an article, "Fit for Duty? The Need for Physical Fitness Programs for Law Enforcement Officers." The article was written by Sergeant Adrienne Quigley, Arlington County, Virginia Police Department. The article reported on a ten-year study conducted by the Cooper Institute for Aerobics Research (Cooper Study), which randomly sampled approximately 1700 law enforcement officers from around the United States.

The Cooper Study revealed that when examined in relation to the population in general, the fitness levels of law enforcement officers were below that of the general population in areas involving aerobic fitness, body fat, upper body and abdominal strength, and low back flexibility. According to Sgt. Quigley, "the data show[s] that law enforcement officers are less fit in most areas than at least half of all U. S. citizens despite the fact that the physical demands of their profession require that they be more fit than the average person."

Sgt. Quigley reports that low levels of physical fitness in the on duty law enforcement community have extremely **negative long-term consequences.** These negative consequences include a higher mortality rate for law enforcement officers when compared to the general public due to cardiovascular disease, colon cancer, and suicide. Moreover, she reports that law enforcement officers suffer more job-related stress than persons in other occupations. Sgt. Quigley states that job-related stress has been linked to cardiovascular disease, high blood pressure, low back pain, and stomach disorders.

Lack of excellent physical fitness has the potential of severe **negative short term consequences** for law enforcement officers as well. Sgt. Quigley observes that law enforcement officers are often involved in situations that require them to run, climb, jump, lift/carry, drag, push, and use force. These requirements call for cardiovascular endurance, anaerobic strength, flexibility, and agility. Fitness deficiencies will result in short-term but potentially life-changing consequences. Consider a foot pursuit over fences and through back yards that results in an officer catching a suspect from behind. Consider the officer who is so tired from the pursuit that the suspect is able to overpower him, take his weapon and shoot him. Was this a predictable result? This was a rhetorical question. The answer is self-evident.

In 2007, Kathleen D. Vonk, Ann Arbor Michigan Police Department wrote an article entitled "Police Performance Under Stress." In the article, Ms. Volk examines the value of physical fitness for law enforcement officers. She observes that a regular fitness program: (1) causes endorphins (i.e., endogenous morphine) to be released into the body; endorphins act as a natural pain killer; (2) helps in weight control, which allows for efficiency in movement during emergency circumstances; (3) produces more efficient heart and lung capacity during stressful situations; (4) permits the cardiovascular system to recover quickly after physical demands; (5) permits the respiratory system to shuttle more oxygen to the brain and muscles; (6) builds muscle, tendon, and bone strength; (7) results in higher tolerance of pain and stress which might be the difference between winning and losing a life-threatening encounter.

The bottom line here is simple. Common sense tells us that physically fit law enforcement officers have a significantly greater chance to not only survive but win a deadly force encounter. Regular aerobic and anaerobic fitness training is a must for the "objectively reasonable" law enforcement officer. If your department does not offer regular fitness training, required or voluntary, it is incumbent upon each officer to engage in his/her own program. Simply put, stay fit and stay alive. Your family has the right to see you come home at the conclusion of every tour of duty.

Physical Exhaustion—Officer Survival— Use of Deadly Force

In September 2010, the Force Science Research Center, under the direction of Dr. William Lewinski, conducted a study concerning how long an officer who is engaged in a physical fight with an adversary can continue before becoming exhausted and unable to defend him or herself. The study, reported in "Transmission 159 of the Force Science News," involved 52 officers between the ages of 23 and 51 (42 males and 10 females). The officers were instructed to individually launch a full-scale physical attack on a 300-lb hanging water bag. Each officer was fitted with a heart rate monitor and a VO2 mask to measure oxygen consumption and gas exchange. They were permitted to use punches and kicks; along with elbow, palm, and knee strikes during their assaults on the bag.

According to Dr. Lewinski, the bag-assault drill "realistically replicated a full force fight by a moderately trained officer to control a strong dynamically resisting suspect." The participants were instructed to continue the assault until they no longer had the strength to go on. After the test was completed a blood sample was taken from each participant.

The heart rate monitors, oxygen monitors, and blood tests revealed that the participants all reached an intense level of energy output during the bag-assault. For example, the heart rate of participants rose to an average of 179 bpm. Blood lactate levels, which reflect the degree of exertion in a human body, rose to 13 times their normal level. According to Dr. Lewinski, **"Most dramatic and alarming was the speed at which [participants] depleted their physical resources. On average, the officers spent 56 seconds hitting the bag."**

The average number of blows delivered to the bag was 183. The vast majority of blows delivered were punches. Each assault was videotaped with time-coded video. **The average officer peaked in their assault of the bag in 15 seconds. According to Lewinski, "After that, the frequency of strikes fell in a sharp and steady decline."** Lewinski reported that "by 30 to 40 seconds, most [officers] were significantly weakened. They were not able to breathe properly, their cadence dropped; their strikes scarcely moved the bag, if at all." These weak blows would have had little impact on a violent adversary.

Lewinski also reported that surprisingly, the same thing happened to the officer participants who were highly fit and had better fighting skill. One commentator on the study opined that the more fit officers were able to use greater strength to deliver quicker and more powerful blows. In the process they expended more energy and used up their greater energy reserves "in roughly the same time as those less fit and skilled." This takes nothing away from the notion that fitness matters because common sense tells us that delivering quicker and more powerful

Deadly Force—The Body's Physiological Response

blows would have greater negative consequences for the recipient of those blows.

Once an officer's level of exhaustion is reached (the study demonstrated an average of 56 seconds), the officer will be in trouble. **The officer will at that moment face a life-threatening loss of the ability to defend him/herself from physical attack.**

Force Science News, Transmission #155, reported on July 30, 2010, regarding an article authored by Jeffrey Johnson, Training Commander, Long Beach, California Police Department. The article, entitled "Force and the Fatigue Threshold: The Point of No Return," appeared in the *Monthly Law Journal*, an online publication of the Americans for Effective Law Enforcement. In the article, Commander Johnson explains that officer fatigue and exhaustion in a street fight is due to excessive anaerobic activity. He states that anaerobic activity involves the body's fast-twitch muscle fibers. He explains that fast twitch muscle fibers are "capable of faster, more explosive motion, but they burn much more energy and are insatiable for fuel." Johnson instructs that fast-twitch muscle fibers are required when a person becomes involved in a physical altercation where it becomes necessary to punch, kick, block, grab, and hold.

Commander Johnson tells us that in a physical altercation, the fast-twitch muscle fibers contract so rapidly and powerfully that oxygen entering the body is inadequate to sustain them for very long. The body will attempt to compensate for the lack of adequate oxygen by drawing on glycogen (sugar) but this process is not sufficient long term. The consequence involves a rapid build-up of lactic acid. This lactic acid buildup will result in muscle shut-down. Johnson explains that the shutdown is temporary but may take as long as 15 minutes for the body to recover.

It should be obvious to readers that fast-twitch muscle fiber shutdown is not a position that an "objectively reasonable" law enforcement officer wants to be in. Particularly, if that officer is alone and grappling with a younger and stronger adversary. It is at that point that the officer's life is directly threatened. The suspect may now be able to disarm the exhausted officer, or reach for a knife, firearm or other weapon that was not available to him seconds before and put an immediate end to the officer's life.

Chapter 11

The bottom line here is obvious. When an officer engaged in physical combat nears the point of physical exhaustion, the officer must be able to resort to an escalation of force in order to save his or her life. The only option available to the officer at that point may well be use of a firearm. An "objectively reasonable" law enforcement officer in this situation should not be required to sacrifice his/her life to a stronger, fitter opponent because he/she is unable to defend him/herself due to exhaustion. At this point, deadly force may be used to preserve the life of the involved officer. Failure to use this last option is likely to result in the officer being disarmed and shot to death. This outcome is not acceptable.

Chapter 12

POLITICS AND THE PATROL RIFLE

In December 2013 the newly elected Mayor of the City of Boston was presented by the Boston Police Department (BPD) with a new plan to equip certain designated patrol vehicles located strategically in specific sections of the City with AR-15 rifles. As I understand the plan, the Boston Police Department (BPD) was not advocating for an AR-15 rifle in every patrol vehicle. Instead, as described previously, the plan was limited to certain specific vehicles within designated sectors. The officers assigned to the designated vehicles were to receive specific training on the function and use of the rifles. The new Mayor, as reported in Boston newspapers, was reported to be opposed to adopting the newly presented BPD plan unless convinced otherwise by the BPD. The outgoing Mayor, who decided not to run again in 2013, had previously rejected an earlier more broad recommendation by the BPD in 2009 to equip all BPD patrol vehicles with AR-15 rifles.

After learning about the new Mayor's misgivings, I decided to write him a letter with a copy forwarded to the Boston Police Chief. Although I cannot speak to the underlying rationale for the new Mayor's hesitation to adopt the new BPD plan, I can say with no equivocation, that in general, outright rejection by public officials of such otherwise eminently reasonable plans has its genesis in political fear of negative public reaction. In fact, the outgoing Mayor's decision to reject the earlier BPD plan in 2009 was made in the face of spirited opposition from certain segments of the community. In 2009, it was apparent to any reasonable observer that the personal well-being of patrol officers was considered less important than silencing expressed public opposition to the plan.

The letter I wrote to the new Mayor follows:

Chapter 12

1/5/14
Honorable Martin J. Walsh
Mayor of Boston
1 City Hall Square, Suite 500
Boston, MA 02201
Dear Mayor Walsh:

    I am writing to express my deep concern for the safety of Boston police officers after reading a recent article in a Boston newspaper concerning your consideration of rejecting a Boston Police plan to place a limited number of AR-15 rifles in designated Boston Police cruisers. In the summer of 2009 the Boston Globe reported in an article titled "A Call to Curb a Lethal Trend" a disturbing rise in the number of high powered assault rifles on Boston streets. At that time, several of these weapons have been discovered in Boston and one was used in the shooting of a young girl apparently caught in the middle of gang firefight. These weapons in the hands of untrained and undisciplined shooters place the public at large at high risk for serious injury and death. Likewise, law enforcement officers who take an oath to protect and serve the public are placed in grave peril when confronted by felons in possession of this kind of weaponry.

    I was involved in law enforcement for 44 years. During my career, I served as a Special Agent in United States Naval Criminal Investigative Service (NCIS), the Federal Bureau of Investigation (FBI) for 30 years and a Deputy Inspector General for Massachusetts Inspector General Gregory Sullivan, in charge of his Investigations Division. At the time of my retirement from the FBI, I held the position of Supervisory Special Agent and Chief Division Counsel. During my time in the FBI and after retirement, I taught the legal aspects of the use of deadly force and officer survival to hundreds of law enforcement officers at the FBI Academy, Quantico, VA, across the State of Massachusetts and around the United States. Since my retirement, I have published a book on this subject and have recently signed a contract to publish a second book on the topic of officer Involved Shootings. During my FBI career, I was

Politics and the Patrol Rifle

involved in two shooting incidents that resulted in the deaths of two felons and the wounding of a third.

In order to understand the magnitude of the threat that assault rifles in the hands of violent offenders pose to police officers and the public, one must first understand how they work. Most police officers in the United States today carry .40 caliber semi-automatic pistols. These weapons fire bullets at a velocity of roughly 900 feet to 1000 feet per second. The rounds fired by these weapons will not penetrate the soft body armor commonly worn by the average police officer serving the public on the streets of America today. Likewise, they will not penetrate soft body armor worn by armed felons on our streets. Conversely, automatic/semi-automatic shoulder rifles such as AK-47, AR-15, M-16, and M4 carbines fire at a rate of approximately 3000 to 3200 feet per second. The rounds fired by these weapons will go right through police soft body armor. Unlike semi-automatic handguns, these high velocity rifles are deadly accurate and easy to fire. Police officers confronting armed felons in possession of these weapons are obviously in serious and real jeopardy.

The average police officer in Boston is armed with a Glock .40 caliber semi-automatic pistol and clothed with soft body armor. These are the officers who arrive first at the scene of an armed bank robbery with shots fired, a gang firefight or an active school shooting in progress. They do not have the time or luxury to wait for the arrival of tactically trained special operations units, e.g., SWAT. Lives are immediately endangered and officers are currently trained to move right in and engage the armed perpetrators. After Columbine, Virginia Tech, Newtown and countless other active shooter episodes, waiting for 'SWAT" is not a viable option. Thus, officers called to enter into high risk situations such as these are operating at a palpable disadvantage. They are ill equipped to confront felons armed with high velocity weapons. The body armor they wear will be quickly defeated by rounds fired from these weapons and their hand guns are greatly inferior to the high powered rifles being fired at them by the felons. Law enforcement history

Chapter 12

contains numerous examples of real life situations which support the validity of my opinion. Some of these situations are described below:

Facing deadly and violent offenders armed with high powered rifles is nothing new for Boston Police officers. For example, on 9/23/70, Boston Police officer Walter A. Schroeder responded to a bank robbery silent alarm within the City limits. (Boston Police Headquarters is located at One Schroeder Plaza in honor of Walter Schroeder). At the time, he was unaware of what he was about to face. Several convicted felons had joined together with two anti-Vietnam War radicals (Susan Saxe and Kathy Power) to form a bank robbery gang. One of the gang members, William "lefty" Gilday, waited across the street from the bank to ensure a smooth get-a-way for the gang members who entered the bank. As Patrolman Schroeder moved toward the bank to intercept the bank robbers, he was shot in the back with a high powered semi-automatic rifle. He fell to the ground severely wounded and the remaining gang members were able to escape the scene. Patrolman Schroeder was rushed to St. Elizabeth's hospital and underwent four hours of surgery. During surgery he received 77 pints of blood. He died the next day from the devastating wound he received during the robbery. As mentioned above, the possession and use of high powered rifles by violent felons on the streets of Boston and across America is much more prevalent today than in 1970 when Officer Schroeder was mercilessly gunned down.

Police officers should not be outgunned on the streets of Boston. The value of AR-15 rifles in the hands of well-trained police officers cannot be overemphasized. For example, on August 5, 2012, Wade Michael Page, a person with White Supremacist views, arrived in the parking lot of the Sikh Temple at Oak Creek, Wisconsin during the middle of a worship service. Page was armed with a 9 MM semi-auto pistol and numerous rounds of ammunition. He exited his vehicle and immediately shot two Sikhs in the parking lot. He quickly entered the Temple and began systematically executing Sikh worshipers. He ultimately killed six persons and wounded four

Politics and the Patrol Rifle

more. Terrified Sikhs ran for cover and called 911. The first Oak Creek officer on the scene was Lt. Brian Murphy. Lt. Murphy was by himself but this did not deter him from bravely doing his job. He saw two bodies lying in the parking lot and approached to give aid. Suddenly Page appeared from inside the Temple and immediately began firing at Lt. Murphy. Page's first shot hit Lt. Murphy in the throat and he went to the ground. Now unable to protect himself, Lt. Murphy was easy prey for Page. Page quickly approached Lt. Murphy and shot him 12 more times from close quarter range. Seconds later a second Oak Creek officer arrived at the scene. He wisely stopped his vehicle before entering the kill zone, jumped out with an AR-15 rifle in hand and observed Page reloading his weapon. He told Page to drop it from a distance of 60 yards but Page ignored the order and began firing. The second officer raised his AR-15 rifle and returned fire, hitting Page in the stomach with his first shot. Page went to the ground, seriously wounded and shot himself in the head, ending the conflict.

The second officer, not only saved the lives of many Sikhs who were hiding from Page in the Temple but also saved the life of Lt. Murphy who, despite being shot 13 times, survived the ordeal. There is no doubt that Page would have finished Lt. Murphy off if not immediately engaged and shot by the second officer. It is highly improbable that the officer firing the AR-15 could have successfully put Page on the ground and out of the fight without the AR-15 rifle. Shooting Page with a handgun from a distance of 60 yards, when Page was a moving target would have required extraordinary skill or pure luck. The AR-15 in the hands of a well-trained officer saved numerous lives on that fateful day, including the life of a brave police Lieutenant and most likely, the life of the second officer as well.

There are numerous additional examples of police officers confronting violent and deadly offenders without the benefit of proper weaponry. For example, on February 28, 1997 two heavily armed men entered the Bank of America in North Hollywood, California. The men carried fully automatic assault rifles with 100 round magazines, 3,300 rounds of soft armor

Chapter 12

penetrating bullets and wore homemade hard body armor with metal plates. They had been involved in previous bank robberies and murdered an armored car guard. During the robbery on February 28, they fired 100 rounds inside the bank. They exited the bank with over $300,000 dollars and were immediately confronted by several uniformed LAPD patrol officers. The responding officers were armed with hand guns and some had shot guns.

None of the initial responders were in possession of high powered rifles. Police officers fired over 650 rounds at the robbers. Almost all of these rounds either missed the targets or failed to penetrate the hard body armor worn by the robbers. The robbers, in turn fired 1,100 rounds at the responding officers. Ten officers and 7 civilians were wounded in the shootout. Miraculously no officer or civilian was killed. Although outnumbered many times over, the robbers continued to pin down the surrounding officers with automatic gunfire for at least 18 minutes before the first SWAT officers arrived. The first responders were no match for the bank robbers. First responders went to a nearby gun store and obtained some high powered rifles while the fire fight was in progress. Once SWAT officers arrived, armed with AR-15 rifles, one of the bank robbers killed himself rather than surrender, and the second one was shot and killed by means of AR-15 rifles operated by SWAT officers. The arrival of officers with AR-15 rifles turned the tide of the battle but sadly not before 17 innocent persons received serious wounds from the violent offenders.

A second incident involving FBI agents is also instructive. It happened in Miami Florida on April 11, 1986. Seven FBI agents confronted two heavily armed suspected armored car robbers who had previously murdered one man and severely wounded a second. After a vehicle pursuit and car crash, a deadly firefight erupted between the robbers and the agents in a residential neighborhood. The agents were armed with handguns and a shotgun. One of the robbers had a shotgun and the other was armed with a military style assault rifle. Although outnumbered by the FBI, the robbers were clearly not outgunned and had the

Politics and the Patrol Rifle

tactical advantage of superior fire power. The robber with the assault rifle responded to the arrest attempt with savage and devastating fury. In the process, although he received a non-survivable wound early into the four minute gun battle which included severance of the brachial artery and penetration across most of the inside of one lung, after being shot, he was able to shoot and kill two FBI agents and seriously wound several more. Before dying, both robbers received a total of 18 bullet wounds. All told, seven agents were shot that day, the worst day of carnage in FBI history. Later on the surviving agents recalled the devastating affect that the robber's assault rifle had on them. In this case, the FBI agents were simply outgunned by a violent offender in possession of a high powered assault rifle. FBI policy dramatically shifted after the "Miami Shootout" and regular field FBI agents have much greater access today to AR-15 style rifles than they did prior to April 11, 1986.

On May 9, 1980 five heavily armed men robbed a Security Pacific bank in Norco, California. Upon exiting the bank, the robbers armed with an assault rifle, shotguns and handguns, were confronted by a single Riverside California Deputy Sheriff. The Deputy, armed with a handgun and shotgun, was immediately fired upon by the fleeing robbers. They fired over 200 rounds at him and hit him 5 times. The Deputy survived but the windshield of his police vehicle was blown out and the vehicle was hit 47 times. The deputy bravely managed to return fire and killed one of the robbers. Other officers engaged the suspects in a high speed pursuit. During the chase another Deputy was shot and killed by the robbers. Eventually, the tide of battle turned in favor of the police but only after another Deputy arrived on the scene with an assault rifle. In all, a total of 9 deputies were shot during the incident. The suspects were apprehended but the price paid was high indeed.

Who can forget the McDonald's restaurant active shooter incident on July 18, 1984 in San Diego California that resulted in 21 innocent deaths with 19 others wounded. In this incident, a lone gunman armed with an assault style weapon, entered the restaurant and began to methodically murder innocent patrons

Chapter 12

and employees, including defenseless women and children. The first responding officer bravely tried to engage the suspect, armed only with a handgun. The suspect fired 30 rounds at the officer and drove him back. The suspect spent over an hour inside McDonald's in a reign of pure unadulterated terror until a police sniper killed him with a high powered rifle. Had the first officer been armed with a shoulder weapon, i.e., an AR-15 rifle, innocent lives would clearly have been saved.

The above mentioned incidents are examples of many more situations in which police officers have been killed and wounded by felons in possession of high powered firearms. Boston Police Officers have already faced the kind of devastating and deadly situations described herein. I can say with a high degree of certainty that it is only a matter of time before they face them again. Unless City officials have the courage and fortitude to permit patrol officers to have immediate access to the kind of weaponry necessary to give them a fighting chance in the face of a high risk incident, the City of Boston will soon be once again mourning for brave police officers who attempted to protect the public from armed and dangerous felons and sacrificed their very lives in doing so.

Sadly, their funerals will be attended by all the politically powerful, and their eulogies will be eloquent and respectful. Officers will no longer come home to their families and instead American flags will adorn the living rooms of the departed. However, no one will have the courage to mention that the dead officers were outgunned during the firefight because it was not politically correct to give them the equipment they needed to protect themselves and the public from deadly harm.

One wise and seasoned FBI agent once told me that if you're smart, you'll never enter a gunfight with a knife. Likewise, no courageous police officer should be required to enter a rifle fight with a handgun. He will lose every time. We trust our officers enough to arm them with semi-automatic pistols. We train them in the split second decision making of when to use them. We know as fact that they are now going to confront felons with

Politics and the Patrol Rifle

> *more powerful weapons. How can we ask them to go out and risk their lives without the right equipment? The time has come to trust Boston Police officers with the weapons they need to protect the public and themselves from serious bodily harm and death. Nothing less is acceptable.*
>
> *Respectfully Submitted,*
> *Michael Callahan Esq.*

Chapter 13

"THE OBJECTIVELY REASONABLE LAW ENFORCEMENT OFFICER" — SUMMATION

Some years ago well-known country & western singing artist Billy Ray Cyrus gave us a song titled "Some Gave All." It was intended as a tribute to the men and women of the US Military who fought so valiantly for our freedoms across the world and gave their lives while serving our country. The song concludes with the poignant words, "And if you ever think of me. Think of all your liberties and recall. Some Gave All." This song, which has always touched me, is equally applicable to all of the men and women of American law enforcement who have paid the ultimate price to protect us here at home from violence and mayhem.

To all of the brave men and women of the US Military and American law enforcement who have died and sacrificed everything they had for our safety, I salute you and profoundly thank you for what you have done. To all of the soldiers and law enforcement officers who are survivors of violent encounters, to those who have been wounded physically or psychologically or both, I likewise pay tribute to you and thank you for what you have done to keep us safe.

This book was intended to reflect on the many sacrifices that the police officers who have gone before us have made, to closely examine those sacrifices, and to learn what we can from them. My primary goal in writing this book was to prevent as many future deaths and serious injuries of law enforcement officers as possible. A second important goal was to protect officers who confront violent offenders in the future from the negative collateral consequences of such encounters, including criminal prosecution, civil liability and departmental discipline.

Accordingly, I have set forth the constitutional requirements for the use of deadly force by police officers in America. Officers who read this book will have no doubt about the meaning of the U.S. Supreme Court decisions on this vital topic. The Court has spoken decisively and its rulings are clearly set forth herein. Similarly, I have carefully examined decisions from the Federal Courts of Appeals across America pertaining to law enforcement use of deadly force. Officers familiar with this book will know

Chapter 13

with certainty what the highest federal court in their geographical region has ruled concerning officer use of deadly force. Knowledge is power, pure and simple.

America is a nation of laws. Clear legal standards establish the paradigm and the parameters which become the road map for officers to follow. Doubt about the law will inevitably lead to hesitation in critical life-threatening encounters. Hesitation is likely to result in death or serious injury for officers. Officers who have read this book will know with certainty what the law permits and what it prohibits. Hesitation caused by legal confusion will be substantially reduced or eliminated.

Readers of this book will clearly understand the "Qualified Immunity" legal defense available to officers in countering frivolous law suits. This book will enable police defense lawyers to better represent their clients and educate judges and jurors about the nature and scope of the law. Officers should never presume that lawyers, judges, jurors, the media, and the public have any realistic knowledge of who the "objectively reasonable" law enforcement officer truly is.

Accordingly, a third major goal for the book was to identify and define the "objectively reasonable" law enforcement officer. I have accomplished that goal. The "objectively reasonable" law enforcement officer is no longer simply a term of art used by the Justices of the Supreme Court. The definition of the "objectively reasonable" police officer is no longer so deficient in clarity that it is vulnerable to the often uneducated opinions of plaintiffs' lawyers and their "expert" witnesses.

This book clearly defines who the "objectively reasonable" law enforcement officer really is. The "objectively reasonable" law enforcement officer is the officer who comprehends and takes seriously the inherent danger of the law enforcement profession. The "objectively reasonable" law enforcement officer is well trained, well equipped and well prepared to face that danger in order to protect and serve.

The "objectively reasonable" officer has been well trained in the law and departmental policy pertaining to use of deadly force. This officer has been well trained in the skill of using firearms and has put that skill into practice in video simulation and force on force training. This officer has a full understanding of the

The Objectively Reasonable Law Enforcement Officer

concepts of "the Reactionary Gap" (i.e., action v. reaction), "Wound Ballistics," "Hide and Ambush," and "Shooting to Incapacitate."

The "objectively reasonable" law enforcement officer understands the physiological changes that will occur in his/her body during a firefight and will not be surprised when they happen. These officers will not be surprised that they have been shot during a violent encounter and will continue to battle their adversary until they have prevailed. The "objectively reasonable" officer will determine long before a violent encounter materializes that they are capable of using deadly force in defense of their own lives or the lives of others.

The "objectively reasonable" officer will be ever vigilant and ready for the possibility that a "routine" encounter can turn quickly into a life threatening one. This officer recognizes the importance of physical fitness and makes a real effort to stay in good condition.

Officers who study this book will increase their chances of not only surviving but winning a violent encounter with a deadly adversary. Likewise, they will enhance their chances of prevailing against civil lawsuits, criminal prosecution and departmental discipline. To all of the "Objectively Reasonable" officers out there who protect our freedoms and liberty, May God Bless you all and May God Bless America.

Index

20/20 vision of hindsight 5
21-foot rule 147
42 U.S.C. §1983 .... 20, 43, 47, 49, 52, 65, 78, 83, 119, 140, 179, 188, 196, 199, 204, 209
A fool's errand 175
Abraham v. Raso 19
Absolute immunity 68
Action v. reaction .... vii, 37, 50, 114, 115, 129, 135, 143, 190, 237
Adrenaline vii
Alcohol, Tobacco, and Firearms Department (ATF) 59
Alexander Jason study 133
Allen v. City of West Memphis 203
Allen v. Muskogee, Oklahoma 125
Americans for Effective Law Enforcement (AELE) 89
Anderson v. Creighton 72, 86
AR-15 rifles 99, 225
Ashcroft v. Iqbal 121
Assault rifle 231
At the moment 17, 18, 22, 23, 33, 206
Auditory exclusion vii
B-Pillar 101
Beanbag shotgun 52
Bennett v. Wainwright 29
Berube v. Conley 31
Billington v. Smith 19
Blair Reaction Time Study 136
Blood loss 153
Body armor 103
Bordanaro v. McLeod 121
Boston Globe newspaper ix
Brachial artery 164, 168
Brockington v. Boykins 42
Brooks v. Gaenzle 12, 16
Brosseau v. Haugen 77, 207
Brower v. County of Inyo 8, 11, 13
Bulger, James "Whitey" 187
Bullet penetration 169
Bullet wounds; non-survivable 154
Bullet-resistant vests 163
California v. Hodari D. 8, 14
Campbell v. City of Springboro, Ohio 121

239

Index

Carnaby v. City of Houston 44
Carr v. Tatangelo 14
Carter v. Buscher 48
Central nervous system 152, 153
Childress v. City of Arapaho Oklahoma 10
Circulatory collapse 152
City of Canton, Ohio v. Harris 120
Clearly established law 74
Cole v. Bone 50, 80, 188
Colston v. Barnhart 182
Colt M-4 rifle 157
Condition Black 216
Condition Gray 216
Condition Red 214
Connick v. Thompson 122
Constitutional standard for use of deadly force 5
Davis, Ed 95
Deadly force standards 118
Deadly force training 107
Deadly force; constitutional standard for 2
Deadly reactionary gap vii
Decision time 130, 135
Defendant's motion 86
Departmental deadly force policy 93
Dewgard, Egbert 87
Dicta 14, 15
Dinkheller, Dep. Kyle 97
Dobos v. Driscoll 121
Dodds v. Richardson 121
Edged weapon attacks 149
Eleventh Circuit Court of Appeals 15
Elizondo v. Green 42
Espinosa v. City of San Francisco 19
Excessive force 3
Exculpatory evidence 122
Expert testimony 126
Failure to train 125
FBI agents xiii
FBI firearms instructors 107
FBI Miami shootout 158, 166, 172, 177, 231
Federal Bureau of Investigation (FBI) ix

Index

Felony car-stop procedure 159
Firearm & Injury Center at the University of Pennsylvania 151
Firearms marksmanship skills 110
Firearms skill, mandatory 107
Firearms training 107, 110
    inadequate 118
First Circuit Court of Appeals 11, 23
Fleeing felon context 2
Fleeing felons 120, 179, 186
    armed 190, 193
    dangerous 183, 188
Forbus, Ken 108
Force Science Institute Ltd 27
Force Science Institute Study 38
Forrett v. Richardson 112, 183-185
Fourth Amendment . v, vi, 3, 10, 21, 30, 40, 50, 65, 72, 78, 83, 86, 178, 185, 187, 197, 201, 207, 210
Fourth Amendment "seizure" requirement 7, 13
Freedom of movement 13
Friendly fire 26
Fyfe, Dr. James 24
George v. Morris 138
Glenn v. Washington County 19, 51
Glock semi-auto pistol 132
Glock training pistol 136
Graham v. Connor 3, 5, 16, 27, 29, 42, 43, 47, 50, 61, 79, 87, 90, 91, 200, 201, 205
Grossman, Lt. Col. Dave 111
Gunshot wounds 151, 153
Gutierrez-Rodriguez v. Cartagena 121
Hall, John 37
Hard body armor 230
Harlow v. Fitzgerald 68, 71, 74
Harris v. Serpas 23
Hayek v. City of St. Paul 50
Hegarty v. Somerset County 31
Hide & ambush 188
Hide and ambush .... vii, 50
Hide and ambush strategy 191
Holster; three levels 134
Hostages, innocent; shooting of 9

Index

Immediate incapacitation 152, 156
Imminent threat 201
Involuntary physiological changes 94
Jean Baptiste v. Gutierrez 19, 66
Judge Trott 141
Kill zone 57, 96, 101, 117
Knife and edged weapons attacks 147
Kolski v. City of Brooklyn Park, Minn. 50
Krueger v. Fuhr 50, 194
Laboratory v. Reality 135
Lamont Estate of Quick v. New Jersey 33
Landol-Rivera v. Cosme 11
Landol-Rivera v. Cruz Cosme 207
LAPD officers 105
Lateral aggressive movement 144
Law Enforcement Officers Killed and Assaulted 188
Law Enforcement Officers Killed and Assaulted (LEOKA) .... ix, 94
Lee v. Anderson 48
Legal knowledge 1
LEOKA 151
Lewinski, William 36, 89, 101, 136, 221
Livermore v. Ellsworth 19
Lluveras v. Merced 121
Loch v. City of Litchfield 50
Malley v. Briggs 74
Marion v. City of Corydon 19
Marion v. City of Corydon, Indiana 46
Marking cartridge 102
Marksmanship training 107
Marquez v. City of Albuquerque 188
McGrath v. Taveras 208
Mechanical time 130
Medina v. Cram 20
Messerschmidt v. Millender 81
Miglietta, Dr. Maurizio A. 154
Milstead v. Cooper 207
Mitchell v. Forsyth 67, 70
Mitigation Zone (MZ) 101
Monell v. New York City Department of Social Services 119
Montoute v. Carr 193
Moore v. Indehar 14

Index

Motor skills; fine and complex	vii
Move and shoot	114
Moving laterally	149
Napier v. Town of Windham	181
Napier v. Windham	31
New York v. Tanella	89
Noel v. Artson	40
Objective legal reasonableness	74
Objective reasonableness	v, 65
Objective Reasonableness standard	5, 27
Objectively reasonable	vi, 4, 16, 86, 92
defined	91
Objectively reasonable officer	30, 91
On Combat	111
Owen v. City of Independence, Missouri	119
Paint bullet	102
Patrick, Urey	37
Patrol rifle	225
Pearson Court	76
Pearson v. Callahan	76, 84
Penley v. Eslinger	64
Pepper ball gun	22
Physical exhaustion	221
Physical incapacitation	153
PIT maneuver	202
Plakas v. Drinski	20, 48
Plumhoff v. Rickard	203
Pre-battle precautions	100
Precision Intervention Technique (PIT)	199
Probable cause	2, 4, 5
Qualified immunity	67, 77, 199
development of the defense	70
Qualified immunity defense	vi
Qualified Immunity Doctrine/Defense	85
Reaction time	130
Reactionary gap	129, 135, 188, 190
deadly	136
Realistic targets	111
Reasonable belief	2
Reasonableness standard	4
Regular firearms training	116

Index

Reichle v. Howards 81
Remsburg, Chuck 27
Respondeat superior 119
Response time 130
Rifle slug xi
Rivas v. City of Passaic 19
Rockwell v. Brown 19, 22
Roy v. Inhabitants of the City of Lewiston 31
Ryburn v. Huff 81
Ryder v. City of Topeka 197
Salim v. Proulx 19
Saucier v. Katz 76
Schulz v. Long 19
Scott v. Harris 86, 141, 199, 203-205
Scott v. Henrich 59
Seizure .... vi, 9, 10
Seventh Circuit Court of Appeals 21
Sheehan v. City & County of San Francisco 20
Shooting to wound 175, 178
Simmonds v. Genesee County 44
Smith v. Freeland 46
Smith v. Freland 80, 188
Spaulding, Dave 115
Speer LE ballistic tests 172
Split second judgments 5
St. Hilaire v. City of Laconia 31
Starr v. Baca 121
Stress inoculation 217
Substantive due process 3
Summary judgment 84
Suspects, police shooting of 12
T.E. v. Grindle 121
Tactical breathing 218
Tandy, Karen P. 87
Tanella, Special Agent Jude 87
Taser 52
Tempe Study, The 131, 132
Tennessee v. Garner ... 2, 4, 7, 16, 29, 43, 47, 50, 79, 98, 141, 179, 194, 200
Tenth Circuit Court of Appeals 10, 13
Thomas v. Durastanti 20, 59

Index

Thompson Submachine gun 157
Thompson v. City of Chicago 188
Thompson v. Hubbard 196
Thompson v. Mercer 208
Threat of death; significant 2
Time lag 146
Tolan v. Cotton 82
Totality of circumstances .... vi, 16, 17, 19
Totality of circumstances test 19
Tunnel vision vii
United States v. Davis 2
United States v. United States District Court 70
Vasoconstriction vii
Vehicle video cameras 203
Vicarious liability 119
Video simulator training 110
Video simulators 112
Videotape evidence 205
Violent Encounters 95, 133
Waterman v. Batton 19, 42
Wilkinson v. Torres 59
Wilkinson, Office James 104
Wound ballistics .... vii, 39, 57, 151
Young v. City of Providence 25
Young v. City of Providence Napolitano 19, 23
Zuchel v. City of Denver 125

OTHER TITLES OF INTEREST FROM LOOSELEAF LAW PUBLICATIONS, INC.

Reasonable, Justified & Necessary
Exploring the Professional, Physical and Psychological Complexities of Deadly Force
by Dan Bernoulli

Legal Issues in Homeland Security
U.S. Supreme Court Cases, Commentary & Questions
by Terrence P. Dwyer

Real World Search & Seizure – *2nd Edition*
by Matthew J. Medina

Use of Force – *2nd Edition*
Expert Guidance for Decisive Force Response
by Brian A. Kinnaird

Conflict Resolution for Law Enforcement
Street-Smart Negotiating
by Kyle E. Blanchfield, Thomas A. Blanchfield, and Peter D. Ladd

Improving Motivation and Morale
A Police Leader's Guide
by Jody Kasper

(800) 647-5547   www.LooseleafLaw.com